THE
Precious Birthright

A VOLUME IN THE SERIES
Black New England
EDITED BY
*Kabria Baumgartner, Kerri Greenidge, Jared Ross Hardesty,
and Nicole Maskiell*

THE
Precious
Birthright

BLACK LEADERS
AND THE
FIGHT TO VOTE IN
ANTEBELLUM
RHODE ISLAND

CJ MARTIN

University of Massachusetts Press
AMHERST AND BOSTON

Copyright © 2024 by University of Massachusetts Press
All rights reserved
Printed in the United States of America

ISBN 978-1-62534-838-8 (paper); 839-5 (hardcover)

Designed by Jen Jackowitz
Set in Adobe Jenson Pro
Printed and bound by Books International, Inc.

Cover design by Sally Nichols
Cover art by S. Lewis, *Map of Rhode Island*, 1804, engraving by Alexander Lawson.
Courtesy David Rumsey Historical Map Collection.

Library of Congress Cataloging-in-Publication Data
A catalog record for this book is available from the Library of Congress.

British Library Cataloguing-in-Publication Data
A catalog record for this book is available from the British Library.

For Shannon, Hallie, Macie, Mom, and Dad
and
All the leaders in the long Black freedom struggle

Contents

Acknowledgments ix

INTRODUCTION
1

CHAPTER 1
"To Promote One Common Good"
Black Leaders in Revolutionary Rhode Island
15

CHAPTER 2
"Dignified Abeyance"
Evolving Black Leadership and Disfranchisement
43

CHAPTER 3
"Forever and Hereafter a Body Politic"
New Leadership and Organization, 1819–1824
64

CHAPTER 4
"The Clouds of Evil"
Survival and Organization, 1820–1831
83

CHAPTER 5
"How Long Will the Lord Suffer Us to Remain as We Now Are?"
Activists and Citizenship in the 1830s
119

CHAPTER 6
"The Mustard Seed"
Part 1: Black Leaders, Allies, and Escalation of the Suffrage Movement
147

CHAPTER 7
"The Mustard Seed"
Part 2: Citizenship
175

EPILOGUE
"Friends to Social Order, True to Our Fellow Man"
202

Notes 213
Bibliography 237
Index 253

Acknowledgments

I would like to first thank my professors and mentors in the Du Bois Department of Afro-American Studies at the University of Massachusetts. Dr. Manisha Sinha first believed in this project and graciously decided to continue advising me after moving on to the University of Connecticut. The advice of one of the most eminent historians of the nineteenth century has been instrumental in the molding of this work. Dr. Traci Parker then took me under her wing, directing this dissertation and lending me valuable support, both professional and personal. Her encouragement, constructive feedback, and guidance through the process has made me a better historian, as she has been truly inspirational as a teacher and scholar. I would also like to thank Dr. James Smethurst for lending his broad expertise of African American history and literature to this project. I am grateful as well to Dr. Barbara Krauthamer for taking the time out of her busy schedule as dean of the College of Humanities and Fine Arts to serve on this committee.

I have been intellectually motivated by many others in the Du Bois Department. The ways in which Dr. John H. Bracey narrated and conceptualized history, and Drs. A Yemisi Jimoh and Toussaint Losier inspired me to delve deeper into the connections between critical race and political theory inspired much of the framework of this project. I am also grateful to have been part of such a vibrant intellectual community of graduate students. The hours spent around the seminar table with my cohort—especially Kiara Hill, Chloe Hunt, and Kourtney Senquiz—have been vital to my development as a scholar. To those with whom I served on committees and taught, or who otherwise helped shape my professional development—Olivia Ekeh, Paul Fowler, Keyona Jones, Cecile Yezou, Leydi Rodriguez, Bob Williams, Candace King, Erika Slocumb, Mtali Banda—I thank you.

I would like to thank the staff at the Rhode Island Historical Society, particularly Michelle Chiles and Jennifer Galpern, for their assistance in the research portion of this project, and Rick Ring for facilitating the publication of part of this book in the *Rhode Island History* journal. Thank you to Ken Carlson at the Rhode Island State Archives, and the staffs at the John Hay Library at Brown University and the American Antiquarian Society for all the help and support. Thank you to Heather Olson at Rhode Island's Public Archaeology Laboratory for sharing much of her research and digitized versions of directories and maps, and to Erik Chaput, the premier authority on the Dorr Rebellion, for adding his blessing at the beginning of this project.

The professors in my master's program at UMass Boston, particularly the late Dr. James Green and my thesis advisor, Dr. Julie Winch, also provided much of the early encouragement I needed to pursue history as a career.

Most importantly, I would like to thank my family for their boundless support. My mother, Diane Martin, first inspired my love of reading and learning and always pushed me to fulfill the potential she saw in me, and my brother, Andy Martin, always believed in me. My father, Rob Martin, not only offered encouragement at every step but also lent his proofreading and editing expertise to the entirety of what follows. My in-laws, Dianne and the greatly missed Fraser McNeilly, always cheered me on and provided countless hours of babysitting so this could move forward. My daughter Hallie Martin, born just as this project was getting off the ground, has inspired me in all the ways a happy, curious, and energetic toddler can. Macie has now taken on that responsibility. Finally, this could not have been completed without the love and support from my wife, Shannon Martin, who—unlike me—never once wavered or doubted.

THE
Precious
Birthright

Introduction

Robert Vorhis probably wanted to be left alone. Instead, the fifty-six-year-old formerly enslaved man found himself the subject of a biographical booklet published first in the Providence *Literary Cadet* and then by a young Providence printer in 1829—the second printing purportedly "published for his [Vorhis's] benefit." Apparently quite a curiosity to "mischievous" white Providence boys, Vorhis lived in a hut he had built just east of the Seekonk River, in what is today East Providence, on land owned by Tristam Burges. A voyeuristic tale, "Robert the Hermit" tantalized the white imagination, its sordid protagonist emerging from "his cell . . . decorated with various shells and bones" to "rove around" the surrounding woods, curiously forbidding any crops to grow on his land and "quietly look[ing] forward for the arrival of that day when he shall 'bid the waking world good night,' and find in countries unexplored, that happiness which life has denied him." Vorhis lived outside the city limits in self-imposed exile, had no pretentions to assimilate in society, and with no (free) children, no discernible future to hope for or to offer. Everything about him fit perfectly the mainstream white ideal of the African American place in the body politic.[1]

Despite the impression contemporary readers must have gotten or curiosity the story might have piqued, a closer look may leave modern readers with a sense that he was not "eccentric, if not insane."[2] Vorhis was born enslaved in New Jersey in 1769 or 1770 and grew up in Georgetown (in what would become Washington, DC). After spending his teenage years as a gardener, marrying a free Black woman named Alley, and starting a family, he worked toward saving for his freedom for an agreed-upon price with his enslaver. When he was almost there, his enslaver turned on him and had him kidnapped and sold to Charleston, South Carolina. Vorhis immediately escaped (just three hours after he was "purchased," he was stowed away on a ship for Philadelphia), was recaptured nine days later, and lived enslaved in Charleston for the next eighteen months. He escaped again, this time on a ship captained by a Quaker who gave him safe passage to Boston. His freedom came with a steep price, as he would never again see Alley and their children, a fact that still weighed heavily on the older Vorhis. He then took to the sea, the safest job he could think of; married a Boston woman; and had a child with her—but the sailor's life proved too much for his new wife, and she and their son (born while he was away) left him. He then removed to Providence and obtained steady work on a packet that sailed between there and New York. Upon finally feeling safe enough to attempt seeing his first wife and children in Georgetown, he traveled there only to find that his wife had committed suicide and his children had not survived long after. He then, in a bout of deep despair, "formed the determination to retire . . . to become a recluse, and mingle thereafter as little as possible with human society."[3]

By twenty-first-century understanding, we may now perceive that Vorhis probably made a more calculated decision to withdraw from society than the author of the story let on. For Vorhis's world was one that sent mixed messages to people of color: on the one hand, he was supposedly "created equal" and entitled to the "inalienable rights" of "life, liberty, and the pursuit of happiness"; on the other, because of the color of his skin, his life was expendable, his liberty contested and circumscribed, and his happiness stolen. Living in Rhode Island might have given Vorhis a sanctuary from slavery, but even there the promises of U.S. citizenship were beyond his grasp: he was still unable to vote, he was mostly barred from accessing the wealth that Providence was generating as a mercantile and manufacturing center, and his individuality was subject to changing tides of race ideology.

Although Vorhis never ascended to the leadership ranks of Providence's Black community or even sought historical recognition, there is a lot more symbolism in this story that can help us understand how race and citizenship functioned in antebellum Providence. In addition to existing in a precarious place outside the body politic, Vorhis lived on land owned by Tristam Burges, a Federalist congressman, during the period in which the Federalist Party had all but ceased to function. The original New York and New England Federalists had been modest allies for northern Black communities. Federalists championed gradual abolition laws, helped set up schools for children of color, and their preference for a social hierarchy based on property ownership over that of a strict racial caste meant that where African Americans could vote, Federalists could largely count on their support.[4] After the party became defunct, the citizenship rights of Black people became vulnerable to gutting by their opponents, who increasingly in the country's early years championed the rights of poor white men.[5] The limited protection Burges's estate offered to Vorhis reflected this alliance. Responses to the rising tide of white supremacy in the early nineteenth century were wide-ranging; many Black people were forced to seek partnerships with philanthropic whites, and like Vorhis, they could gain for themselves a modicum of protection or individual benefit. Black leaders forged these alliances as a way to ensure for their communities a voice in the body politic and used them as weapons in the fight for more equitable citizenship—and often, Black activists were not shy about holding whites accountable for living up to their speeches and writings on equal rights.

Also like Vorhis, despite severe proscriptions on their freedom, African Americans determined for themselves what they wanted their futures to look like. Some sought to carve out a comfortable place for themselves and their families by going their own ways, most often through capital accumulation outside of the bourgeoning industrial sectors. Many others came together to build community institutions like mutual benefit societies and churches to foster the kind of collective respectability they felt was necessary to overcome white prejudice. Respectability in the early nineteenth century was a survival strategy. African Americans were at the forefront of antebellum campaigns for temperance, missionary work, and especially the movement to abolish slavery and shelter those who escaped from the South. They often mixed in with, but sometimes worked apart from, alongside, or ahead of, whites. From a strong base of community support and armed with the political acumen to deal with the conservative white elite class, Black leaders chose the exact right moment to intervene in the Dorr Rebellion—the political crisis precipitated by the state's Suffrage Association—earning a metaphoric seat at the table when it came to distributing the spoils of victory.

Black men were unceremoniously disenfranchised by the state in 1822, when the word "white" was inserted into the voting qualification section of Rhode Island's digest of laws. Over the next few decades, Providence's Black community put together a multifaceted campaign of self-liberation that included a unique combination of agitation and accommodation to republican ideals in order to achieve for themselves the ultimate right of citizenship— "the precious birthright of freedom," in their words—the right to vote, which they won officially in 1843.[6] Their campaign brought out issues that the Black freedom struggle has long had to grapple with in its response to persistent white supremacy, particularly respectability and the refutation of the color line as a social, economic, and political barrier to self-determination. In the end, Providence's Black leaders were able to both articulate and act on successful arguments for their inclusion in the body politic.

Several books have centered Providence's Black community, the Dorr Rebellion, and other aspects of the city's (and state's) history, but little scholarly work has yet analyzed the city's Black leaders and their fight for citizenship rights. This is a gap in the academic literature made even more stark by the fact that Providence's Black leaders offer the story of a remarkably successful victory in at least one arena—the right to vote. Perhaps this is because an honest look reveals some of the sacrifices they had to make in order to achieve their victory, drawbacks that may have blunted the national and regional impact of the movement's success. Providence's Black community's absorption into the conservative world of Rhode Island politics also, at first glance, seems to have put them outside the radical and progressive tradition in Black intellectualism. However, their carefully constructed campaign for the right to vote so complicated the white power structure that, though having occurred in the smallest state in the union, it deserves analysis as part of the larger story of Black liberation.

What Black leaders did not accomplish as a result of their success is also quite telling and warrants attention. In order to win and then maintain their position as agents within the body politic, Providence's Black leaders closely allied themselves with the Whig Party of the 1840s. Keen on keeping the Whigs in power lest Black votes for third parties lead to a Democratic takeover and possible loss of the franchise, Rhode Island African Americans largely shunned the Liberty Party and Free Soil movements. They also broke somewhat with radical abolitionists like Frederick Douglass, many of whom championed the Black suffrage cause during some of its darkest days. Providence's Black leaders, after enfranchisement, participated in antislavery associations but eschewed the movement's more public criticisms of the national political parties, perhaps lessening their influence. They were also unable to get the state to abolish race proscription in other areas, most notably school segregation in the 1850s. Despite winning the right to vote, the color line, as it did everywhere in the United States, remained strong right through the civil rights movement of the 1960s, when the cause of inclusion was again taken up by Brown University students of color.

In their seminal work *In Hope of Liberty*, historian James Horton and sociologist Lois Horton wrote, "The voice of Black America between the Revolution and the Civil War was the voice of America's conscience."[7] Providence's antebellum Black leaders reflected this sentiment as well as any individual or organization of the time period. They fashioned the language and spirit of the Declaration of Independence, particularly its ideas of self-governance, taxation without representation, and equality, into a campaign that, though overlooked, on further reflection offers a recipe for what successful movement can look like in the American republic. The following pages will help to deepen our understanding of the interplay of race, society, and politics in antebellum America, and complicate and inform our notions of how disfranchised people have been able to win concessions from a society in which so many were hostile to their very presence.

Republican Citizenship and Leadership

There are two phrases I use often that are central to this work: "republican citizenship"—which I also mean when I use "citizenship" by itself—and "leadership class." I use "leadership class" because the people I introduce to the scholarship do not fit comfortably into the notions of traditionally white or Black socio-capitalist structures, but in a way they carved out a status distinct unto itself—one tied to laboring for community uplift as opposed to achievement of personal wealth. A full explanation of what I mean by "republican citizenship" is crucial in order to properly understand the rights that African Americans were striving for, the place in the body politic they envisioned for themselves, and the tactics they were using to do so.

Ideas about who was eligible for citizenship and what the privileges of citizenship entailed came directly out of the Enlightenment philosophy imbibed by the founding framers of the government. The Declaration of Independence and Constitution are largely made up of paraphrases from works like John Locke's *Second Treatise of Government* and Jean-Jacques Rousseau's *The Social Contract*. The framers used this philosophy accordingly to rationalize their supposed right to separate from a government that they claimed had abandoned their "common interest" or "general will," and also to establish the "common interest" on which the new government would be based. The founders claimed that they represented men who were no longer in a "state of nature," what Locke defined as the original condition of humanity, capable only of forming associations to survive and feed their base passions, a state in which war was a constant and in which blind obedience to a monarch was the expected form of government. A critical mass had applied the reason and logic they accumulated to the amassing of property and becoming independent agents of their own future, the ultimate expression of conquering the natural world according to the philosophers. That property needed protection, and so the next logical step would be, for those who were capable of obtaining and maintaining property, a desire to protect it. These rational and logical people would then be bound by the common interest of protecting their property from those susceptible to the base passions of man (who were, though they lived among the rational, still in a "state of nature") to come together and form a government and set of laws. All would have their say in what that would entail; in effect, they would be ruled by a "social contract." The "signatories" to that "contract" would be the people with the power to establish it, alter it if need be, have the ability to speak freely about it, and, most importantly, vote on their representatives tasked with implementing its protections.

As European men conquered, plundered, and enslaved Indigenous people and resources on other continents, and developed their self-fulfilling ideas about the supremacy of people with light-colored skin and other European features, it became clear who they thought of as "rational": white people, and men in particular. The pursuit of military glory and, in America, the discipline of militia life would become incorporated into American republican idealism. European family and gender norms antiquatedly elevated men and commodified the lives and bodies of women, applying to them the qualities of irrationality and passion, thus allowing them and children (boys had yet to learn rationality) to be seen as needing to be controlled. Women, children, and people of color, because they supposedly did not have the capacity to own and control property, or even themselves, were in a "state of nature," dependent on rational white men and susceptible to however white men wished to control them.[8] Therefore, the right to vote was universally withheld from children and nearly so from women, while Black men, despite being property holders, were severely circumscribed from this right across the country.[9]

John Locke himself was a stockholder in the Royal African Company, which trafficked in slavery, and a member of Great Britain's Board of Trade and Plantations, which ensured the profitability of colonies like Virginia and Barbados by providing for laws that allowed the arbitrary punishment and execution of enslaved people, laws banishing free people of color who dared interdict the property of whites from the bounds of colonies, and laws to prohibit people of color from marrying or procreating with whites.[10] Thus, it is fair to assume that the founding philosopher's vested interest in white supremacy was largely the entire rationale behind race and citizenship—a circumstance that starkly mirrors that of the founding framers of the U.S. government. Because of all this, and despite property-owning Black men and women not being explicitly barred from voting in some states, we can see that this was to be a government of, by, and for elite white men. In effect, "citizens," "the people," and "the body politic" would all be synonymous with "white men" in this supposedly representative form of government.

Of course, despite white men's best efforts, people of color owned and controlled property. They were capable of using reason and logic, and found ways to contest slavery and free themselves all around the country, winning general emancipation in all northern states. They "proved" their manhood and rationality by enlisting in huge numbers in the American Revolution, serving admirably wherever they fought. When the country was swept up in religious revivals, and Protestant Christianity became part of the fabric of "the people's" idealism, African Americans played a major part in its spread and influence. They spearheaded the movement for temperance in the 1820s and 1830s, in what can be seen as an ultimate affirmation of self-control. Campaigns for "respectability" were attempts to prove to the powerful that Black people were worthy of citizenship—that the color of the skin was no impediment to rationality and capability in the Enlightenment tradition. They used a wider, egalitarian interpretation of the principles set forth in the Declaration and Constitution as their ideological base, and in doing so confronted these ideals' often-understated white supremacist underpinnings. This was the beginning of the American version of the Black freedom struggle.

Recent scholarship has moved Black civil and political rights to the very center of the evolving definition of citizenship in the first four score and seven years of the American republic. Kate Masur has shown how Black men and women, using localized struggle, gave the public discourse a vocabulary through which citizenship could be defined and extended. Van Gosse argues that Black men's "collective practice" in political activism—if not at the polls, at least in setting the terms of public discourse—was central to pre–Civil War notions of citizenship politics. Christopher Bonner notes astutely that "by claiming rights as citizens, Black people therefore helped make citizenship more important, pushing the status toward the center of lawmaking discussions, arguing that it should be a cornerstone for individuals' rights and their relationships to American governments." Further, he states, "through their political work, Black people built a new republic." While it may have taken the Civil War to ultimately bring that "new republic" to fruition nationwide, Black Rhode Island leaders did so in their state a full two decades earlier.[11]

The Providence story in some ways complicates our ideas of who the leaders of movements were. I call them a "leadership class" partly because they operated largely before a "Black middle class" emerged in the state, and the cadre was much smaller than that of, for instance, Philadelphia, where an "elite" could rise. Black people in Providence often did not adhere to Leon Litwack's notion that the leadership in Black circles was determined by "wealth, occupation, family, nativity, color, and education."[12] As the historians of particular Black communities have shown, defining "class" in antebellum Black communities is fraught—perhaps because we typically define it, as Litwack seems to have done, without acknowledging the racial proscriptions that affect social hierarchies. Black people could project all the elements of good republican citizenship—they could accumulate wealth, show their capacity for independence, and so on—but the color of their skin still placed them outside of the white republican body politic in most areas, and outside its social hierarchy nearly everywhere. This is, in my view, why the endless debates of the Suffrage Association about the place of African Americans in the movement, debates that historians have mostly ignored, tore the movement apart. Were Black people a part of the same working class as their white neighbors, or did the color of their skin, their perceived dependence, and their alleged inability to reason place them beyond the bounds of citizenship? Could they be *citizens*? Or were Black Rhode Islanders just *denizens*, people who lived among the citizenry but did not have the same civil and political rights accorded citizens? One historian has shown that many white leaders sought to resolve the issue of race and citizenship by designating Black residents as "denizens."[13] The supporters of the Dorr Rebellion never could unite on an answer, and continued Black leaders' and allies' attacks on them over this point severely undercut their movement.

Leadership in Providence's Black community had little in common with that of their white neighbors. Providence's Black leaders hewed more closely to those of Philadelphia, whom Julie Winch stated frequently lacked "wealth and social position[;] they were eloquent, skilled organizers and devoted to social reform; ability . . . propelled them into the ranks of leadership."[14] Many Providence leaders were listed in city directories as laborers, traders, or barbers, or frequently changed occupations. They achieved their status within their community by their activist labor, not necessarily the money they accumulated. Most were literate, and some were not. Some had lighter skin, and some were "unusually black."[15] What they had in common was the resolve and desire to articulate a vision for inclusion that, at least nominally, adhered to all contours of republican citizenship but one: white supremacy. As it was then and has always been since, that was the most difficult to barrier to break down.

* * *

Robert Vorhis's pain and ostracism may have been caricatured for the pleasure of white Providence residents, and the image of the lonely old man with no free children may have earned him curious approbation. When white individuals in Providence considered the ideal Black citizen, they imagined their own farcical portrayal of Vorhis—not the leaders who would put forward a successful movement to win back the right to vote. This was the age that saw the birth of minstrelsy and disappearance narratives imagining free people of color (of either African or Native descent) as bumbling tricksters, futureless and placeless inhabitants of the new nation. "Bobalition" broadsides received heavy circulation in the northern cities, ridiculing Black speech, exaggerating physical features associated with Black people, and shaming them for "imitating" elites in an effort to gain citizenship.[16] Rhode Island was fertile ground for this type of literature. Poorer white residents there were anxiously pressing for their own inclusion into the body politic, and there, as elsewhere, the shifting political landscape and race ideology allowed them to differentiate themselves from their Black neighbors, imagining for themselves a place among the elite by elevating whiteness as the principle condition for citizenship. Where Federalist influence waned, white people were granted the space to expand their rights; states began to relax property requirements while implementing, in most places for the first time, the word "white" into their voter qualifications.[17] Rhode Island's failure to include poor whites along with its proscription against Black voting in 1822 set the stage for the dramatic climax in the early

1840s, as the parallel Black and white movements to win (back) the franchise collided with a staunchly conservative state government. Whites had their own obstacles to overcome, many of which they placed in front of themselves, but Black Rhode Islanders had to figure out how to overcome the "affliction" of race.

This book tells that story, adding the Providence leadership class's voice to the already rich scholarship regarding Black protest in the antebellum North. It begins by discussing the first people who laid the foundation for African Americans' claims to citizenship, the revolutionary soldiers of the First Rhode Island Regiment and the formerly enslaved men who fostered ties to white religious allies in Newport and Providence. The professed manliness in battle of Black revolutionary soldiers, their willingness to defend the body politic from taxation without representation, were, in addition to the personal ventures for freedom, assertions of collective positioning for more equitable treatment as citizens. In the years surrounding the war, it was the early leaders in Newport, tied in many ways to Africa and slavery, who breathed life into their brethren in Providence. In the late 1780s and early 1790s, the African Union Society was dominated by emigrationists who, while maintaining a traditional mutual benefit society, also raised money to repatriate themselves. The failure of one such scheme in 1794–1795 and the loss of philanthropic and community support doomed emigration as a strategy for race uplift, and shifting demographics meant the leadership center of gravity moved from Newport to the mainland. Most of the Providence residents discussed here did not necessarily see themselves as permanent community leaders, though their visibility in the city helped entrench the notion that, despite emigrationism and the shift from the spirit of revolutionary egalitarianism to one of white supremacy, African Americans were part of the Providence and Rhode Island social landscape.

In the first years of the nineteenth century, the first Black leadership class coalesced in Providence. It was a leadership cohort born out of the struggle against ascendant white supremacy, disfranchisement, and the correlated abandonment of their Federalist Party allies. The committee nominated to plan the building of the African Union Meeting House, Providence's first Black church, offers us our first glimpse of a community, a "body politic," united in motivation, if not tactics, to gain greater access to the citizenship rights their parents had sought in the Revolution. The meetinghouse was multidenominational and housed a school in its vestry, its "warm and commodious" rooms envisioned as a cultural and political space.[18] Initially conceived by

Black members of white churches who chafed under the discrimination they endured during worship, the building became the first communally owned space in the town, and the springboard from which the subsequent movement would be launched.[19] As they took this forward stride, however, a shift in the political landscape meant the sweeping out of power of the philanthropic Federalists and the addition of the word "white" into the state's voter qualification statute. Although it appears that African Americans very rarely voted because of the "freeman" system in Rhode Island, this was a huge blow to the leadership—and one that Black communities experienced all over the country. Behind this lay the overheated rhetoric of the Missouri Crisis and the national questioning of the place of the future of the country's hundreds of thousands of free people of color; properly contextualizing Rhode Island's internal and external debates means that we can more fully understand what the Black leadership was up against, and would be again when race became a major part of the national conversation.

Black leadership and rank and file grew even more resilient under disfranchisement and launched a multipronged offensive in order to win (back) citizenship rights. The decade after disfranchisement saw two ugly pogroms in majority-Black neighborhoods, one in "Hard-Scrabble" in 1824 and the other in "Snow Town" in 1831. Black leaders during this period began petitioning for the right to vote based on taxation and education. Their resistance through these crises, along with their organizing during this period and willingness to portray a republican brand of respectability, helped put them in a position of strength when the time came to make their case for re-enfranchisement.

A flurry of organizing activity took place throughout the 1830s, as Black leaders joined the growing abolitionist movement, inviting abolitionists to speak in the African Union Meeting House and attending regional and national antislavery conferences. In these years, the social became the political. A professed commitment to temperance meant a separation from the white rabble violently rioting against abolition across the country, public displays of educational attainment implied the ability to reason like any free person, and the organization of new churches reflected a piousness that combated the supposed susceptibility to vice in Black neighborhoods. Activism in the convention movement among people of color and abolitionism created avenues for an articulation of self-liberation philosophy with or without adhering to republican norms, though most denounced the separatism of early Black nationalism in favor of cooperation with white allies.

By 1841, Black leaders had swung into action as suffrage agitation among white Rhode Island boiled over into all-out crisis. Alfred Niger, a veteran of the Colored Convention movement and agent for the antislavery *Liberator* in Newport and Providence, tried to vote in the white Suffrage Association's call for a constitutional convention, and then was nominated as a trojan horse candidate for the association's treasury position in order to make it finally discuss whether or not African Americans were to have the right to vote. Niger was rebuffed twice, and then the association rejected a petition from young Alexander Crummell to omit the word "white" in the qualifications for voting in their constitution. Consequently, the movement, now led by Thomas Dorr (a former abolitionist), ceased to be a viable avenue for the franchise. The Rhode Island Anti-Slavery Society, along with the national branch, excoriated both the Suffrage Association and the state government for their white-only provisions, holding up the contradictions in the messaging on both sides, and especially the association's selling of their souls for political expediency. Providence's Black leaders made the politically savvy decision to protect the city during the seemingly impending violence, reminding their white neighbors that their ancestors fought alongside whites for the Declaration's ideals. This invocation, made frequently by Black leaders and then put into action in 1842, made them equally eligible for the right to vote. With this in mind, the state government decided to put the question of Black voting to a public now grateful for the service of Black men in their protection of the city. It passed easily, and African Americans officially became members of the body politic.

While the right to vote was an important achievement for Providence's Black community, and Black voters were largely incorporated into the Whig Party machinery, their skin color still proved an impediment to fully equal citizenship. The movement for equal access to education was ultimately unsuccessful until after the Civil War, and the color line remained on statute books in other areas. However, the city's first Black elected official would come out of this leadership class when Thomas Howland was elected to a ward captainship in 1857. Again, this step forward was tempered by a nationally important step back, as the *Dred Scott* decision the same year undermined any claim to citizenship rights African Americans were making in Rhode Island and elsewhere. Howland subsequently challenged the decision by attempting to obtain a passport; he was utterly defeated, and shortly after he emigrated to Liberia given the odds stacked against him and his fellow Black Rhode Islanders. The pendulum then swung back in the opposite direction with the outbreak of the

Civil War, when once again Black Rhode Islanders responded to the call in a contest over the meaning of citizenship.

While Robert Vorhis and Thomas Howland decided to live out their days outside the bounds of the body politic that had rejected them, the stories of the community leaders who infiltrated the bastions of republican ideology are worth telling for a variety of reasons. First, these leaders achieved arguably the largest collective success before the Civil War. The ways in which they both accommodated to a system of oppression but also were able to resist and change it can tell us a lot about what it means to be a citizen of a country whose founding mythology is one of egalitarianism but whose real foundation rests on white male supremacy. The history of people of color challenging the established racial hierarchy is entering an exciting new phase, and recent developments in the twenty-first-century political world have made an understanding of both the system and how it can be successfully challenged paramount to making meaning out of our past. It is crucial to not only recall successes but to evaluate their impacts and limitations, to learn the vocabulary of the oppressors and the agents of change, and to understand the forces that create and alter society. Who is citizenship for? What does citizenship entail? These are questions that have plagued the country since its founding, and we must use this history to enable ourselves to better articulate what it means to be a citizen of this republic.

CHAPTER 1

"To Promote One Common Good"

BLACK LEADERS IN REVOLUTIONARY RHODE ISLAND

"By the assistance of the most merciful GOD," wrote Salmar Nubia in July 1789, "we may be able to prosecute this grand design for the welfare of our Oppressed brethren, And the best interest of our poor, suffering nations of Affrica."[1] Nubia, a "person of good genius," had been kidnapped from the African continent and taken as a slave but now was the secretary of the Free African Union Society in Newport, one of the first mutual benefit societies of, by, and for African Americans to record their proceedings.[2] The letter that contained these words was sent to "all the Affricans in Providence" and included a suggestion that those on Rhode Island's mainland form their own society in order to "promote one common good"—an idea that in the 1780s could mean several different things for African American communities.[3]

On one hand, it could mean strengthening community bonds by supporting its members and their families in various ways. Mutual aid societies were a hallmark of early free Black communities and were necessities in towns and cities where, in the days immediately following slavery, exclusion from artisan and mercantile trades and increasing hostility from white neighbors forced most African Americans into economically precarious situations.[4] The Free African Union Society, like others across the North in the late eighteenth and early nineteenth centuries, indeed paid for and organized funerals for their members and members' families, and loaned money and goods to those who petitioned that they had fallen on hard times. The society, for example, lent money to member Newport Wanton when he was sick in April 1792, and reimbursed his wife for the expenses incurred at his funeral the following year.[5]

To men like Nubia and many members of the society, the promotion of the "common good" could also mean a return to their homes in Africa. Nubia and some of the most influential members of the society, including Newport Gardner, Bristol Yamma, and Zingo Stevens, were all born in Africa and, in various ways, expressed their desire to repatriate themselves there. Most of their efforts at fundraising in the early 1790s pointed to this end, and they would briefly ally with white ministers interested in spreading the gospel to the "heathenish" continent in attempts at making this return home come to fruition.

The American Revolution's upheaval of the colonies' social, political, and economic order, and its consequences for Black communities around the North, were interpreted and acted on in a variety of ways. Black (and Native American) men enlisted in the armed forces on both sides of the war, most often depending on which offered the greatest chance at freedom. In Virginia, where the royal governor Lord Dunmore offered freedom to enslaved and indentured people who took up arms for the British, and across the southern lowcountry, where the war upended plantation life, tens of thousands of Black men and women escaped their captivity for British lines.[6] In the North, where free and enslaved people of color had been active Minutemen and fought in battles at Lexington, Concord, and Bunker Hill, the Continental Army, despite Washington's declaration against the enlistment of "any stroller, negro, or vagabond," offered the surest avenue to freedom for many.[7]

The strength of the colonial slave regime in Rhode Island largely prevented the coalescence of a leadership class among African Americans, which meant that Black response to the Revolution was anything but monolithic. The abolition of slavery in the state was a marked victory, as despite its painful limitations (discussed below), Black people could look toward and discuss what freedom would look like for them and their children. Would it take place inside or outside the new American republic—a republic that stated its foundational ideals as freedom and equality but still held slaves almost everywhere? Would union in the cause of liberty break down old distinctions of color and allow for Black participation in the body politic? To African Americans eager to taste the fruits of victory, the future was at the same time promising and treacherous. It is important to examine this era of Black leadership because the conversations around emigration, colonization, and devotion to the evolving American political order were foundational to the formation of the nineteenth-century leadership class. The alliances with elite whites fostered here afforded critical access to the wealth and power necessary for community advancement. Finally, the establishment of organizations in which leaders emerged provided the space necessary for ideas to develop, strategies to be honed, and the "common good" for Black Rhode Islanders to be more clearly defined.

Black Kings, Governors, and Soldiers

A search for the first Black leaders in Rhode Island should perhaps begin in a colonial-era tradition known as "Negro elections." Analogous to the more well-known "Pinkster" festivals in New York, Negro elections were celebrations in which Africans and African Americans met together, usually one day a year, to elect "kings" and "governors" to serve as, according to historian William Pierson, "enforcers of social propriety."[8] Enslavers would pay for food and drinks and allow enslaved people to borrow clothing, horses, decorations, and anything else deemed proper for the day. Votes would be cast and "kings" elected in crown colonies, "governors" in the more autonomous colonies that elected their own governors and legislatures. The leaders would be paraded to open fields and give addresses, appoint ceremonial sheriffs and military positions, and lead goodwill toasts for the upcoming year. These gatherings offered space for families to celebrate together and people of color to socialize outside the purview of whites (though the latter often attended). The authority and responsibility of the kings and governors could vary widely, but the position was nevertheless an important status symbol for the governor and his family.[9] Election Day was also a space for people of African descent to gain and maintain some sense of control over their own destinies and those of their communities. Governors like Prince Amy of Newport could serve in both the ceremonial post and as a high-ranking member of the Free African Union Society, a mutual benefit organization. Elsewhere in Rhode Island, Black elected leaders appear to have developed their own court system and proscriptions for punishments and fines. Black kings and governors, given their positions as elected administrators of ceremonies, were community leaders in a very real sense—but when the merrymaking and socializing was over, they most often returned to their stations as captive servants, laborers, sailors, and so on.[10]

Celebrations and cultural expressions such as this were possible as long as, James Horton and Lois Horton remind us, "whites were convinced that it operated in their best interest."[11] A common historical interpretation of these election days is that they allowed enslaved people an escape from the suffocating control under which they toiled, a "safety valve" through which the will to rebel or escape could be mollified by the seeming generosity of white enslavers. While whites reassured themselves that "Negro elections" were necessary diversions to keep their captives happy, or that they were just imitations of white elections, Pierson also notes that participants "were creating an important celebration of Black awareness," particularly as many enslaved people were either born in or one generation removed from one of many African communities.[12] Elections may have functioned as ways to acknowledge the royal lineages from which some enslaved people were taken captive. They also seemed to have served as affirmations of a common identity rooted in the African continent: many participants spoke languages indigenous to African communities and nations, wore traditional clothing, and carried cultural symbols. Instruments and drums native to Africa often accompanied the ceremonial proceedings, and the folk traditions of singing satirical songs and putting on plays in sarcastic imitation of whites—perhaps a cultural antecedent of the "cakewalk"—could be seen and often drew large crowds.[13]

In Rhode Island, it seems as though most of the "Negro election" activity took place in Newport and the plantation country of King's (then Washington) and Kent Counties. These towns had the heaviest concentration of people of African descent and therefore the most opportunity for community building. In 1755, Newport's population of color numbered 1,234, a full 18 percent of all the port's residents and over a quarter of the state's whole population of color. That same year, one-third of the plantation-heavy South Kingstown's population was nonwhite. By the eve of the Revolution, Newport's population of color had increased only slightly, to 1,292 from twenty years before, though it remained at 14 percent of the whole population.[14] These figures also undoubtedly included Native Americans who, when living inside the bounds of the colony, were most often counted as "Black" or "mulatto" when census-takers attempted to make the distinction. Although, as historians Joanne Pope Melish and John Wood Sweet have noted, the realities of conflicting ideological currents about race were more fluid than the binary census designations suggest, these are nevertheless the best figures we have to determine the numbers of people who might make up the population of participants in "Negro elections."[15]

In Providence by 1774, there were only 371 people of color, including 68 Native Americans, enumerated—about a quarter of the number residing in

Newport—and they made up about 8.5 percent of the town's overall population. There were roughly half as many people overall in Providence as Newport, making the former a distant second to Newport's statewide dominance. "Negro elections" do not appear to have taken place in Providence, though according to Black Providence memoirist William J. Brown, African Americans there would participate in the festivities in nearby Warwick, most often on the third or last Saturday in June. Without its own leadership, Providence's Black community, most of whose residents were enslaved themselves, was cementing ties with enslaved and free African Americans in Kent and King's County plantation country—in effect, helping to forge a uniquely Rhode Island Black identity. The tradition's importance seems to have waned by the early nineteenth century, though it would continue on the mainland until 1840, by which time Providence's African American leaders were spending their activist energy on gaining the right to vote in official national, state, and local elections.[16]

When the revolution that gave birth to the United States came, new avenues toward citizenship opened up, inspiring hope in Black communities across the North. The rhetoric of liberty and equality that was shouted from all corners—mobs and legislatures alike—convinced many African Americans across the North that their own freedom was now in reach, and that slavery, which had been so central a part of the Black experience in New England and the mid-Atlantic states, could no longer be rationalized in an atmosphere that championed the natural rights of man. Also galvanized by the Declaration of Independence's allusions to "unalienable rights" and its declamation of taxation without representation, free born or potentially free African Americans could look toward the possibility of inclusion in the body politic writ large, not just inside their own circles. The many Black Rhode Islanders who freed themselves; the influence of Quakerism in Newport and Providence; and small, already free and well-connected Black communities in the state's two principal towns all combined to kick off the movement toward citizenship in earnest.

African Americans very early in the contest showed that they were willing to play a major part in the struggle over American liberty. After the famous 1772 burning of the HMS *Gaspee*, a British revenue cutter that was the bane of bigwig colonial Rhode Island traders' profits, an enslaved Rhode Islander, Aaron Briggs, suddenly seemed to have been gifted a weapon with which he could win his freedom. A "mulatto" most likely having Native and African ancestry, Briggs was picked up by the British ship *Beaver*, having run away from his "indenture." What he had to say was potentially explosive. In sworn testimony given in January 1773, six months after the incident, he claimed that he was forced to row one of the boats to the *Gaspee*, which had beached itself on a sandbar, so he had intimate knowledge of who was in on the plot to destroy the king's ship. He proceeded to implicate five of the most powerful Rhode Islanders, including John and Joseph Brown, the former a well-known trafficker in slaves.[17] To counter his claim, two enslaved men who slept every night in the same bed as Briggs claimed that he was in bed all night and not on the *Gaspee*. Other witnesses accused Briggs of orchestrating his story to receive the hefty reward being offered by the crown for anyone who could bring the perpetrators to justice.[18] Did Briggs see cooperation with the British as a way out of slavery? Did the other two enslaved men counter his claim to boost their own chances at freedom from grateful Rhode Island elites?

The evidence seems to favor the idea of Briggs seeing an opportunity and putting his life on the line to seize it. His indenture was set to run out at the age of twenty-four, and he claimed he was eighteen while his master claimed Briggs was sixteen.[19] Without an official birthdate, and knowing that indenture agreements could be revoked at the behest of the enslaver, he must have been aware that even his eventual freedom—not to mention potential citizenship—was far from a guarantee.[20] Further, the deputy who first took Briggs's statement hinted that his superior should see to it that "the King will have justice done him."[21] Three years later, after the violence broke out in and around Boston, this notion that turning against one's enslavers could bring about the "justice" was set to writing when Virginia's royal governor, Lord Dunmore, issued a proclamation that promised freedom to anyone enslaved or indentured who took up arms for the British. Wherever hostilities broke out between whites, freedom for African Americans was suddenly part of the conversation. The stakes were as high for them as anyone in the coming war.[22]

Black men were serving alongside whites in the famous Minuteman companies of Boston in 1775, most as substitutes for able-bodied white men unwilling to do the hard labor they were accustomed to having people of color do for them. While Black soldiers may not have drilled with white militias, they presented themselves at the early battles and their services were accepted.[23] These men seized their opportunity, seeing the patriot cause—whether or not they believed in it—as the clearest avenue toward freedom for themselves and their families. Prince Esterbrook was one such man, and he was wounded in action the day the "shot heard 'round the world" was fired at Lexington.[24] Peter

Salem famously shot and killed Major John Pitcairn at Bunker Hill, where it was estimated that over one hundred people of color participated on the side of the rebels. In some areas, it was unclear as to which side would offer the best chance at freedom, as in the case of Connecticut man Seymour Burr. Although enslaved by a patriot master who treated him "with much favor," Burr initially saw his best option for freedom with the British. Caught by his master's posse when he attempted his flight, his master instead offered Burr freedom should he fight with the Americans and forfeit his soldier's compensation to pay for it. Burr accepted.[25] The South was a different story, where up to 100,000 enslaved people, including 80 percent of Georgia's entire enslaved population, took up arms for the British in exchange for their freedom or escaped in the confusion. Local, family, and other circumstances, of course, dictated which side to join or where to flee.[26]

George Washington's announcement that the Continental Army would not enlist Black soldiers was overridden by the constant need for able bodies. By December 1776, Washington began backtracking, allowing "free Negroes" to enlist, and by 1777 no regiment in New England was seemingly without soldiers of color.[27] In Rhode Island, the need for soldiers became more acute as most white enlistments—which totaled only 1,500—ended in 1778, while the British occupied Newport with a force of 6,000 men, choking the economy of the state and impoverishing the city. The General Assembly (the state legislative body), which had moved its headquarters from Newport to Providence, responded to the pleadings of state military commanders, approving a law providing for the enlistment of free people of color and manumission of any enslaved man willing to fight, with compensation for their owners.[28] This engendered fierce opposition by some of the state's leading slaveowners and traders. They contended that this move would send the message that the state needed to rely on people of color to gain independence and that the precipitation of manumission—understood as the natural and legal consequence of service—would have a disastrous effect on the institution of slavery in the state. They were right.[29]

One other thing the dissenters said was also telling, however. Arming "a band of slaves to defend the Rights and Liberties of the country," they protested, was "wholly inconsistent with those principles of liberty and constitutional government for which we are so ardently contending . . . and would also give occasion to our enemies to suspect that we are not able to procure our own people to oppose them in the field."[30] This distinction between "our own people" and those proposed to be enlisted made clear who the new government was intended to benefit. The opposition also included "a Mr. Hazard Potter"—probably Thomas Hazard Potter, the twenty-four-year-old son of a wealthy slaveowner—who told enlistees of color at a recruiting station that they would be placed at the front of the lines, forced to do manual labor, and if captured, sold as slaves to the Caribbean rather than be treated as prisoners of war. The backlash in the General Assembly was quick. The recruiting of people of color for the new, integrated First Rhode Island Regiment started in February 1778, but so many were joining that during the May legislative session, the assembly passed an act forbidding manumission and enlistment of enslaved people after June 10. Apparently, the deluge of those other than their "own people" willing to seize their freedom was upsetting both the social order and the state coffers. Compensated emancipation was expensive.[31]

African Americans, as they had in every war before and would in every war afterward, performed valiantly and to near universal praise in the Revolution. The regiment continued enlisting men of color, most of them enslaved, after June 10 despite the prohibition. In the Battle of Rhode Island, the Black regiment covered a strategic retreat, repelling Hessian forces three times while sustaining few casualties. They were on the frontlines at Yorktown, where they took a strategic redoubt from the British and fiercely protected their commanders, Christopher Greene and Jeremiah Olney, the latter despite his public refusal to endorse the idea that people of color made good soldiers.[32] They also took part in the disastrous Oswego campaign, where, having been greatly thinned out by disease and exposure in northeastern winters since Yorktown, they endured frostbite and permanent disability because of the march through four feet of snow.[33]

Several acts of Black patriotic heroism would live on in Rhode Island lore, resurrected especially when an occasion called for proof that Black Rhode Islanders, because of their defense of the republic, were worthy of citizenship. When the regiment was protecting Pine's Bridge in Yorktown, New York, they were surprised by loyalist forces, who mortally wounded their commander, Colonel Greene. As Greene lay dying, Black soldiers in the regiment formed a human chain around him, suffering heavy casualties themselves while protecting him from further attack.[34] "Prince" Jack Sisson played a crucial part in the 1777 raiding party that kidnapped British general Richard Prescott. Sisson was reportedly one of several people of color to volunteer for the raid, led the rowing team to Prescott's location just outside of Newport, and then led the charge into the house where they found Prescott. For Sisson's act of bravery in defense of the patriot cause, he was one of the few people of color to earn obituaries in several Providence newspapers on his death in 1821, and his memory was invoked in the pages of the *Colored American* as evidence of Black commitment to the republic.[35]

Two incidents involving Black soldiers demonstrate, however, how race could serve to limit the very freedom and equality they were fighting for—early signs that, even when defending the lives and property of the American people, Black soldiers would be held to a different standard. Ideas of freedom, equality, and citizenship for white men were complicated by a reliance on Black participation in the very creation of the republic. At around 1:00 a.m. on April 10, 1781, Prince Greene, a free Black man who had enlisted prior to the 1778 law that allowed him to, was on guard duty near the Continental and French artillery stores when he was apparently harassed by a white man, Edward Allen. Providence had been under martial law and a 10:00 p.m. curfew since 1776, and Greene and others on guard duty at the artillery store were authorized to shoot any intruder who did not obey commands. Whites had long made a "sport" of harassing Black people on the streets of Providence, but Greene was charged with defending the property of the U.S. military, and with martial law supposedly backing him up, he had to treat this as anything but "sport." He shot Allen as he and a companion were attacking Greene with stones and wooden sticks. Greene, though in uniform and on duty, was tried in the civilian court in Providence County and convicted of manslaughter. His hand was branded with an "M" as a permanent reminder of his conviction, and he was returned to duty. Allen received a monument that read, in part, that he had the "misfortune" of being shot by a "Negroe soldier." According to John Wood Sweet, this acknowledgment was Rhode Island's only commemoration to Black service in the Revolution for many years afterward.[36]

Later that year, on December 22, 1781, Private Fortune Stoddard of Newport faced a similar circumstance. Having just seen action in the trenches at the Battle of Yorktown, Stoddard was in Head of Elk, Maryland, with his comrades, many of whom were recovering from disease that had swept through the regiment. A drunk white mob of sailors, led by their captain, James Cunningham, had assaulted Stoddard the night previous in the same building that housed many of the sick men. Perhaps Stoddard was protecting those who could not protect themselves. Cunningham had to be restrained at the point of a loaded musket with fixed bayonet, but he returned the next day. Upon being refused liquor by the building's owner, he and the sailors began ripping up floorboards and using them as weapons against the unarmed soldiers who had come to investigate the nuisance. Having left and returned armed, one white soldier of the regiment had Cunningham cornered with his loaded musket and bayonet when Cunningham snatched it out of his hand and beat him with it. Stoddard fired at Cunningham, likely saving his white brother's life. Cunningham died within two hours. Like Greene, Stoddard was convicted of manslaughter and branded on the hand—however, because he could not pay the court costs, Cecil County wanted to sell him into slavery. Jeremiah Olney, though no supporter of Black soldiery, intervened to have the Continental Congress pay the court costs, and Stoddard was spared the worst of fates, though the veteran of Yorktown had to face the rest of the war in a Cecil County jail.[37]

Gradual, *Post-Nati* Emancipation

The abolition of slavery would be the most immediate and significant outcome of the war for Providence's Black community. The Rhode Island General Assembly in 1784 passed an act freeing the children of all enslaved people—girls on their eighteenth birthday and boys at age twenty-one. Although painfully gradual, *post-nati* (after-birth) emancipation prompted a precipitous decline in the institution statewide, but its legacy—like Black service in the Revolutionary War—was complicated, and its limitations would shape the social and political contexts in which Black community leaders operated for the next eight decades. In order to unpack the abolition of slavery, it is important to understand exactly why it came about, where the "abolition impulse" came from, and who some of the major players were. From the examination that follows, we can see why the early Black leadership class was based in Newport but also why Providence came to overshadow its island counterpart as the legacy of the Revolution was being established.

Part of the reason abolition had so many limitations was the fact that the institution of slavery was central to the development of the colony and state. As historian Christy Clark-Pujara has shown, Rhode Island shipping magnates not only enriched themselves by making Newport one "corner" of the famed Triangle Trade route, but the duties collected from slave imports added so much to the public coffers that they financed roads, bridges, and other public works projects that quite literally built the state. The rum, candles, and other materials that were traded for slaves on the coast of Africa provided the state with jobs, as did shipbuilding trades (ropemakers, caulkers, carpenters, etc.) and maritime work.[38] The farms of Rhode Island's plantation country provided food to the West Indies, feeding enslaved laborers where every available acre of fertile soil was used for staple crops. This also reinforced the institution of slaveholding in the state, as increasingly throughout the eighteenth century enslaved people themselves were forced to produce the goods that sustained slavery elsewhere.[39]

In Rhode Island, the urban maritime areas of Newport and Providence contained nearly as many enslaved people as did the countryside.[40] Reflecting a pattern that emerged throughout British North America, enslaved people in the towns were forced to be more versatile in their occupations, working as domestic servants, day jobbers, helpers on small farms, errand runners, and numerous other duties. Some apprenticed for artisan jobs, often either owned by an artisan in that trade or rented to an artisan to learn a particular skill. The fluidity in daily life, proximity to a dynamic commercial environment, tantalizing potential of escape aboard ship, and overall more frequent contact with whites and free people of color often left room for negotiations for working conditions or the opportunity to free oneself through purchase. Early community leaders largely emerged from the alliances made by those either enslaved to or working or studying under the elite white merchants and clergy. The short distances the smallest mainland colony allowed for travel also meant that ties with those enslaved on plantations were more easily maintained than they could be elsewhere—especially as evidenced during Negro Election Day, in which people of color from Providence traveled to the Warwick countryside to partake.

However advantaged urban enslavement may have seemed, the reality was that those who endured it lived as captives. Enslaved people had to face the drudgery of menial work and forfeit most, if not all, of their pay to their owners. Long days of serving white families typically gave way to uncomfortable sleeping quarters in the garrets above, basements below, or closets next to their enslavers. Apprenticeships for people of color often meant service in the home rather than valuable skilling or networking, and indentures were frequently extended or ignored because of minor infractions or municipal authorities' fear of African Americans becoming public charges. Aside from the slave market in Providence's Crown Coffee House serving as a daily reminder of their commodification, the threat of being sold southward—or kidnapped for that purpose if free—was an ever-present reality unique to people of color in Rhode Island and elsewhere in the North.[41]

Most harmful to subsequent generations, the idea that Black people were conditioned because of their nature for enslavement—an idea put into theory by Enlightenment philosophers and carried out in actuality all over the New World—was planted firmly in Rhode Island early on.[42] Laws on the statute books created the category of "negroes, Indians, and mulattoes"; all were at some point during the colonial era and after the Revolution banned from purchasing liquor, being out after a certain time, or liable for (re-)indenture or (re-)enslavement. People of color, the authorities implied, needed to be policed for their perceived temperamental deficiencies, while the only things whites were barred from doing because of their race was marrying and providing liquor to people of color.[43] Ideas about Black and Native inferiority were so firmly entrenched that they able to survive the revolutionary rhetoric around liberty and equality, but as the upheaval was getting underway, Black Rhode Islanders were able to begin chipping away at the walls that race theory had erected around whiteness.

Outside of Black resistance but directly related to it, the first rumblings against the institution of slavery were mild, conservative, and religious. The Quakers were the most famous group of early abolitionists, having spoken out against it because of the violence required to maintain it and its abrogation of the "Golden Rule."[44] Black Providence residents found perhaps their staunchest white ally in one such Quaker after he converted to the faith: Moses Brown. Born into a family of merchants, partner in various successful business ventures (some of which involved the slave trade), and an active politician, Brown's conversion to Quakerism and espousal of abolition on the grounds of Quaker philosophy immediately had a tremendously positive impact in the 1770s and beyond.[45] African Americans in Newport could count on Congregational minister Samuel Hopkins, who held that slavery was sinful and that Africans and other people of color were the "brethren" of whites, that all the enslaved should be freed and their souls saved through conversion. Brown and Hopkins were perfect allies for potential Black leaders. Brown had major cachet in both the business and political communities (which usually overlapped), access to wealth, and a genuine interest in shepherding the Black community as a whole into freedom and a more equitable form of citizenship. Hopkins teamed up with Ezra Stiles, another prominent minister whom Hopkins convinced to sponsor the education of Black Newporters selected for a mission to spread the gospel to Africa.[46]

The rhetoric of liberty, combined with Quaker and evangelical "New Divinity" sensibilities to demonize the trade and ownership of slaves in the decades before the war, put the whole idea of the institution on the defensive. Starting in the early 1770s, Moses Brown waged a campaign using his prestige and business connections to employ Quaker arguments against the institution as a whole. He began publishing letters critical of slavery in the *Providence Gazette*, a newspaper popular among the merchant elite and which was largely supported by his firm's advertising money. In November 1775, a contingent of prominent Brown-allied Providence lawyers and businesspeople, in an effort to halt the traffic in enslaved people, petitioned the General Assembly, asking it to prevent the introduction of "negros" into the colony. If any enslaved person of color was in fact brought to Rhode Island, they requested the assembly immediately free that person. "Those who are desirous of enjoying all the advantages of Liberty themselves," the petitioners reasoned, "should be willing to Extend personal Liberty to others."[47] The petition was read into the record and adopted: Black citizenship had officially come up for negotiation in the state's highest seats of power.

By 1779, over two hundred Black soldiers, most of them formerly enslaved, had enlisted. Black men in uniform were guarding Providence's arms stores and formed a large contingent of those charged with protecting the town from possible British invasion. Add to this that enslaved people were also using the chaos of the war to free themselves by running away—doing so at twice the rate they had before—and we can see that Black resistance was making the collapse of the entire institution of slavery seem possible.[48] In May of the same year, an enslaved woman named Abigail got the General Assembly to go on record formally opposing the institution. Along with her three children, Abigail escaped her captor when his intent to sell them all to North Carolina was uncovered, and she sought legal protection from the assembly.[49] That October, the General Assembly showed that it had begun mobilizing against the institution when it passed an act forbidding the sale out of state of any enslaved person, calling such an action "against the rights of human nature" and declaring slavery itself a condition that "this General Assembly are dispos'd rather to alleviate, till some favourable Occasion may offer for its total Abolition."[50] All three drafters of the 1779 act were mainlanders, and two of them, Welcome

Arnold and David Howell, represented Providence, which was rapidly becoming the epicenter of the ideological countercurrent against slavery.

The Revolution also precipitated a dramatic decline in Newport's prominence within the state. This shift largely occurred because of Britain's controlling Newport throughout much of the war, choking off economic activity and depleting the city's entire population by nearly half—from 9,209 to 5,530. The slave trade was no longer functioning there, having moved inland to the coffers and ships of Bristol's D'Wolf family. The economic and political center of gravity had dramatically and quickly shifted to Providence, which overtook Newport in customs house receipts by 1790, and where closer connections with inland towns, farms, and factories fueled a temporary shipping boom.[51] There, the rhetoric of liberty had been allowed to flourish among its merchants. The collapse of the geographic center of slavery in the state was the last pillar propping up the institution.[52]

By the time the war ended in 1783, the *Providence Gazette* was seemingly persuading its readers to accept the end of slavery. It reprinted editorials from around the country, like one by "Justice" in Pennsylvania, who addressed a letter to his state's legislature at the request of "B" (Moses Brown?) and called the enslaving of others due to the color of their skin a practice that was "repugnant" and "tyrannical."[53] The *Gazette* then printed a petition from the Quakers of Providence, led by Moses Brown, that offered text for an act of gradual abolition—something that sought middle ground, assuring those who hated slavery on its face but feared Black freedom that the transition would be calculated and smooth. The proposal only offered freedom to those born after a certain date (January 1, 1784, in the original petition, which was written in December 1783), and then only after a period of forced apprenticeship until the ages of eighteen for girls and twenty-one for boys.[54]

The petition made its way to the General Assembly, which moved remarkably quickly. Regrettably, the assembly did not record the debate on Thursday, February 26, 1784, but the act proposed in the petition passed both the lower and upper houses (which would later be named the House of Representatives and Senate, respectively) and fixed the subsequent Monday (March 1) as the date the law would take effect. It was essentially, word for word, the same text as the Quaker petition, a manifestation of the influence the Brown contingent had in the legislature. A second and important clause of the gradual emancipation act was one that required towns to see to the education of the free children born to enslaved mothers, as "Principles of Morality and Religion . . .

reading, writing and Arithmatic" were crucial requirements for the independence envisioned for them by the assembly.⁵⁵

After a political backlash weakened the influence of Brown and the merchant elites, the October 1785 session of the General Assembly passed a new act repealing this second clause. The new law instead forced the mother's owner to ensure the care of the free child, along with any enslaved person manumitted voluntarily by an owner. This set the stage for the nature of independence—an essential contour of citizenship—to become an ideological battleground where race, rights, and republican principles were weaponized in competing visions of American citizenship. One, led by people of color, Moses Brown, and his ideological heirs, saw the structure of government and philanthropists (many of whom were one in the same) assuming responsibility for the protection and education of the formerly enslaved and their children, so that at a later time distinctions of race might be dissolved and people of color would hold the same privileges and immunities as anyone else. After all, people of color had played a vital role in the defeat of tyranny and victory of personal liberty, and as such, "humanity require[d]" they be "entitled to Life, Liberty and the Pursuit of Happiness," the original emancipation act stated in an echo of the Declaration of Independence.⁵⁶

Another vision, however, encoded in the law by the October 1785 act, professed a deeply rooted anxiety about the perceived dependence of people of color and the "extremely burthensome" cost predicted to even start the project of emancipation.⁵⁷ By that year the state was coming to grips with the debt incurred by the Revolution and the dislocations of thousands of people during the chaos of the previous decade. The economic insecurity blunted the Providence faction's power in the legislature, most of whose members were antislavery, pro-urban mercantilism, and in favor of centralizing authority; their adherence to a collective view of prosperity was the most likely inducement for them to proactively ensure the smooth transition out of slavery for people of color, despite the painful limitations they agreed to. The backlash ushered in by recession led to the creation of the Country Party, which held personal liberty and decentralization of authority sacrosanct. Their ascendancy meant Rhode Island would be the last of the original thirteen colonies to ratify the Constitution, but their individualism also placed the burden on African Americans themselves to elbow their way into the body politic—one that, for nearly two centuries, had relegated most to slavery. Black leaders would have to operate in this environment, as they had in the decades before the

Revolution, but the narrow opening emancipation provided meant that Black leaders could at least establish themselves and begin searching for ways to break down the stubbornly resistant obstacles that slavery and race had placed in front of them.

Emigration, Colonization, and Black Leadership

Before abolition and even the Revolution, whether through "Negro elections" or closer alignment with the colonial power structure in general, Black leaders worked to improve the lots of their communities. The Black men associated with Samuel Hopkins and his missionary plans were perhaps the first class to undertake organizational leadership in the newly forming country. Two who showed early promise in leading the effort were John Quamine and Bristol Yamma. In 1773, Hopkins identified them to Stiles as members of Hopkins's congregation who, if all could engage the funding and support from other elites, were eligible candidates to spread the gospel in Africa. Quamine was born on the Gold Coast of Africa (present-day Ghana) and kidnapped by a ship captain at the age of ten in 1754 or 1755. The captain had secured schooling for him for a few years before the treachery, but Quamine was able to retain a fluency in his native Fanti language. After being sent to Rhode Island in 1773, he freed himself by winning a lottery split with a friend. He showed an interest in religion, and the combination of his education, language proficiency, and Christian zeal appealed to Hopkins's missionary mind. Quamine was also recommended to Hopkins by Reverend Philip Quaque, the first person of African descent ordained in the Church of England, who knew of Quamine's family in Africa and his desire to return to them.[58] Little is known about Yamma's early life except that he was born in Africa, was still enslaved by the time Hopkins determined to send him to the College of New Jersey (later renamed Princeton University), and that he too retained some fluency in his first language. Both men were married with children in Newport, a fact that must have given each pause as they contemplated returning to the lands of their birth.[59]

It was most likely around this time that Hopkins befriended someone who was to become a community leader later in the eighteenth and then early nineteenth century: Newport Gardner. Gardner was born Occramer Marycoo in Africa around the year 1746 and sold into slavery in an eerie echo of Quamine's story: at age fourteen, he was promised an education by a ship captain who kidnapped him instead. He was bought by Caleb Gardner in Newport (who renamed him), and recognizing the young man's capacity for learning, saw to it that he received an education in the city.[60] A self-starter and born leader, Newport Gardner quickly learned English and music on his own. He also came to the attention of Hopkins, again most likely attracted to the young man's capacity for learning, his retention of his own language, and the desire to return to Africa as a missionary—though missionary work may have just been the avenue toward his real goal, returning to his home. Regardless, Hopkins later proclaimed that Gardner was "a discerning, judicious, steady, good man," and was second in many things only to Bristol Yamma.[61]

In 1774, Quamine and Yamma sailed for Princeton, and by 1776 Salmar Nubia had been engaged to join the two missionaries in the scheme. Nubia, like Quamine and Yamma, was born in Africa and taken from the Windward Coast (in present-day Côte d'Ivoire), though he grew up in the African interior. The whole plan, however, collapsed within three years. The Revolutionary War took away the attention and funding of the mission's sponsors, as well as potential support from the state's Black communities, much of which had mobilized for the patriot cause. This included John Quamine, who decided at some point that the war was perhaps a better avenue for freedom, at least for the time being. He enlisted to serve aboard a privateer, hoping to secure prize money enough to free his wife. Instead of saving souls as a missionary, he died trying to save his family in 1779.[62]

Gardner, Yamma, and Nubia, along with Caesar Lyndon, an enslaved man who was so shrewd in business that he became wealthy enough to loan money to free white men, and others formed the core of the Free African Union Society, founded in Newport on November 10, 1780. While most of its records for the 1780s are missing, by 1787 the group was partially a mutual benefit society—paying its members' families for expenses incurred during sickness, death, or other hardships and seeking to record births, marriages, and deaths of the Black community—and partially an African emigration society.[63] Benefit societies had existed everywhere from the African continent to the New World plantations to the American cities, but this one was, according to many historians, the first to record its proceedings.[64] Meetings took place in the homes of its members, most often that of Abraham Casey, a formerly enslaved man who purchased his freedom by becoming a chocolatier for merchant Aaron Lopez.[65] It appears that most members probably had similar backgrounds, with many bearing names commonly associated with enslavement:

classical names like Prince, Caesar, or Cato; those of places like Bristol, Newport, and London; or those of powerful Rhode Island families who held slaves like Lyndon, Gardner, and Casey. African names and naming patterns, like Zingo, Quarm, and Cuffe, also predominated in the society's record books. By 1787, the prominence of emigration on the agenda suggests that those who were African-born made up a powerful bloc within the organization.[66]

On July 27, 1789, Newport leaders Anthony Taylor and Salmar Nubia wrote to their "affectionate brethren" in Providence, urging them to form their own chapter of the Free African Union Society and partake in a new emigration scheme. They wrote specifically to Cato Gardner and London Spear, about whom little is known, except that their names suggest similar backgrounds to the Newport leaders. Gardner and Spear wrote back a week later, saying that they had "assembled [their] brethren together" to consider Free African Union Society's proposal, and that it was met with enthusiasm, though the meeting was cut short by a storm. The next day, August 5, Bristol Yamma, who had since moved to Providence, and James McKenzie (about whom very little is known before this point) wrote back, saying that Gardner and Spear had forwarded them the letter and they were happy to form their own chapter. By September 22, Providence had formed a society with McKenzie as secretary, Cato Coggeshall as president, Bristol Yamma as "moderator," and Bonner Brown as treasurer. "Representatives" were London Spear, Bristol Olney, Cudgo (in other places spelled "Cudge") Brown, Cato Mumford, William Stober, and Felix Holbrook. The first leadership class in Providence's Black community had etched their names into posterity.[67]

The Providence chapter, like that of Newport's, would be a mutual benefit society, with members paying dues in the expectation that should any member's family become destitute or in need of money, they would have access to the common pot. Members would have to pay two schillings at every quarterly meeting, and no one would be able to continue without having already put in eighteen schillings in the first three years. Each applicant to the society was also to be "examined" and approved by two-thirds of the representative committee. The financial requirements ensured that the society would remain under the control of those in the community with money to spare, and the examination each prospective member had to go through meant the society was looking for more than just monetarily successful people—perhaps this was an affirmation that they wanted to keep the society respectable. They decided that the society was to be a subordinate auxiliary of the parent one of Newport, requesting that they have access to the Free African Union Society's pot of money should their treasury be unable to support a destitute member but offering that their officers would be of inferior rank to those of Newport.[68]

The Providence society was certainly made up of the Black elite in one important regard: most headed their own households and were owners of their own homes. An achievement that showed the kind of independence and control necessary for republican citizenship, heading one's own household was, according to historian Robert Cottrol, "the first step in the building of Black institutions." With 27 percent of Black Providence residents living in Black-headed households in 1790—an increase of only 10 percent since 1774—but only 16 percent of all Black residents still enslaved, it was clear that, despite the precipitous decline in the institution, slavery's social legacy was still holding strong. Few had yet been able to work their way out from under white control.[69] Of this group of ten leaders, eight headed their own households at some point before 1810, and six of them owned their own homes.[70] At least five of them were formerly enslaved.[71] Most, like their counterparts in Newport, bore names associated with slavery—including surnames of prominent Rhode Island families to whom they may have been enslaved and places they may have been born—or African naming patterns ("Cudge" or "Cudgo" especially were most likely corruptions or pronunciations of some West African societies' name for boys born on a Monday).[72] Some also had connections with white elites—whether through work relationships that offered avenues for deal-making, physical proximity, or possibly even familial relationships—links to power that Providence's Black leaders would exploit in the future as well. The members' wide variety of occupations, places of origin, and skills meant that the primary elements uniting them were their personal prosperity in a state that sought to limit them, and their goals for improving the lots of each other and their community.

For four of these men, very little information exists in the archives. What we do know is that Cato Coggeshall, London Spear, William Stober, and Bristol Olney all owned their own homes by 1798. Spear, a cooper by trade and also a huckster, owned a home on Benevolent Street, near Rhode Island College (now Brown University), on the large hill east of the Providence River. Stober, a seaman from South Carolina, lived nearby on the East Side. He was not listed as a head of household until 1810; perhaps his life on the ocean kept him away when earlier census-takers came canvassing. Coggeshall, a teamster, owned his home on Charles Street, which would have been at the northern edge of the town in a popular mixed-race neighborhood surrounding Olney's Lane. There, Bristol Olney owned a small home (valued at only $70) and also rented one from a Mary Simmons. Olney, who worked as a laborer on municipal projects, must have made enough to support a large extended family, renting two other houses in which twelve people lived in unspecified locations in the town. He most likely had to work extra hard as well: records indicate that for hauling a load of stone for use in building a fountain in town, he was paid only three-quarters of what a white man was paid for the same task. According to historian Jay Coughtry and colleagues, the Black Olneys were one of the oldest families in Rhode Island. Bristol had a relative of the same name who died in the Revolutionary War in 1781, and his son William would carry on his father's work in the Providence branch of the Union Society as a representative of the branch to Newport meetings.[73]

Cudge Brown and Bonner Brown had both been enslaved to the firm Moses Brown and his brothers ran; they had the good fortune of being selected by Moses to work for him personally, and he freed them after his conversion to Quakerism. Cudge was born in Africa and enslaved with his brothers in the white Brown brothers' firm. He worked as a teamster, driving between Moses's farm and another. Before his emancipation, Moses allowed Cudge to live with his wife, Phillis, on property set aside for him, and offered to pay for his education, an opportunity he took advantage of for eight weeks. The lot granted to him was on Olney Street, and he eventually saved enough money to buy that lot and part of an adjacent one, build a house there himself, and raise his four children with Phillis. He continued to work for Moses and had his sons work for Moses also. Bonner, it appears, also received a lot from Moses and farmed on it, though he was not listed as a head of household until 1820.[74] Little is known about Bonner, but he had ascended to the Providence branch of the Union Society's presidency by 1794.[75]

Cato Mumford was enslaved before and during the war to Nathaniel Mumford, a ship captain who engaged actively in the slave trade during the 1760s. Cato had become acquainted with the wealthy merchant Joseph Nightingale, probably having served in the regiment Nightingale commanded during the war. Mumford's freedom was apparently more precarious than most veterans, as he was forced to earn it by working for Nightingale for two years—the result of an agreement between Mumford's master and Nightingale.[76] Later, despite having taken on a community leadership role and passing the Union Society's respectability tests, he was nearly "warned out" of Providence after being labeled a transient. Nightingale wrote to the town council on Mumford's behalf, vouching for his character.[77] Mumford also lived for a time in Newport, where he may have met Bristol Yamma; the two were probably special links between the Newport and Providence organizations, having spent time in both towns.[78] Mumford and Yamma were listed as subscribers to Samuel Hopkins's *System of Doctrines Contained in Divine Revelation*, evidencing another valuable ideological and personal connection to both the society and its missionary aim.[79] Yamma had also been acquainted with Moses Brown through Hopkins and John Quamine during the original emigration planning, delivering messages to the Providence philanthropist from Newport.[80]

Felix Holbrook brought a history of activist zeal to the society, having been a part of the society that petitioned the Massachusetts legislature for their "civil and religious liberty" in 1773. Holbrook and his enslaved compatriots cited the ways in which white Massachusettsans "have made such a noble stand against the designs of their fellow-men to enslave them," and how "the divine spirit of freedom seems to fire every humane breast on this continent," before claiming that it was their "natural right" to wish to alleviate their condition as well. Well-versed in the founding republican ideology of the country, Holbrook, having been born in Africa, nevertheless signed off on the petition's later stated goal of raising enough money for a joint venture between white and Black people to settle a designated area of coastal Africa.[81] Like the Providence society he would join, he saw that the racial proscriptions in the province overheating with liberty fever were too entrenched to overcome his perceived "natural rights." His time in Boston might have put him in the antislavery circles of the more well-known Prince Hall, the founder of Black freemasonry, and poet Phillis Wheatley, both of whom had acknowledged the emigrationist goals of the Rhode Islanders but neither of whom offered much support.[82] After leaving Boston to fight in the First Rhode Island Regiment, Holbrook settled in North Providence where he was listed as the head of a household in 1790. Like Mumford, he lived on the edge of freedom, having had a warrant drawn up to forcibly remove him from Providence to Boston because of supposed vagrancy.[83]

Another person who put action behind his words was James McKenzie. Little is known about McKenzie's life before his service in the African Union Society, except that he came to Rhode Island on a prison ship from Charleston, South Carolina, near the close of the Revolutionary War. McKenzie and Yamma were the two who responded most enthusiastically to the call to form a society in the late summer of 1789 and seemed the most committed to the emigration plan. McKenzie then led a failed mission to start a settlement in West Africa in 1794–1795, an event that proved to be the fulcrum on which the balance of ideological power in Providence's Black community turned away from the emigrationists and toward those advocating liberation inside the American body politic.[84]

Emigration as an avenue toward freedom had been resurrected in 1787 with the founding of the British settlement for free people of African descent in Sierra Leone in West Africa. William Thornton, a Quaker planter from the Virgin Islands and proponent of the new free colony, spent much of that year in Newport drumming up support for a voyage of settlers, and with many of the Newport and Providence Free African Union Society members having been kidnapped from homes in Africa and showing a desire to return, he saw a welcoming audience.[85] The societies and their white allies, Moses Brown and Samuel Hopkins, paid close attention to the progress of the colony over the next few years, and Yamma and McKenzie traveled back and forth between Newport and Providence in preparation for the mission. In early 1793, Yamma expressed interest in leading a mission to the prospering community of Freetown in Sierra Leone, but by the summer he had contracted an illness and Hopkins urged him to go to North Carolina, thinking that the warmer weather there would help him recover. He died there in January 1794 before the revived emigration plans could get underway.[86]

This time, the seeds of its failure had been sown earlier than the death of one of its core proponents. In 1789, Newport and Providence had reached out to other Black community leaders in the northeastern United States and garnered a stunning lack of support for the mission from them. From Boston, Prince Hall, who had recently committed to fostering African American leadership through his Black freemason lodge, responded to the Newport society's overtures for support of emigration with a simple reply claiming he had received it but had little to say in response. This may have been due to the Rhode Islanders' reliance on the support of William Thornton—who had himself expressed doubts about the motives of other white benefactors—rather than their own leadership. Hall and the Bostonians had petitioned the Massachusetts legislature for funding for a similar mission but had always couched their ideas in more self-determinist, perhaps early Black nationalistic language. From Philadelphia's Free African Society came a reply that appealed to their brethren to strive for respectability at home, to "continue daily in fasting from sin and iniquity" in order that "the Lord thereby may be pleased to break every yoke and make the oppressed go free." "With regard to the emigration, you mention, to Africa," the society wrote, "we have at present but little to communicate on that head, apprehending every pious man is a good citizen of the whole world."[87] Reflecting the ideology of the group's founders, ministers Richard Allen and Absalom Jones, and dominated by formerly enslaved men born in nearby Delaware and New Jersey, the Philadelphia society professed an early evangelical abolitionism aimed at improving the lives of African Americans in the only home they knew.[88]

The Providence and Newport societies' other means of support, their white allies in the state, also began to retreat from the mission. Moses Brown and his Quaker companions in Providence had set up the Providence Society for Abolishing the Slave Trade in February 1789, a few months before the Providence branch of the African Union Society was organized. The Providence Abolition Society, with its profession that "it having pleased the Creator of mankind to make of one blood all nations of men," vowed to assist those who, "by fraud or violence are or may be detained in bondage."[89] As Brown had been doing in the years since his conversion to Quakerism, the Abolition Society dedicated itself to using the legal system and its coffers to free the victims of the slave trade, for a time in legal limbo in Rhode Island, and other refugees from the violence of slavery.[90] However, it made no mention of (re)patriating African Americans—a break from Samuel Hopkins's and even Moses Brown's prior activist leanings. With Brown embroiling himself in a public fight against the slave traders, including his brother John, and concentrating his efforts on the legal system, Hopkins was left as the main white supporter of the mission. In a General Assembly dominated by Anti-Federalists, who stood opposed to Quaker moralism and looked the other way in the face of the reemerging Rhode Island slave trade, the support Hopkins hoped to garner there would not be forthcoming.[91]

On January 15, 1794, the Providence branch of the Free African Union Society wrote to Newport to propose sending one Black man each from Providence, Philadelphia, and Boston to Sierra Leone as emissaries to secure land and support for a new settlement there. The Newport society's Newport Gardner, who had been holding onto the hope of returning to his home, wondered why the Providence society should have made such a move without either consulting the Newport branch or seeking a representative from there. The Providence branch replied, acknowledging their overreach but happily reporting that James McKenzie and William Olney were excellent candidates, possessing "extensive knowledge of land affairs." They asked if the Newport branch had anyone that they wanted to send on the mission, to which the island branch replied naturally proposing that their representative be Newport Gardner. Funding the mission remained a complicating factor, however. The Providence branch discussed how enthusiastic their white neighbors seemed, writing, "It is impossible for you to form any Idea of the incouragement we meet with. Every white person in Town seem to be forward in promoting the matter." The Newport branch deemed white support there less forthcoming despite Hopkins's zeal, writing tentatively that they wanted to keep the matter quiet before laying it before their town's abolition society. Besides, they reminded Providence, the mainland branch needed to await word on state funding or the approval of Moses Brown; no outreach to or from Boston and Philadelphia was saved in the society's records.[92]

By late 1794, a way had opened for the mission to get started without much funding. With the British and French distracted by their ongoing war and unable to carry on their West African trade, the firm of Brown, Benson & Ives (owned by Moses Brown's nephew Nicholas) outfitted one of their ships, the *Charlotte*, to ply the West African coast with Rhode Island wares, concentrating on the Sierra Leone area. James McKenzie, with his experience as a seaman, was able to secure a spot on the ship as second mate, most likely at the behest of Moses Brown. The *Charlotte* entered Freetown in January 1795. While the captain was negotiating the value of the ship's commodities with the settlement's white governor, Zachary Macauley, the governor was also meeting with McKenzie and discussing the terms of a proposed settlement of Rhode Island's Black families. Apparently, the Providence branch of the society had been given bad information that the colony was looking to attract "all & every Householder that will or shall arrive within the space of six years" by offering free land. The timing was also off; the French had sacked and burned Freetown in December 1794, while the *Charlotte* was on its way there. It arrived just as the town was struggling to recover from that trauma. Nevertheless, Macauley agreed to provide land for twelve families so long as they had certificates from Samuel Hopkins acknowledging their sobriety, honesty, and industry. McKenzie returned on the *Charlotte*'s home voyage, perhaps with the hope of seeing the mission through, especially because the governor apparently believed McKenzie's behavior to have been "proper and becoming."[93]

Nothing ever came of the plan to have six Black families emigrate, however. Samuel Hopkins wrote to Macauley in September 1795 but apparently did not endorse any families for emigration—either from Providence or Newport. While his abandonment of the scheme after endorsing it for so long puzzled historian George E. Brooks, who wrote about the failed mission, its undoing was probably more rooted in the fact that it was managed by whites people rather than the prospective Black settlers themselves. Hopkins, after all, had himself been suspicious of other white collaborators.[94] Macauley's strict requirements and his need for another white man to certify prospective settlers may have signaled to Black Rhode Islanders that their liberation was still contingent on the whims of whites and not their own self-determination. This mission's failure was an early manifestation of the related, but divergent notions of emigration and colonization as solutions to the "problem" imposed by Black freedom in a country that contradictorily professed liberty as its basis while continuing to profit from enslaved labor. Emigration, or voluntarily leaving the country, was a strategy that African Americans would employ throughout the history of the republic, and according to Manisha Sinha, was "based on a vindication of Black equality." Colonization, by contrast, was a tactic employed by whites to send freed African Americans abroad under whites' patronage for purposes ranging from ostensibly providing freedom for Black people in a land that refused to recognize them as citizens, to "Christianizing" non-Christian societies abroad, to ridding the white republic of a perceived nuisance. Black people, however, nearly universally refused to participate in colonization schemes—they often saw such plans as disruptive of their own or their collective self-liberation, especially when it was understood that a major underlying motive was to perpetuate and strengthen the institution of slavery. While the situation in 1794–1795 was a bit muddier than the emigration and colonization plans of the nineteenth century, especially since some of the correspondence among the Providence branch of the Union Society, Hopkins, and Moses Brown is missing from the records, it certainly foreshadowed Black resistance to any plan that did not include their own visions of freedom and citizenship.[95]

A Lone Voice

The immediate post-Revolution years represented a high tide for the leadership of the emigrationists, most of whom were African-born and had endured capture and slavery in their earlier lives. The desire to return coupled with the lack of opportunity the new republic promised for them, the latter being particularly evident when Rhode Island's political climate underwent a conservative swing away from Federalism, resulted in a leadership class that prioritized self-liberation outside of the body politic. In the coming years, the idea of seeking citizenship elsewhere would wane dramatically, especially when the motives of the American Colonization Society were laid bare and rejected by most Black and white abolitionist Rhode Islanders. If the Revolutionary War veterans of color lived to see their pensions as largely the only fruit of their labor, and the formerly enslaved saw only severely circumscribed freedom, they in their old age and the subsequent generation would build on the Negro Election Day governors' and Free African Union Society branches' more pragmatic aims—community sustenance and a commitment to improvement of their condition where they were.

Anthony Kinnicutt's action of self-liberation stands out during this period as perhaps the clearest attempt to become part of the body politic, one that would be emulated by the subsequent generation, and it occurred even before the republic officially came into being. Kinnicutt, "free born, although not wholly of White blood," was a prosperous victualler on Providence's wharf, where he supplied ships with wares and liquor—the latter of which he had to purchase a license to sell. Although he did not fight with the First Rhode Island Regiment in the American Revolution, he had pledged to support the war effort along with other men of Providence in 1775, and he invested $35 to sponsor a quarter of a share in a privateering venture undertaken by the sloop of war *Sally* in early 1778. Kinnicutt then decided to test whether the rhetoric of liberty and equality was really as universal as it seemed, or if "White blood" was one of the necessary prerequisites for citizenship in the proposed country.[96]

By 1778, with shipping at a standstill and capital almost entirely diverted to the war effort, Kinnicutt's business had most likely taken a hit. That may be why, in addition to connections with ship captains and merchants, he thought to invest in a privateer. That may also be why he decided to petition the town council, asking it to either make him a voter or relieve him of his tax burden. Regardless of his reasoning, the petition he submitted to the "Freemen of the Town of Providence" assembled for their March 1778 meeting was a starkly worded affirmation of the position he perceived for himself in the republic, one that urged the town to disregard the color of his skin and focus on his independence, industry, and ability to acquire and maintain property. His assertion of being born free distanced himself from slavery and his apparent allusion to partial white ancestry may have been a hedge against a potential negative reply because of his skin color. "By his Attention to his Business," his petition stated, "he hath been enabled many years ago to purchase a small real estate or lot joining to Power's Lane in Providence, which he will prosseseth, and further to render great Assistance to his family and children." With that as a basis, he asked for "the Privilege of being a Freeman of the Town like another Man if his real estate should be of sufficient Value," or if rejected, that "he ought to be exonerated from the Payment of any Rates and Taxes." He too felt that taxation without representation was tyranny.[97]

Kinnicutt's appeal to "freemanship" through possessing enough real estate points to an issue that would become a flashpoint not just for Rhode Island's people of color but also later for its poor whites. When the state's charter in 1663 created the General Assembly, the royal government authorized it to create a body of "freemen" who were to be "men of competante estates and of civill conversation," and who would "have the liberty to choose and be chosen as officers both civill and military." The freemen were the only people authorized to vote, and by 1760 the General Assembly had fixed the minimum real estate requirement at £40 (or $134). As historian Patrick Conley pointed out, one needed not only to possess the minimum amount of real estate but also to apply to the assembly or be nominated by the town's chief officer—a fact often neglected by historians of the state. Town councils like that of Providence also required applications for freemanship. This essentially created two tiers of citizenship: colony (subsequently state) and municipal. The right to choose representatives—a privilege that lay at the heart of republican citizenship—was closely guarded.[98]

In a way, Kinnicutt was doing nothing different than his white neighbors who were as successful as he had been. His attempt to downplay his ancestry and the color of his skin signals that whiteness was an implied requirement for freemanship, or citizenship, even though no such proscription was explicitly written. Otherwise, Kinnicutt might not have bothered to apply. What he was up against was race ideology, the brand that slavery had cast on all New World settlements dominated by Europeans—Rhode Island included. His petition also shows that people of color now had a new weapon to fight against racism: the rhetoric of liberty, the founding philosophy, which included the exploitable contradictions of natural, "unalienable" rights theory and race ideology.

Anthony Kinnicutt was never admitted to freemanship. Instead, after a second petition later in 1778, he was granted an exemption from taxation. Apparently dissatisfied with the outcome, he left town a few years later—though not before loaning the town one hundred dollars to pay its bounties for forty-three military volunteers. One of the beneficiaries of Kinnicutt's action was Felix Holbrook. Like his emigrationist counterpart, he was forced to seek his citizenship elsewhere.[99]

However, Kinnicutt's petition would serve as the blueprint for later campaigns for the right to vote. In the late eighteenth century, the state could sacrifice one man's contribution to its coffers in exchange for keeping the contradiction between freedom and race ideology alive. The next generation of leaders, this time based solely in Providence and operating with more ideological and economic firepower, would begin making similar arguments that Kinnicutt made in his petitions. In the early nineteenth century, Providence's Black community would face a rising tide of white supremacy but also build on existing alliances and foster a leadership class capable of undertaking a collective effort like the one Kinnicutt took by himself.

CHAPTER 2

"Dignified Abeyance"

EVOLVING BLACK LEADERSHIP AND DISFRANCHISEMENT

As Providence's William Jones, Speaker of Rhode Island's General Assembly, was about to be elected governor in 1811, his servant Claude Gabriel apparently grew frustrated with his life in the growing town. Gabriel was born in Portugal, most likely to enslaved people of African descent, and had taken up life as a ship steward in the French West Indies before settling in New York City; Stonington, Connecticut; and finally Providence—where he came "highly recommended" to the Jones family. Gabriel decided to return to sea aboard a ship bound for Russia, despite having two young children with his wife, Prudence, and a secure job serving an elite family. His move was emblematic of the political situation African Americans in Providence—and all over the North—faced. Jones was a Federalist, and apparently cared for Gabriel's family's wellbeing, but the realities of the hardening color line meant that Gabriel could hope for little more than generosity and goodwill—on Jones's terms and, in the years before a leadership class more fully coalesced, as long as his prosperity remained his alone and not his community's.[1]

By 1811, almost thirty years after the close of the Revolution, Providence had drastically changed. Its population of people of color had more than doubled; according to census data, there were 371 people of color (303 "Blacks" and 68 "Indians") in 1774, and by 1810 there were 871. They remained just above 8 percent of the total population of the town throughout this period. The population overall had also more than doubled—from 4,321 to 10,070, overtaking

Newport as the state's most populous town.² By 1810, a full 65 percent of African Americans lived in Black-headed households, signifying a shift in the power dynamics that slavery had wrought.³ While many still worked for white employers, relationships between whites and people of color were much more transactional in nature—and as the latter became more independent, numerous, and increasingly crowded into tenement neighborhoods with poor whites, interactions could be quite hostile. Alliances with elite whites, some of which held over from slavery and many of which were sustained through the presumption of benefits for each side, provided the Black communities growing around Benefit Street, Power Street, Olney's Lane, and "Hard-Scrabble" (an impoverished neighborhood near Olney's Lane) a modicum of protection.⁴ It helped that many Providence elites, including William Jones, were Federalists, who around the country were clinging to a relatively more inclusive understanding of liberty than were the proslavery Jeffersonians—the latter of whom dominated Newport, Bristol, and the rural areas of the state that were declining in population.⁵

Like Anthony Kinnicutt, Claude Gabriel's intellect, ambition, and ability to maintain his family's prosperity would certainly have afforded him a more equitable citizenship if he had been born in different skin. Gabriel spoke fluent French and spent much of his earnings in Providence learning to speak and read English. While one account says that he returned to sea in 1811 in the capacity of cook, another says that he was either a doctor or the ship's "foremost hand."⁶ Regardless, once in Russia, Gabriel apparently sought out or mutually agreed to work as a body servant to Russian tsar Alexander I. We know this because William Jones wrote to the U.S. minister to Russia and future president John Quincy Adams, himself a Federalist transitioning to the Madison-Monroe wing of the Democratic-Republican Party, under the assumption that Gabriel had been detained by the Russian government against his will. "He is perfectly well satisfied with his condition here," Adams replied to Jones, "which is a very advantageous one." Gabriel's only disappointment was his wife's refusal to join him in Russia with their children. The next year, the tsar sponsored Gabriel's return trip to Providence to convince his wife to emigrate to Russia. While there, he initially received a hero's welcome, perhaps in part due to now-governor Jones's influence. Just thirty years after they would have been a common sight in Providence, the town marveled at the festooned and uniformed Black man, adorned with "well filled pockets" and dress sword sheathed at his side.[7] However, according to Adams, upon his return to Russia (which he made with his wife and children), Gabriel "complain[ed] about having been ill treated in America, and that he was obliged to lay aside his superb dress and sabre, which he had been ordered to wear, but which occasioned people to insult and even beat him."[8] The visible signs of his success abroad, along with his exhibiting the traits that should mark someone for republican citizenship, was threatening to the racial order of the American republic.

Adams then relayed something Gabriel said that reflected the reality of the position of African Americans all over the North as the slow transition out of slavery failed to carry with it the freedom promised by the Revolution. Gabriel told Adams that he was "not a citizen of the United States, but considers himself as a free man, and best qualified to judge of the manner in which he is to provide for himself and his family."[9] Legally, he was right. As someone not born in the United States, he could not, per the Naturalization Acts of the 1790s, become a naturalized citizen because he was not a "free white person," the first requirement laid out for naturalization. The insertion of the word "white" into naturalization law had far-reaching effects on race and citizenship, including Chief Justice Roger Taney's rationale for his claims that citizenship was a privilege meant only for white men in his famous *Dred Scott* decision.[10] For Gabriel, his assertion falls in a long line of those made by the Newport and Providence branches of the Free African Union Society before him, as well as the more cohesive (but not monolithic) leadership class that would develop by the close of the 1810s. By then, the leaders were hoping that the exposition of race being the only factor preventing their access to the rights of citizenship would help remove that obstacle. Collectively, the leaders in the generation from 1790 to 1820 were forced to confront a rejuvenated spirit of white supremacy, which had recombined quickly after the rhetoric of personal liberty and Black service in the Revolutionary War felled slavery in the region. This time, most emigrationist sentiment was dropped. While Black leaders were able to build on the foundation laid by the Revolutionary generation, they had yet to unite around a strategy or cause. But from what we can reconstruct about this largely forgotten era, we can see that community uplift and inclusion into the ranks of citizenship were high priorities. They could do little to stop the political sea-change that swept the word "white" into the state's statutory voting qualification in 1822, but the unfavorable climate provided the impetus for a more concerted push for citizenship.

Leadership before Disfranchisement

The northern and southern power brokers worked out a compromise over the meaning of liberty in the new republic, leaving intact the racial proscriptions inherent in the founding philosophy despite African Americans' and Native Americans' playing an important role in the war for independence. In effect, the country doubled down on its commitment to white supremacy. As the three-fifths clause enshrined the power of proslavery officialdom for the foreseeable future and naturalization laws required foreigners to be "white" if they wanted to become citizens, the barrier of whiteness was officially applied to another important avenue of citizenship. The Militia Act of 1792 outlined that the country's defense would be undertaken by state militias, which were to be organized and composed of "every free able-bodied white male citizen of the respective States."[11] This put the Revolutionary War veterans of color in Rhode Island in the unusual position of being officially acknowledged for their services by receiving federal pensions while being told that their and their descendants' service was no longer desired. More importantly for the descendants of the First Rhode Island Regiment, the line drawn around being white and male for future soldiery undermined claims to citizenship based on their fathers' service. As outlined in Enlightenment republican philosophy and brought up in future debates about Black citizenship, this even implied for Black men a status equal to that of women and children.

Colonial laws that had evolved in slavery and severely proscribed freedoms for people of color were carried over in the new state, whose General Assembly was dominated by the Anti-Federalist and Democratic-Republican–allied Country Party. The Rhode Island digests of laws well into the nineteenth century contained statutes written before the Revolution and gradual abolition, including one from 1770 that allowed authorities, after breaking up a "disorderly house" kept by "Free Negroes and Mulattoes," to "bind out" to servitude its residents for a period of time of up to two years. Newer laws included proscriptions on interracial marriage (something even abolitionists like Samuel Hopkins refused to countenance), a prohibition on town councils' granting liquor licenses to any "colored or Black person," and a clause in the same law preventing the employment of any "Black or colored person" to sell liquor.[12] If specific curfews and laws limiting the movement or assembly of people of color did not make it into the new digests, custom certainly marked people of color for stricter policing.[13] Taken alongside the anxiously written 1785 addendum to the gradual abolition law, which removed the responsibility of freed people who became "chargeable" from the municipality to the former owner, we see both a pattern of distrust in African American liberty and a formal acknowledgment of their supposed inability to act as independent agents of their own lives—a crucial element in the denial of their citizenship.

The paranoia about "chargeability" and African Americans' lack of independence was also manifested clearly in the idea behind the "warning out" system. As historian Ruth Wallace Herndon has pointed out, the warning out system was adapted from English common law, specifically the custom that local authorities were charged with taking care of their indigent poor. The "transient" poor, or those who had not yet become permanent legal residents of a town, were liable to being "warned out," or removed legally to the place assumed to be the town of their origin or permanent residence. With the end of chattel slavery and the dislocations wrought by war and economic depression, the postrevolutionary period was one that saw African Americans especially moving into more urban areas like Providence, trying to reconstitute their lives with family and social networks, and away from decimated Newport and the plantations of the southern counties. As such, they were much more vulnerable to this system. While they received a smaller percentage of warnings out before the war, following the war, despite being only about 10 percent of the state's population, they made up about 40 percent of the warnings out between the end of the war and 1800. Further, Herndon has shown that complaints about "disorderly" behavior were often coupled with the idea of someone "likely to become chargeable," and therefore became reasons for warning out. Under scrutiny already by the doubt surrounding the abolition of slavery, minor infractions or misunderstandings could lead to people of color especially being removed from their new homes, potentially back to the same towns and plantations in which they had been enslaved.[14]

The tenuousness of the entente between African Americans and elite whites also could put the former in precarious positions—even for those in business with such an esteemed abolitionist and friend to free African Americans as Moses Brown. Cudge Brown, one of Moses's former slaves and member of the Providence branch of the African Union Society's executive committee, had worked on land that Moses had set aside for him, assuming that he was working toward owning it. Moses had often promised to hand over the deed for it, but as Cudge's health began to fail in 1812, Cudge's son Noah was alerted to the fact that he needed the deed to settle the estate. Moses never provided the deed and instead sold the plot that had Cudge's family home and a small farm on it to a Mr. Angell, who turned around and sold part of it back to Noah. Moses offered a pittance of a strip adjoining the part Noah had bought, and so what was once a 150-foot-wide lot with the Brown family homestead was reduced to a 40-foot-wide lot, which nonetheless stayed in the possession of Cudge Brown's family for a few generations. African Americans were forced to endure setbacks in these uncomfortable times, taking small victories as they came and bearing the inequalities in their alliances with elites. Few alternatives had yet presented themselves.[15]

Some African Americans found financial success and were notable in the collective memory of the city by people looking back at the early nineteenth century. For the most part, however, their successes were short-lived, narrow, or incomplete before 1820. They were largely barred from artisan trades, both because of the labor patterns carried over from slavery—in which African Americans were mostly employed in farming, manual, or servant jobs—and because whites held a near monopoly on those trades and would apprentice their children or other whites by custom. This left many entrepreneurial African Americans in Providence to turn to more creative ways to achieve better conditions for their families. Such improvements in circumstance required, perhaps, engaging in the underground economy by opening one's home to boarders, sailors, or people willing to pay for alcohol, dancing, and sexual services; utilizing the transactional alliances built with powerful whites; or finding a niche or skill with which one could build patronage from white or Black clientele.[16]

One person who found such a niche was Scipio Brenton, one of the more famous people of early nineteenth-century Providence, largely because of the popularity of his oyster cellar at Vinton's Corner, where North Main and Market Streets met on the Providence River. Using a picture of Sir Walter Raleigh as his logo, the "aristocratic" Brenton catered to an elite white clientele, including a dinner given in honor of Rhode Island's Revolutionary War veterans. Although he was infamously rebuffed by Claude Gabriel during the latter's brief return from the Russian court, Brenton continued his occupation into the 1820s and 1830s, setting up a stand in the town's most popular theater. Still, his earlier successes may have eluded him later in life: he was listed simply as a "laborer" in the city's directories in the 1830s. Catering, while a potentially lucrative occupation, could also be hypersensitive to market fluctuations, and especially because Brenton's clientele consisted of Providence merchants, the job could reproduce the racial inequality of the master-servant relationship. Brenton, whether his success lasted, most likely helped pave the way for the more famous George T. Downing, who used the inherited and earned wealth his family catering business produced to vault himself to the forefront of Providence's Black leadership in the 1850s.[17]

George Thomas was also able to achieve some individual success as a barber, an artisanal trade that offered social mobility in many cities largely because, like catering, it could reproduce the inequality of the master-servant relationship while providing an avenue toward monetary success. Thomas, the former slave of Colonel Jeremiah Olney, deemed himself an aristocrat, using a gold figure of Achilles instead of a barber's pole as his business's logo and dressing in knee buckles and a powdered wig. Perhaps using his connection to Olney, he served exclusively customers of "quality"—mostly white—charging much more than other barbers in the area to distinguish himself. He also managed "African Balls," large celebrations that most likely evolved from Negro elections, and did so quite tyrannically, often beating his Black servants, according to a later white observer. He eventually moved to Boston seeking higher-paying clientele but was forced back to Providence after not finding success there. He returned to the town having alienated both his white clientele and, notably, the Black community—who, as would soon become evident, looked for leaders who prioritized community uplift and not individual power.[18]

One of the people George Thomas held in "dignified abeyance" was one of the last "Negro governors," Prince Whitman. A bridge between the revolutionary age and the early nineteenth century, Whitman, like John Quamine, Bristol Yamma, and Newport Gardner, was born in Africa and there enslaved and brought to Rhode Island. At some point in his life—whether during his capture, his enslavement, or his service as a solider in the American Revolution—he lost most of his nose, a fact that led to torment from white schoolchildren. Despite apparently living an impoverished life after slavery, he was elected "Negro governor" after the war. Perhaps it was the community rallying around a man in his condition that led George Thomas, a man who had wealth and connections with elite Providence whites, to disdain people like Whitman. Whether or not Whitman's "royal blood" played a part, his election to a position of prominence made clear that the community sought from its leaders something different than what Thomas was offering. Whatever it was they looked for in their leaders, Prince Whitman had it, signaling that wealth was not the most important characteristic, as it was in white circles, but also that ties to elite whites meant little if they did nothing to uplift the community. Whitman lived into old age despite his infirmity, and though he left little record behind and died in poverty, he clearly helped provide an early precedent for future leadership.

Another bridge between the revolutionary era, and similarly functioning as a community leader in the absence of a leadership class, was Bristol Rhodes. He was born enslaved and freed himself by serving with the First Rhode Island Regiment. It was a freedom for which he paid a dear price, losing a leg from a cannonball at Yorktown. He was never as prosperous as the flamboyant Scipio Brenton and George Thomas but had a steady income from his work at an iron foundry, to which he limped over four miles from his home in Cranston, and his Revolutionary War pension. Repeatedly shortchanged by Congress and the state, Rhodes had enough backers in the General Assembly to make sure he was paid in full whenever the government he fought for fell behind. He was a rare person of color feted at military parades and Brown University (Rhode Island College until 1804) commencement exercises, and delighted children with his war stories. Not everyone from the body politic appreciated his sacrifice to the cause of liberty, however, as in 1794, shortly after moving to Providence, his white neighbors tried to get him warned out. The town authorities investigated but determined there was no cause to warn out the war hero.

The stated reasoning for the investigation was Rhodes's holding of gatherings for a "large number" of African Americans on the Sabbath in his family home.[19] He was most likely holding church services for those people who may have felt uncomfortable with the discrimination in the First Baptist, First Congregational, or St. John's Episcopal Churches. The same year that Richard Allen was founding the African Methodist Episcopal denomination in Philadelphia, all churches in Providence were run by whites, and though many African Americans were members, according to William J. Brown, "many attended no church at all, because they said they were opposed to going to churches and sitting in pigeon holes, as all the churches at that time had some obscure place for the colored people to sit in."[20] Inside churches, the white class structure evolving around wealth had crept into worship practices: pews were commodified and sold, their price determined by proximity to the front and center of the church. Wealthy whites flaunted their status by purchasing expensive pews, and African Americans' positions on the margins of society were reflected by their relegation to these "pigeon holes."[21] Rhodes's house seemingly offered a space where people of color could gather and worship how they wanted—as equals and outside of the oppressive racial and social hierarchy that whites had set up.

Rhodes, who had apparently become a leader for Providence's Black community outside of the Providence chapter of the Free African Union Society, derived his status from his commitment to the amelioration of oppression of African Americans on their own terms. This was especially true because Christian sensibility and independence had been hallmarks of Rhode Island's self-consciousness since its founder Roger Williams left Massachusetts. Unlike the strongest faction in the Union Society, Rhodes's small act suggested self-liberation inside the geographic bounds of the republic. He had the credibility of wearing the struggle to create the republic on his body, having been injured in the most famous and consequential battle, and made a comfortable and consistent living with which he provided for his family and community. By the time he died in 1810, the event that sparked the creation of the first, more permanent Black leadership class was still nearly a decade away—though his holding of a church in his home for Black community members may have shown later leaders a template for success when it came to collectively approaching the problem of race in the new republic.

Race and the Politics of Disfranchisement

When Bristol Rhodes died on July 3, 1810, his obituary in the *Providence Gazette* read, "Died: in this town, Tuesday last, in an advanced age, BRISTOL RHODES, a Black man, of the late revolutionary army, in which he long served with deserved reputation. At the siege of York-Town he was severely wounded, having unfortunately lost a leg and an arm, and has since subsisted on a pension."[22] A Federalist newspaper, the *Gazette*'s lauding of the leading African American citizen of the town symbolized the ways in which the Federalist Party still held fast to the ideals of the Revolution, granting someone who clearly exuded republican respectability a due sendoff, regardless of their color. The next decade, however, would bring periodic changes of political circumstance in the state that tested the alliance between African Americans and conservative whites, with one result being formal disfranchisement of the state's nonwhite residents. Another major result was the strengthening of the Black community with the birth of its first permanent leadership class and space of its own—the African Union Meeting House, discussed in the next chapter.

The first of these changes was the concerted push for the broadening of voting rights in Rhode Island, which came in early 1811. For the previous twenty-five years, the Country Party, with allegiances to the Jeffersonian/Republican branch of national party politics, had ruled the state with little opposition. Party lines were often quite blurry, however, as Federalist-allied General Assembly representatives ascended to the legislature's Speakership, and the same Federalists often supported the governorship of Republicans Arthur Fenner, until his death in 1805, and then Arthur's son James Fenner two years later. However, as manufacturing took off in and around Providence by the turn of the nineteenth century, and the 1807 embargo on foreign goods weighed on the state's merchant elite and farmers alike, Federalists and their local allies saw a resurgence of support, regaining many legislative seats and mirroring the same trend throughout New England. The Federalist ascendancy achieved a major breakthrough with the narrow election of William Jones in 1811 on the "American Prox"—"prox" being the list of candidates each party printed on its paper ballots. This realignment held steady for the next six years, with Federalists guiding the state through the War of 1812, the Hartford Convention on secession, and the aftermath of each.[23]

The Republican Party fiercely contested this new order, alleging in 1811 that wealthy Federalists were temporarily subdividing their land, renting it out to loyal supporters, and thereby creating new freemen specifically to allow them to vote.[24] Two new newspapers emerged in Providence in the resurgent partisan atmosphere—the *Providence Patriot, and Columbian Phoenix* for the Republicans and the *Rhode Island American* for the Federalists—and in the absence of reports on debates in the General Assembly, they formed the arena for public debate about politics. The *Patriot* in February 1811 began running editorials advocating for a relaxing of the property requirement as a way not only to prevent fraud but also to honor all who fought for and defended the republic yet did not own the requisite amount of property. Race was not explicitly mentioned early on, but by the time an act was brought to the legislature, it suggested allowing suffrage for "every white male citizen of this state, who has attained to the age of twenty-one years, and who has rated for a poll or property tax, or who is or has been enrolled in the militia of this state."[25] While color had been the basis for several provisions in the Rhode Island law digests over the previous century and a half, this would, for the first time, insert "white" into the law regulating the most sacred right of citizenship in the republic. The "white" provision, coupled with an extension of the franchise, became the definition for "universal suffrage" or "general suffrage," depending on what the political circumstances dictated. The proposed act passed the senate but was rejected by the Federalist-dominated house thirty-eight to twenty-eight.[26]

This initial addition of "white" to the voting requirement and the commentary around it is indicative of several things. First, there was no discernible outrage on behalf of the town's or state's Black communities, most likely because the freemanship required for voting had excluded them anyway—as shown by Anthony Kinnicutt's petition in the revolutionary period. Second, its failure to define exactly what "whiteness" was—something that Kinnicutt claimed was part of his ancestry, and was certainly a part of others listed as "Black," "mulatto," or "colored" in censuses—meant it was probably up to town meetings to define who was "white" and who was not. Interestingly, an 1814 list of Providence voters does contain one Thomas Thompson, and the only person by that name in the censuses of 1810 and 1820 is listed as a person of color. There was a Thomas Thompson on a committee made up of African American men planning to build the African Union Meeting House 1819, and this same Thompson was listed as a Black head of household in an informal 1822 census, so it is feasible that he or other Black men were admitted as freemen from time to time. Outside of this, however, there is little evidence or discussion of Black voting, and so adding "white" may not have seemed so groundbreaking in 1811.[27]

During the early 1810s, after this preliminary push for widening the franchise was made, the partisan presses took off in Providence and race became grist for the political mills. In January 1813, when Federalist domination was clear enough that Republicans failed to even nominate a "prox," the *Providence Patriot* ran its first opinion piece speculating on the horror Black voting would cause for the state. This was prompted by accusations that Federalist Caleb Strong's extremely narrow victory in Massachusetts's 1812 gubernatorial race occurred because African Americans' votes pushed him over the top, and the publication of "Slave Representation," a collection of essays in the *Connecticut Journal* that urged northerners to "fight" for the repeal of the "three-fifths clause" in the Constitution. "Slave Representation," written anonymously by Sereno Edwards Dwight under the pseudonym "Boreas," argued that including three-fifths of enslaved African Americans in congressional apportionment meant that, even though they could not vote, the enslaved were responsible for fifteen extra seats in the House of Representatives. The Federalist Dwight made the salacious claim that without it, John Adams would have had a majority of electors in 1800—that Jefferson in fact owed his presidency and that Republicans owed their national prominence to the slave system. The editor of the *Patriot* rebutted that the Federalist majority in Massachusetts being the product of free Black people was worse and antithetical to the Constitution, which explicitly implied that white freemen should speak for the community. The election of Strong, he claimed, was usurped by those who were formerly slaves—a potentiality "Washington endeavoured against." He then launched into a vicious attack on northern free Black people, offering a "large pumpkin" to anyone who could write a "dissertation" on the intellect of free Black northerners and a squash to anyone who could prove that Black Massachusettsans deserved the vote more than southern slaves.[28] Anti-Blackness was becoming a valuable political currency for Republicans across the country.

Federalists, for their part, had argued during the debate over the 1811 voting rights proposal that the charter granted citizenship to "purchasers of the soil" and duly accepted freemen. Their professed fears that "bog-trotters" from Ireland and "frog-eaters" from France would supplant native-born farmers, while eschewing mention of African Americans, shows how blurry the "color line" actually was in the first decades of the nineteenth century—something historian Noel Ignatiev has shown in his *How the Irish Became White*.[29] Federalists' proposed dividing lines between citizenship and non-citizenship—property ownership and nativity—meant that possible pathways to citizenship for Black Americans ran through them. Elsewhere in the country, prominent Federalists like Alexander Hamilton and John Jay had sponsored African Free Schools in New York City, and one of that city's Black leaders, Joseph Sidney, was at this time ardently urging African Americans to support the Federalist Party.[30] In Boston, the *Providence Patriot* sarcastically noted, Federalist Josiah Quincy was "their [African Americans'] representative," lending credence to the idea of Black support being the deciding factor in Federalist power in Massachusetts.[31]

Further, the Federalist Party had largely begun advocating for the gradual emancipation of the nation's enslaved people. In part a political strategy to oppose the Republicans' base of support, southern slaveholders, and in part philanthropic in nature, antislavery was another connecting point between elite white Federalists and Black communities.[32] In Rhode Island, the Federalist *Rhode Island American* began tacitly sending signals of antislavery leanings, first by sarcastically commenting on the "humanity" Republican and ruthless slave trader James D'Wolf showed by supposedly having a diseased African woman thrown overboard to save others from dying. Soon after, the paper published a sermon by Timothy Dwight, president of Yale College, in which the minister "charged" whites with the duty to help African Americans change the behavior supposedly learned in slavery—the paternalism nevertheless offering a milder view of race ideology than the *Patriot*. The *Rhode Island American* even reprinted a Baltimore paper's plea for public help in finding a "respectable" Black family who had gone missing—in a way, an anti–fugitive slave advertisement.[33]

The potential for alliance between Providence's Black community and elite Federalists, however, was clouded by the politics of race as well. During the debate surrounding the voting rights bill, new Speaker of the House William Hunter, who would soon be elected by the General Assembly to serve in the U.S. Senate, asked rhetorically, why not include "negroes, women," or recently arrived immigrants if the principle the franchise rested on was simply residency and age? Hunter, who had been steeped in British governing philosophy and was an enthusiastic watcher of parliamentary debate, gave an answer that showed Federalists too had drifted from the revolutionary ideals of liberty and natural rights. The answer, he said, was that governments needed to pass laws based on *expediency*, not necessarily principle.[34] Hunter's positioning of the idea of African Americans or women voting as ridiculous was indicative of how Federalists viewed their role as republican superiors in their relationships with anyone who was not wealthy, male, and white—something that would plague Black alliances with the Whigs and Republicans for the rest of the nineteenth century. Unwittingly perhaps, he was handing the future, Democrat-dominated Suffrage Association their prime argument for disfranchising Black people.

By 1814, the direct threat of the War of 1812 being waged in New England generated a brief hiatus for the state's Black residents' status as negative components in the political rhetoric. On February 8, 1814, Quom, a volunteer aide-de-camp with a fifteen-member unit of Black soldiers known as the "Division of Rhode-Island Veterans," wrote to the adjutant general in Boston, a letter that was later published in the *Providence Patriot*. Recommended as "the most efficient for the contemplated purpose," the small unit was ready to march to Boston to assist in the defense and "recovery of the long-lost *maritime rights* of New-England," especially should white troops desert, as they had in other warfronts. That September and October, as Providence anxiously awaited an expected British invasion from Narragansett Bay, the "Committee of Defence" publicly thanked the town's free people of color for providing seventy-six days of "voluntary labor" building breastworks and other defensive infrastructure. As they had in the Revolution, Black residents *en masse* offered their labor for the benefit of a body politic that occasionally recognized their service but refused to acknowledge them as members of its citizenry. They were, they knew, like the previous generation did during the Revolution, helping to build a case for their inclusion.[35]

Political race-baiting, dormant during the war, returned in 1817. As a very close election season dawned in April, the *Providence Patriot* claimed that a Federalist–African American alliance had begun as a result of the war, ridiculing governor William Jones for supposedly elevating the fifteen Black soldiers of the Division of Rhode-Island Veterans as guardians of the entire coastline of the state when he could have used the state's financial resources for a more formidable (white) defense force. Further, the writer said, Federalist James Burrill, who had recently been sent to the U.S. Senate by the General Assembly, would have made "slaves" out of ordinary men had his push for secession at the Hartford Convention been enacted—a similar argument that Republicans would use around the country to discredit the Federalist Party's perceived treason. Federalists would "make a lord of Burrill and a prince of Black Ben" if they were to continue in power. One of the last holdouts of Federalist power, Rhode Island's branch of the party was defeated by sixty-eight votes in the governor's race and ousted completely from the state senate (losing every seat), though it retained a small majority in the house.[36]

The movement to expand the suffrage among whites also returned with the new Republican surge. Familiarly, it began with Republican outrage over an election they felt was swung toward the Federalists by Black voting. The *Providence Patriot* ran an editorial in which it accused a Black man, later identified as Primus Bailey, of voting in an election in the small farming town of Little Compton, giving the Federalist candidate a one-vote majority. The author declared the election unfair because, according to him, African Americans didn't vote in other towns.[37] Despite this "evidence," the near-annihilation of the Federalist Party in the state over the next four years, the General Assembly managed to keep any liberalization efforts at arm's length. A "general suffrage" bill came up for discussion again in the assembly in November 1818, perhaps taking some inspiration from Connecticut's newly enacted law that relaxed the state's freemanship requirement while inserting "white" into its qualification statute, and the bill was referred to committee. In February 1819, the committee tasked with considering the bill wrote to each town asking for their input but then decided against acting on it. The state's disproportionate representational system, which favored the rural but wealthy elite, did not have to respond to any grassroots movements; Federalists were absorbed on multiple sides of the Republican Party, temporarily killing a unified response.[38]

Rhode Island politics were then seized by the tentacles of the Missouri statehood debate, which reached every corner of the country and made race a front-page issue. An 1819 bill to admit Missouri as a slave state came before the U.S. House of Representatives, and shortly after freshman congressman James Tallmadge from New York offered an amendment halting the further introduction of enslaved people and freeing those born to enslaved women at age twenty-five. The halls of Congress rapidly turned into an arena for clashing visions not only of the future of slavery in America but also of the prospect of African Americans' citizenship and place in the body politic for those who were free.[39] In Rhode Island, slavery had been a dead issue for thirty-five years. However, when Henry Clay authored a compromise that would allow Missouri's constitutional exclusion of free African Americans from its boundaries, the partisan newspapers seemed to fracture and the simmering issue of race became the fault line. The *Rhode Island American* stayed true to its Federalist roots, focusing not on the color line but on the revolutionary principle of personal freedom. It reprinted Christian missionary Jeremiah Evarts's letter to Congress claiming that the Declaration of Independence made no distinction of color between citizens when enumerating their rights, and also editorialized that, because Black people were considered citizens in some states, their exclusion from Missouri would violate the "privileges and immunities" the Constitution afforded them.[40] These editorials further pointed out that their Republican counterparts were doing the bidding of southern slaveholders within their party, labeling Rhode Island's pro-compromise representative Samuel Eddy a "doughface"—an appellation first used by John Randolph of Roanoke to taunt northerners who had supposedly abandoned their principles.[41]

Significantly, in the *Rhode Island American* there was a concurrent uptick in reprints, news articles, and editorials that took a decidedly antislavery stance and portrayed African Americans in a positive light. Even before the Missouri crisis exploded, the paper allowed George McCarty, the African American owner of a refreshment stand in the Market House, to publish a piece thanking his "friends indeed" for helping with the reinstatement of his license, and proclaimed the opening of a "school for coloured people of all ages" in the First Baptist Meeting House—a bit paternalistically asking elite "heads of family" to allow their servants time on Saturday afternoons to attend.[42] The paper published pieces supporting their defense of African American citizenship at home and abroad, with one editorial mirroring one of African Americans' central arguments against slavery, that its continuation in the South had detrimental effects on the country, white and black, as a whole. It praised the building of the African Union Meeting House (detailed below) as a positive step for Providence's Black community and then ran a story about African American "industriousness" on the frontier, profiling one Black man who invested in land and now owned about $40,000 worth of it in Kansas.[43]

On the other side of the political aisle, Black citizenship became a bludgeon Republicans used in their efforts to discredit the Federalist Party once and for all. After exploiting the inconsistencies in Federalist positions on race— namely, their previous compromises with the South on slavery, and the fact that their elites disfranchised Black people as well as white—the Republicans coopted the middle ground sought by Rhode Island's Federalist senator James Burrill.[44] Burrill, while arguing in favor of separating the Maine and Missouri statehood bills, said that he was "not only averse to a slave population, but also any population composed of blacks, and of the infinite and motley confusion of colours between the Black and the white."[45] In the late 1840s, this idea would largely influence bolters from the Democratic Party who made up much of the Free Soil rank and file, but in 1820 the Republican tent was large enough to absorb this faction. For the state's most powerful Federalist to formally concede the idea of Black inferiority to the rival party showed, first, how weak the party had become but also in how precarious a position Black communities could find themselves. In the first major national conversation around the future of African Americans' place in the republic since the Constitutional Convention, they were again sacrificed on the altar of compromise.[46]

Another element of the Missouri debate that brought race to the forefront of politics in Rhode Island was the prospect of the "three-fifths compromise" granting further outsized influence to the proslavery Republicans. In the General Assembly's June session of 1820, therefore, a new push to take up a suffrage bill with the qualification that "every free able-bodied white male citizen of the United States, of the age of twenty-one years and upwards" and equipped and served in a militia be granted the right to vote came up in a context quite different from the one a few years before. That summer, state Republican commentators tried to thread an ideological needle by taking the position that Rhode Island's African Americans, despite not voting, were fully represented in Congress, whereas only three-fifths of their brethren in the South were. In August, after the new voting rights requirements had passed the state senate, editorialist "Constitution and Laws" wrote, "Our blacks count the same as whites, though they have no more concern in our own political affairs than the blacks of Virginia."[47] A week later, another writer tried to lessen concerns about Missouri representation by similarly claiming that free Black people could not vote in Rhode Island, just like they would not in Missouri. In December, as the General Assembly prepared for its January session, two more editorials appeared with that same argument, with the allusions to the lack of Black voting serving doubly to affirm their support for the Missouri Compromise (and Samuel Eddy) but also reinforcing a sort of racial unity among white voters in the renewed push for the white "general suffrage" bill.[48]

Two events in 1821 heightened white Rhode Islanders' racial anxieties and most likely helped push the General Assembly to finally pass the "white" provision. The first was the June publication of the Massachusetts House of Representatives' report on "the expediency of amending the laws of this Commonwealth concerning the admission into, and residence in this state, of negroes and mulattoes." The Republican author of the report, Theodore Lyman Jr., determined the "facts" of the matter to be that, among other things, Black populations were "expensive and injurious" burdens in other states, if the state were to remain lax in its treatment of African Americans then many would flood the state as they fled from more discriminatory states, and that jobs needed to be saved for "native" whites. Reprinting the *Richmond Enquirer*'s sarcastic comment that what was once "heresy [for] Missouri is orthodoxy in Massachusetts," the *Providence Patriot* took its cue and began printing stories of crimes committed by African Americans, including at least one implying that Black people were committing vague "outrages" in Providence and imploring police to surveil this "expensive and injurious population," using the same exact words to describe the Black community as Lyman had in the Massachusetts report.[49] The paper also imported from Massachusetts the "bobalition" trope, which harshly caricatured Black speech, dress, and dance—in one instance, ridiculing the idea circulating around the town of setting up a school for Black children by claiming the only results of that would be to induce Black people to imitate whites and "amalgamate" with them.[50]

The second event in 1821 was the September–October New York constitutional convention, which met to decide on new changes to that state's voting requirements. A fierce partisan battle had been raging there for decades, and Federalists had been, much more openly than in Rhode Island, defending Black voters against Republican moves to get the word "white" inserted into the qualification. The Federalists, by 1821 badly outnumbered in New York's legislature yet in firm control of politics statewide, could not stop the Republican-dominated constitutional convention from adding "white," but Federalist titan Peter Jay, son of founding framer John Jay, was able to win a small concession from the Martin Van Buren–dominated Republican faction that allowed African Americans to vote should they hold $250 worth of property.[51] The national juggernaut that the Republican Party had built meant that the waves from the New York convention were sure to reach Rhode Island. The Federalist *Rhode Island American* could only grumble that it was ironic that those who claimed victory for "universal liberty" were the same people fighting against Black voting.[52] The *Providence Patriot* responded similarly as it did to Massachusetts's report on Black exclusion by ramping up its racist attacks on the Black population and reprinting New York newspaper accounts sensationalizing crimes committed by African Americans. In one case, it published a Republican Party publication claiming that all of the crimes prosecuted in Chester County, New York, were committed by African Americans. In another, the paper reprinted a *New York Advocate* article lampooning a paternity lawsuit between two Black men, saying that the only "benefit" to enfranchising Black men would be whites getting to watch spectacles such as this in which Black men imitated white dress and speech. One reprint from a Bridgeport, Connecticut, paper detailed a case in which a Black man raped a white woman, and ended by the paper's editor advocating only "protection in person, property, and religion and no more for them." Tellingly, he added sarcastically, "let the agitators of the Missouri plot read above and reflect."[53]

Earlier in 1821, another roadblock for Rhode Island's African American population had been put up. That year, the governorship came up for grabs when popular incumbent Nehemiah Knight was sent to the U.S. Senate. The Federalists of Providence allied with the urban Republicans to nominate a "Union" candidate (Providence's Samuel Bridgham), but he was soundly defeated by more traditional Republican William Gibbs, an event that confirmed the lack of influence the Federalists had in state government. While the "universal suffrage" bill was still unpopular with the state's elite freemen, by the February 1822 session of the General Assembly, the Republicans could no longer ignore the anti-Black sentiment that had swept into their party.[54] Most likely, this is why the word "white" was added to section 1 of the "Act Regulating the Manner of Admitting Freemen and Directing the Method of Electing Officers in This State" in Rhode Island's law digest. The regulation now read, *"Be it enacted by the General Assembly, and by the authority thereof it is enacted, That the freemen of each town in this State, at any of their town-meetings, shall and they hereby have full power granted them, to admit so many white persons, inhabitants of their respective towns, freemen thereof, as shall be qualified according to this act."* The only difference between this section in the 1822 digest and that of 1798 (the last time it was updated) was the word "white." No property qualification was changed, so in effect the change made even smaller the pool of potential voters.[55]

Perhaps because so few African Americans voted in the state or because the "universal suffrage" bills kept getting tabled, the partisan newspapers failed to even take notice of this change. Maybe it was because the change seemed redundant in a republic so fully committed to white supremacy. Regardless, while many historians have mentioned Rhode Island as part of the larger pattern of the concurrent movements to widen the franchise for whites while restricting it from Black men, this state presents a unique and challenging case. Some have found in other states evidence that white elites allied with a growing and agitated white laboring class, an agreement that articulated an idea of whiteness as a common bond among citizens and that elevated poorer whites to freemanship in order to solidify their position within the republic. The degradation of Blackness and ascription of nonrepublican traits onto Black men especially—made ever more convincing by the persistence of slavery in the South and discrimination-induced poverty in the North—meant that their disfranchisement was a natural outgrowth of shifting racial ideas.[56] Questions about citizenship rights would emerge more broadly in the subsequent decades, when Black and then interracial groups of abolitionists began circulating a vision for the future that was more democratic, egalitarian, and inclusive, but in the "Era of Good Feelings," white political and class unity presented northern African American communities with calamitous hardships.

In Rhode Island specifically, the few historians who have sought to explore the 1822 disfranchisement of African Americans have done so briefly and abstractly. Joanne Pope Melish posits that disfranchisement was reflective of a "rubric of 'negro' removal," the idea that whites had begun to employ both a discursive attack on Black personhood and a legal attack on Black rights in order to remove them from the body politic because they could not remove Black people physically from the borders of the republic. Christopher Malone more closely links the politics of the state to the actions in Massachusetts and New York but suggests that Melish's analysis of "removal" discourse played a role as well. John Wood Sweet situates the state's disfranchisement of Black voters with politicians' acceptance of poor whites' arguments that Black men, like aristocrats, could not be trusted to support the interests of the growing white working class. Robert Cottrol claims that disfranchisement was a reaction to the growing prosperity and independence of especially Providence's Black community; his position seems less plausible as a *cause of* disfranchisement due to the lack of white anxiety, "replacement," or "white slavery" rhetoric, but his point about the coalescence of a strong community would certainly inform the Black *response to* the racial restriction.[57]

No matter which way it is analyzed, the insertion of the word "white" into Rhode Island's digest does not fit in perfectly with any of the broader analyses for a variety of reasons. First, the racial restriction did not coincide with an expansion to poor whites, as it did elsewhere. This is perhaps because of the domination of state politics by elite landholding Republicans and the persistence of Federalism in Providence—each of these circumstances presenting barriers to potential alliance with urban white laborers, the drivers of suffrage movements elsewhere. Second, though the Federalist Party ceased to function formally, its ideology of the rights of property trumping racial distinction, and its informal alliance with the Black community, were absorbed into the state Republican Party and remained a major factor in the General Assembly. Moses Brown's continuing influence in elite merchant circles, as well as recollection of Black service in the Revolution, which remained strong in the state's collective memory, may have been why the move was done so quietly.

Without debate reconstructions or meeting minutes in the General Assembly, it is difficult to state definitively exactly why disfranchisement occurred. Melish and Malone are probably both right, and their analyses provide a starting point to answering this question. We can see in the public conversation delineated above that ideas about Blackness were becoming increasingly intertwined with politics and visions for citizenship as the republic matured. The concurrent development discussed by Cottrol and deepened in the next chapter also meant that Providence's Black community, having turned their focus away from debating emigration and toward citizenship, was well-equipped to respond to this rising tide of white supremacy. In the battle for "universal suffrage," which to most whites meant employing race as a unifying factor across class and social lines in an effort to gain more citizenship rights, Rhode Island's elites had delivered a solution that no one liked.

The Black community would spend the next two decades working to use this to their advantage. The alliance between Black leaders and elite whites, personified by Claude Gabriel and William Jones eleven years prior to disfranchisement, would be called on again to support the community's acquisition of a social, political, and religious space of its own. The building of the African Union Meeting House, happening concurrently to the debates around white manhood suffrage, gave rise to and institutionalized a new generation of leadership united behind winning a more equitable form of citizenship for Rhode Islanders of color.

CHAPTER 3

"Forever and Hereafter a Body Politic"
NEW LEADERSHIP AND ORGANIZATION, 1819–1824

On the evening of March 9, 1819, representatives from Providence's Black community and the leaders of the city's predominantly white churches met at the town's First Baptist Church. On the agenda was planning for the construction of a meetinghouse and school specifically for the benefit of the city's bourgeoning Black population. Edging close to a thousand members by the 1820 census, Providence's Black community was about to embark on its most significant effort at self-determination since the state's gradual emancipation law was passed in the wake of the American Revolution, despite increasing racism in the national and state political climate.[1] Formal disfranchisement had not yet been enacted, and a destructive riot (1824) and bloody pogrom (1831) initiated by white mobs still lay in the community's future, but on this night the literal and figurative foundations of community consciousness came to fruition, and the meetinghouse became the physical base from which a localized Black freedom struggle engaged. The events surrounding the building of the African Union Meeting House reveal an emerging class of leaders much different from their predecessors; they sought access to the levers of power in the state not to support emigration but to make their lives at home more tolerable and prosperous. They were leaders who sought to harness republican ideals to advance their movement to win citizenship rights that the state government had reserved solely for elite whites—people who heretofore have been largely passed over by scholarship. Some have been hiding in plain sight, and others are still obscure. A closer examination of them and the house they built illuminates just how African Americans, even while a small fraction of Providence's population, were able to establish activist roots necessary for advancement despite the countercurrent the universal suffrage movement was creating.

Only recently have the few scholars who mention the African Union Meeting House posited that it was African Americans themselves who took the initiative. Before the twenty-first century, only Irving Bartlett in *From Slave to Citizen: The Story of the Negro in Rhode Island* did so, while other historians like Julian Rammelkamp, Robert Cottrol, J. Stanley Lemons, and Michael McKenna discuss the role prominent whites played in its founding—though they all note briefly the impact the building had in the organization of Providence's Black community. Cottrol mentions many of the leaders and rank and file by name, but they often get absorbed in his bird's-eye statistical analysis, which, while valuable as a foundational text, perhaps merely scratches the surface. Twenty-first-century historians Mark Schantz and Christy Clark-Pujara especially in her *Dark Work: The Business of Slavery in Rhode Island* have given the Black community leadership the agency it properly deserves in founding the meetinghouse, and they, along with Erik Chaput and Russell J. DeSimone, briefly discuss its centrality to the Black community. None, however, have fully devoted a study to the composition of the Black leadership class and how they used the meetinghouse as a base for their efforts at gaining a more equitable form of citizenship. I argue that this action specifically consolidated Providence's first Black leadership class, helping place the community in an advantageous position to wage its political and social battles against the color line in the near future.[2]

The African Union Meeting House Revisited

The generally accepted story of the founding of the African Union Meeting House appears in the papers of businessman, philanthropist, and abolitionist Moses Brown. *A Short History of the African Union Meeting and School-House* was compiled by Baptist minister Henry Jackson, who played a large part in securing the land Brown bought for the meetinghouse and homolyzed at the plenary sessions at which the building was planned. In Jackson's rendering of the story, it was the "interesting exertions" of white religious leaders and white women teachers—members of a "society for the instruction of the coloured part of the population"—who initiated the call for an African American religious and educational space. "The people of colour were requested to meet at the vestry of the First Baptist Church," and "they assembled as requested," according to Jackson. This narrative fits in with the previously dominant historical trope of philanthropic whites spearheading positive change for Black communities, a rendering that often blots out the "exertions" of Black men and women themselves. The language of the document at times is overly patronizing toward the Black community—the author states that it was the "slavish and gross state of ignorance of the people of colour" that influenced white benefactors to act. A brief foreword to the document reads as follows: "The design of publishing the following pages, is to prevent any misunderstanding among the people of colour, respecting their Meeting and School-House, and thereby laying a foundation of future difficulty."[3] While it is true that white philanthropy was often necessary for Black community institutions to get started—for example, the New York Manumission Society and its funding of Black schools, which produced abolitionists and intellectuals Henry Highland Garnet, Alexander Crummell, and James McCune Smith, among others—this often obscures the role that people of color played in their own liberation.[4] The alliances that African Americans built with elite white powerbrokers were negotiated to be much more mutually beneficial, and as we saw in the failure of the colonization schemes of the 1770s and 1790s, Black communities only offered support for them when tangible benefits were likely.[5] The maintenance of these ties were actions of self-liberation, entered into freely and with considerable thought on the part of African American community leaders and the rank and file. Therefore, while white church elites played an important role in the formulation of the project analyzed here, a closer look at the African American leaders acting on their own behalf is necessary to tell a more complete and accurate story.

There is, in fact, a primary counternarrative that shows Black community leaders advocating for themselves rather than waiting for white leaders to act benevolently. One such example is William J. Brown, a laborer, at times a shoe repairman, and a member of Providence's Black leadership class in the mid- to late nineteenth century who was able to use his thirst for education and ambition to better his community to live a moderately successful life. In his autobiography, *The Life of William J. Brown of Providence, R.I.*, he discusses the agency with which African Americans were able to push for their own church and school. Whereas in *A Short History of the African Union Meeting and School-House*, white church leaders requested that representatives from

Providence's community of color meet, in William Brown's telling it was Black people themselves who decided to "take measures" and discuss the feasibility of building the meetinghouse. It was they who took the idea to Moses Brown, who agreed to buy the land, and they who "notified the different pastors of the several churches and called a meeting in the vestry of the First Baptist Church."[6]

The historical evidence seems to favor William Brown's account. African Americans were increasingly relegated to balconies during church services, whether prohibited economically (due to pew-selling) or socially.[7] Similar circumstances had previously led to Richard Allen's founding of the African Methodist Episcopal Church in Philadelphia following a walkout in protest of the white church's discriminatory practices, meaning there was regional precedent for Black communities seeking their own houses of worship. Additionally, the community already had a history of its own advocacy; the Providence branch of the Free African Union Society had laid much of the groundwork for the development of Black leadership, and though it had largely ceased to function by 1800, it did made a brief comeback in 1811 before the historical archive becomes silent on it once more.[8] A Black lodge of freemasons had formed in Providence in 1797, most likely by Providence leaders having heard Black masonic founding father Prince Hall's speech in Boston. The Hiram Lodge Number 3 lasted only a few years despite its proximity to Boston and continued communication with Hall, but according to an official history of Black freemasonry, a Providence contingent of masons was represented at the 1808 election of a new grand master on Hall's death.[9]

In many ways, the African Union Meeting House can be read as an outgrowth of this mutual benefit tradition. Early Black churches were not just spaces for religious worship; African Americans of several Christian denominations used the meetinghouse, and some even continued worshipping in white churches. Warwick Sweetland and Henry Greene, both men of color and members of the planning committee, continued their membership in Providence's First Baptist Church, and George Willis, another man of color, served as First Baptist's sexton, worshipping there until 1840 when he joined the meetinghouse's successor, the Meeting Street Baptist Church.[10] The African Union Meeting House would also serve as space for education and social and political activism—cultural arenas that were often heavily regulated and restricted where white people could see and hear. In 1820, most members of the planning committee were also signees of a petition to incorporate the African Society, discussed below. The society sought not only to raise money to provide "Christian instruction" but also to allow its members to be "forever and hereafter a body politic."[11] Perhaps such an attempt to present the meetinghouse as a political organization made the addition of "white" to the voting qualification statute two years later more urgent, lest the Federalist-Black alliance cause a reversal of that party's political fortunes.

Who were the members of this new Black leadership class? The most important detail that the *Short History of the African Union Meeting and School-House* contains is the list of names of the men appointed to the African Union Meeting House planning committee. Voted to the committee "by the advice of their friends," all eighteen have remained in relative obscurity in the secondary literature, but what we can piece together about them from the archives can help us understand what it meant to be a leader of an antebellum Black community outside a major population center like New York, Philadelphia, or Baltimore. According to this document, "The following was the committee appointed at this meeing, viz: *Warwick Sweetland, Abraham Gibbs, George M'Carty, George J. Smith, George C. Willis, Joshua Weeks, Derry Williams, Hodge Congdon, Nathaniel Paul, Henry Taber, Peter Waters* and *Thomas Graham*. To which has since been added, *James Harris, Thomas Thompson, George W. Barrett, Henry Greene, Stephen Wolmsly,* and *Asa C. Goldsbury.*"[12]

Perhaps the most significant element that tied these men together is the fact that, like their predecessors in the 1790s, most were heads of households. As more free African Americans became laborers for themselves, opened their own shops, or kept up connections with wealthy white benefactors, they began moving into their own homes and taking charge of family affairs. While African Americans living in Black-headed households reached a peak of over 65 percent in 1810, it dipped slightly to 60 percent by 1820—at least in part due to the general economic downturn of the previous year. Some Black men and women had also invested in real estate, like committee member George McCarty, who owned the land Moses Brown bought for the meetinghouse.[13] As discussed earlier, removing themselves from perceived dependence on whites was crucial for Black men seeking a place in the American republic, and living independently, especially as the head of a family, was a positive affirmation of this.

The conspicuous absence of women in both Cottrol's analysis and on the committee is probably because many women who owned businesses were viewed as outsiders in the strict, masculine notion of republican respectability. The few women of color who did run businesses like nearby Warwick's

Elleanor Eldridge, who owned a domestic service business, had to work extra hard to expand their operations as well as protect them and their property from fraudsters in a legal system dominated by men. Several Black and white women owned homes that doubled as taverns and boardinghouses, places that catered to an interracial group of clientele, and as such these spaces were condemned as hotbeds of "vice" and "disorder"—a development that would lead to violent outbursts in 1824 and 1831.[14] Additionally, the support of white churches, in which men dominated leadership roles and surely expected that Black men would do the same, was crucial to the success of building the meetinghouse. The *Short History of the African Union Meeting and School-House* fits neatly in with prevailing notions of the place of white women as nurturing teachers who could foster "virtue" within the Black community and goaders of elite white men to undertake the project. Black women were expected to be entirely absent from the process (save for Terisa McCarty, George's wife, who cosigned the deed of sale for the property).[15]

Aside from the fact that what these men were planning would serve as a church, the presence of Black ministers Nathaniel Paul and Asa Goldsbury on the committee is an important factor to note. By the 1820s, Protestant Christianity had become a fundamental part of republican ideology in America. This was especially true in Rhode Island, which tied its respectability to its founder Roger Williams and his ideas of toleration toward all Christian denominations. The Second Great Awakening, a religious revival that gave rise to new Christian denominations, ones that democratized American religion by eschewing the vertical hierarchies of the older orders, offered an avenue toward leadership for ministers of color, while at the same time independent Black householders chafed under the segregation they and their families were forced to endure in white churches. Consistent with a pattern spreading across northern cities, Black ministers, as leaders of the religious spaces that offered safe harbor from racism and discrimination, almost always formed an important part of Black leadership in the communities they served.[16]

Four of the men on the African Union Meeting House committee were listed as laborers in at least one of the Providence directories. One, George Barrett, was listed as a "mariner." Two were ministers—Nathaniel Paul and Asa Goldsbury. One, Derry Williams, was listed as a sexton. There was one "trader," George McCarty, who owned the land that was sold to Moses Brown for the meetinghouse. George Smith was listed as a coachman to an elite white man. And finally, an additional seven men were not listed in any occupational directory, though we can partially understand who they were through census records or other directories in which they appear.[17]

While Black men across the North, including in Providence, were striving to live their lives consistent with the American republic's notions of independence, gender, and religion, Black community leadership differed from that of whites especially with regard to occupation. Occupational data in most cases is only available starting in 1824, when the first city directories were published. Therefore, while probable, it is not absolutely certain that all of the men listed above were working the same jobs in 1819 that they were identified as working in 1824. Even with this in mind, we can see that the committee comprised men who held a wide variety of occupations. This fact is somewhat in line with the Black "middle-class" leadership taking hold in Black communities across the North. In other northern cities, prominence in Black communities was determined less by occupation or income and more by the level at which one contributed to the progress of the community, by those who were connected with elite whites, and by ministers in the emerging Black churches.[18] This is because, according to historian of Providence John Gilkeson, while the white "middle class" was increasingly defined by capitalism and monetary gain as a result of the Industrial Revolution, the Black population, long excluded from artisan production and then from factory production, evolved a class structure in northern cities apart from that of whites. Black men more commonly worked as odd-jobbers like wood sawyers, manual laborers, or in the homes and yards of elite white people—taking work as it came along and remaining vulnerable to seasonal or economic fluctuation. Some Black men accumulated wealth, but the lack of access to more regular positions as artisans or operatives meant that occupation was less of a divisive force than it was becoming to their white neighbors.[19]

And so, though the evidence is fragmentary, we can begin to reconstruct the Black leadership class of Providence, long overlooked in both the story of African American class development across the country and in the histories written of their own hometown.

A Closer Look

Nathaniel Paul was a Baptist minister who did much of the fundraising for the project, and he is perhaps the most well-known of everyone on this list. He was a young man in his late twenties when he took to the Baptist circuit in New England and New York, and as agent for this project he was able to raise over five hundred dollars, impressive but far short of what was needed to get the meetinghouse built and put to use.[20] This was just the beginning of Paul's brilliant, if understudied, career; he would go on and fundraise for the Wilberforce settlement for refugeed and freed slaves in Canada, tour the United Kingdom and Ireland to network with abolitionists there and raise money and awareness for the accelerating movement in the United States, and vocally oppose the American Colonization Society from his base in Albany. He (along with his more famous brother, Thomas Paul), helped pave the way for later Black preachers and orators who would become fixtures in the abolitionist movement—Episcopalian ministers Henry Highland Garnet and Alexander Crummell, activist and lecturer Lewis Hayden of Boston, and Frederick Douglass, to name a few.[21]

While white and Black ministers from neighboring churches and states "lectured" on the Sabbath, Asa Goldsbury, a minister in training when he came to Providence, taught at the school and took care of much of the preaching in the meetinghouse's first two years.[22] At several points in the brief appearances he makes in the historical record, Goldsbury seems to present us with issues that complicated and frustrated many Black communities, North and South, and that still exist to the present day. The first is skin color—he was described as an "octaroon," or someone with (supposedly) one-eighth African ancestry.[23] William J. Brown, after praising Goldsbury's preaching and teaching ability, made sure to mention that his light skin made many people take him for white. In addition to the implied biological connection with whiteness, *Short History* compiler Henry Jackson thought it prudent to publish testimonials by white ministers who taught Goldsbury and saw him preach. While testimonials for newcomers to such important positions were common, and Black ministers were for the most part a relatively new phenomenon to New England, Jackson added that the testimonials were published for the benefit of the people of color themselves. This would seem to signal the importance of connections with elite whites in portraying respectability, even among Black people. While this could be read as the author speaking strictly from a white point of view, the fact that they were probably in touch with the Black community—and that this notion seems to be backed up by William J. Brown's constant, if grudging, yearning for elite whites to support his ventures—can lead us to conclude that, in addition to ability, connection and confirmation by elite whites was at least a part of Goldsbury's middle-class respectability. In a way, this proves that

African Americans not only needed to be outstanding at their occupations (as Goldsbury probably was) but they were also burdened by the need to impress people outside of the communities they sought to improve. In 1826, Goldsbury moved to New Orleans—a city in which his light skin color probably played an even more prominent role—to found the city's First African Baptist Church.[24] Other minister-teachers would follow in his footsteps and build on the foundation he laid, including Jeremiah Asher and John W. Lewis—the latter founded a short-lived boarding school for New England's youth of color in the city in the 1830s and was a regional leader in the temperance movement.[25]

The most commonly listed occupation for the men on this list was "laborer." "Laborers" Henry Greene and George Willis epitomized the dynamism with which talented men of color often lived, as both were listed as having other professions in various city directories. Greene was listed as a machinist in 1828, a laborer in 1836, and a "[illegible] maker" in 1850.[26] The multitude of occupations complicates our understanding of Greene, and perhaps those in a similar situation to him; machinery and the making of a certain product were probably specific trades that could lead to a career, so why was Greene relegated to "laborer" status in between these jobs? One explanation may be that African Americans were systematically excluded from many regular jobs, only being hired when the white labor force dried up. Providence's William J. Brown remembered in his autobiography being rejected for a job by an employer "bitterly opposed to hiring a Black boy, while there were so many white boys he could get." Additionally, valuable apprenticeships were often closed to people of color. As Brown recalled, "Other boys of my acquaintance, with little or no education, jerked up instead of being brought up, were learning trades and getting employments, and I could get nothing." Brown's profound exposition is worth quoting in full:

> It seemed singular to me at first. I soon found it was on account of my color, for no colored men except barbers had trades, and that could hardly be called a trade. The white people seemed to be combined against giving us any thing to do which would elevate us to a free and independent position. The kindest feelings were manifested towards us in conversation, and that was all. I was now seventeen years old, and was at a loss to know what steps to take to get a living, for if I possessed the knowledge of a Demosthenes or Cicero, or Horace, or Virgil, it would not bring to me flattering prospects for the future. To drive carriage, carry a market basket after the boss, and brush his boots, or saw wood and run errands, was as high as a colored man could rise. This seemed

to be the only prospect lying in my path. Some of my associates worked for eight or ten dollars a month, but what would that small pittance be to them, settled down in life with a family to support, if they should have long continued sickness to contend with. This wouldn't suit me; I must go somewhere else to find employ.[27]

Perhaps what Brown confronted was similar to what Greene faced: Brown had tried his hand at several different things, at various times sawing wood, accepting a job at sea, and then eventually teaching himself shoe repair (which netted him less than a fully apprenticed artisan) to make a living. Perhaps Greene taught himself machinery and the making of a specific product, but regular work eluded him and he was forced to become a laborer and perform odd jobs to earn money during slack times.

George C. Willis, sexton in Providence's (white) First Baptist Church and then deacon in the African Union Meeting House, serves as an example of someone who was able to parlay multiple careers into considerable wealth, a minor national role in the African American convention movement, a major role in the city's temperance movement, and a major role in the movement to win back the right to vote for Black people in Rhode Island. According to historian Robert Cottrol, he was a laborer, but in the 1840 U.S. Census he is listed as having an occupation in commerce.[28] As both a lay church leader and someone engaged in commerce, his public role would have enabled him to bridge Black and white worlds, as to be successful in both, he likely would have needed the support of white and Black spiritual leaders and white and Black wealth. Unlike William J. Brown and Elleanor Eldridge, who published their life stories because they were impoverished in their later years despite having undertaken lucrative enterprises, Willis had real estate property assessed at seven hundred dollars in the City Council's 1851 tax report, a considerable sum of money for anyone at the time.[29]

Two additional laborers according to the 1832 city directory were Warwick Sweetland and Thomas Thompson. Sweetland shows up elsewhere only in a directory of the First Baptist Church, which indicates he died in 1833. Interestingly, this meant that he might have continued worshipping there despite being a committee member of the African Union Meeting House.[30] Thompson was listed as the owner of his own house in an 1822 survey of people of color who were heads of households, living with his wife and one child. By 1830, in his home eight people of color under the age of twenty-three resided along with him and (presumably) his wife—a tall order for someone heading a household on the commonly irregular pay of a laborer. Six of the young people were female; perhaps they contributed to the household income as domestic servants in others' houses or took in washing, common occupations for Black women to supplement the often meager or irregular incomes men faced in a discriminatory social and economic climate.[31]

One of the most important industries to early Providence was represented in the person of George Barrett: in the 1832 city directory, he was listed as a mariner. Sailing was famously one of the most common professions among African American and Native American men in the eighteenth and nineteenth centuries. While most people of color started as cabin boys or stewards, shipboard life afforded opportunities for upward advancement that were not available on land. With the obvious perils on the sea an ever-present reality, skill trumped race in job distribution; there were even instances of enslaved people rising to the level of captain. However, irregular work, especially during times of war and economic upheaval; the transient lifestyle; sailors' often carefree spending of their wages; and the famous alcohol-infused behavior of sailors on land—in addition to the interracial manner in which they often caroused—meant that even though they were important parts of a mercantile economy, Black and white mariners were often an impoverished, unwelcome presence to the political and moral reformers of the early nineteenth century.[32] Nonetheless, the presence of a mariner on the March 1819 committee is further proof that monetary status was not the most important factor of one's worthiness or respectability in the Black community.

However, one aspect of Barrett's life would certainly have made him worthy of the community's respect—he was a military veteran, having served in the War of 1812. Largely a maritime war, he was possibly in the navy. Even though African Americans were officially banned from joining the armed forces, that law was commonly flouted for largely the same reason Blacks were able to advance in the sailing profession—the necessity of skill in perilous conditions. Barrett also had a military connection by having served with General Edward Carrington, a leader of Rhode Island's militia during the war and in the years following, the architect of a shipping empire.[33] William J. Brown, citing this connection as the cause for Barrett's knowledge of military tactics, wrote about how Barrett was the leader of the African American militia company, the African Greys, that marched in procession at the opening of the meetinghouse in 1821.[34] It is also possible that Barrett used his connection with an elite white powerbroker to secure his job as a mariner, and this relationship undoubtedly enhanced the war veteran's respectability. Barrett's connection to Carrington foreshadowed the events that would play out two decades later, when African American militiamen played a major role in suppressing the Dorr Rebellion in 1842, an act that led directly to their enfranchisement by the Whigs—typically elites in the Federalist tradition, anti-immigrant, and often softer on race than Democrats—who were in control of Rhode Island politics.

Henry Taber was almost certainly a Revolutionary War veteran, native of Guinea on the African coast, and previously enslaved to a Judge Constant Taber of Newport (Henry's name was listed on muster rolls variously as "Henry Taybor" and "Harry Tabor or Taber"). His age may have prevented him from being listed in the city's occupational directories, which began publication in 1824, though he was listed as a laborer in war records.[35] At some point after earning his freedom and his honorable discharge on June 15, 1783, Taber moved to Providence and may have used some of the $302 he earned for his service to purchase a two-story house on Benevolent Street, valued at $200 in 1798.[36] Certainly, his status as a Revolutionary War veteran, like Barrett's as a veteran of the War of 1812, afforded him an air of respectability in both Black and white American circles. His and his comrades' legacy was invoked in the later fight for voting rights, as in addition to the actual military service Black Providence residents provided during the Dorr struggle, the memory of Rhode Islanders of color like Taber serving with distinction in the Revolution was offered as evidence of their fitness for citizenship. By the late 1810s and early 1820s, his service certainly gave him standing enough to be voted to the committee.

George J. Smith had a very close and powerful connection to an elite white Providence resident. He was listed as a coachman and part of the household of John Carter Brown in the 1850 U.S. Census (though he had been the head of a household himself in the previous three federal censuses). John Carter Brown was an heir to the fortune of the Brown family of slave traders, which included Moses Brown in his pre-Quaker days, and later a book collector; his collection was the foundation for the present-day John Carter Brown Library, a valuable space for historical research—a passion of John's. We can surmise that Smith was John Carter Brown's personal driver, as none of the other members listed in his household were coachmen. Moses Brown was John Carter Brown's great-uncle; perhaps this connection played a role in Smith's activities in support of the meetinghouse. Smith also may represent a larger history of personal livery service to elite whites as a marker of social status both inside and outside of Black communities. In later years, the Pullman porters, Black men who served whites in white-only Pullman train cars, could be considered middle class, the "aristocracy of Black labor," though they were often denigrated by being called "George" (after George Pullman) and not their actual names.[37] Richard Wright's famous 1940 novel *Native Son* also quite famously delves into the paradox of livery service to whites as both middle class and degrading. Although George Smith apparently did not leave behind his feelings in writing, and he is silent in the historical record outside of his occupation and appointment to the committee, he does perhaps demonstrate an early manifestation of status in the white and Black community consistent with this larger historical narrative.

George McCarty has perhaps the most fascinating and unorthodox story of anyone in this study. Born on the Caribbean island of Montserrat, his surname makes him a hard person to track through the historical records—at various times, it was spelled "M'Carty," "McCarty," and "McCarthy." We can surmise the person with all these spellings was the same because in each census from 1810 to 1840, the person was listed as a "free colored person" with four people in his household. McCarty owned a "refreshment" stand in the Market House, the center of Providence's economic life in the first few decades after the Revolution, making him a visible part of the community as a whole.[38] He was also apparently a savvy investor, having owned much—and valuable—real estate. It was he who sold the land on which the meetinghouse would be built to Moses Brown for two hundred dollars; he cosigned the deed with his wife, Terisa (also known as Maria Theresa in the record of his death in 1863).[39] Sixteen years after selling that lot, he advertised the sale of several lots on Meeting Street, on which stood "substantial dwellings," and he made sure it was known that his holdings were "free of encumbrances."[40] Interestingly, he was not listed on the tax roll taken in 1851, though he very clearly owned a lot of property—probably more than George Willis, who was assessed a city tax. He also was active in antislavery circles, serving as a delegate to the New England Anti-Slavery Convention in 1836.[41] It was probably the combination of his economic connections within the larger community along with his activism that helped him earn his place on the committee.

Abraham Gibbs left behind fewer records than McCarty but also rented space in the Market House.[42] The 1820 U.S. Census showed him living in Providence with a younger woman and child. In the 1822 directory of all people of color who were heads of households, Gibbs was listed as the owner of a house in which lived five people whose connection to him cannot be determined. In

1830, he was listed as living with a younger woman, a young man, and an older white woman. This last detail is tantalizing: the white woman may have simply been a boarder that the Gibbs family took in for extra income, or even a white immigrant domestic servant—either way, an inversion of most Black-white community ties. Gibbs was the listed author and first signer of the petition to charter the African Society, written the year after the committee was put together and signed by most members, perhaps showing he was viewed as a leader among leaders.[43]

Hodge Congdon never appeared in city directories and only shows up in census data for 1810, 1820, and 1830, as living with his wife and (probably) two sons. He is mentioned in a few narratives surrounding the meetinghouse, however, in ways that can tell us that he probably earned a middle-class living even if we do not know how. First, we know that after the parade through Providence for the meetinghouse's 1821 opening, his Benefit Street house was chosen as the place where the leaders would meet to plan the celebration. And even though Congdon's wife, Jane, apparently had to earn a living as a laundress, at least as late as 1870 when she was eighty-nine years old, the Jane Congdon estate was large enough that it helped keep the African Union Meeting House's successor, the Congdon Street Baptist Church, afloat after it ran out of money in the 1870s.[44] Jane owned a first-run copy of David Walker's *Appeal*, a fiery antislavery tract published in 1829 that helped galvanize the abolitionist movement, perhaps showing that Jane and Hodge Congdon were well-connected with the larger, regional Black community.[45]

Finally, we have the men who left few records behind for historians. There is a James Harris buried in the mostly African American section of the North Burial Ground in Providence; he died in 1829, but his gravestone is weathered to the point of illegibility. William J. Brown mentioned that Harris was involved in a protest against taxation of the African American community while it was disfranchised, though this took place in the 1830s, which would mean the James Harris who died in 1829 either is not the James Harris on the March 1819 committee or Brown was wrong in his recollection.[46] I found Stephen Wolmsly nowhere in a search of the census records (perhaps due to the spelling of his name), though he was listed as the head of a household and owner of his own house in the 1822 survey. Derry Williams, who died shortly after the committee met, was listed as a sexton for St. John's Episcopal Church; his ecclesiastical employment and connection with a white parish qualified him for committee membership. Joshua Weeks was the head of a family of five who at one time rented from an apparently wealthy landowner, Stephen Harris, and may even be the same person as "Josiah Wicks," listed as the coauthor of the aforementioned petition with Gibbs.[47] Peter Waters lived with his wife and two daughters in Providence in 1820, and along with McCarty and Gibbs, rented space in the Market House—but other than that is absent from the historical record. Thomas Graham led a household of seven people in the 1810 U.S. Census but died shortly after the meeting, with the *Providence Patriot* noting that he was "a respectable man of color."[48]

Why would these men have little or no mention in historical records? One explanation may be that one or more of them was a seaman, who lived notoriously transient lives, often settling in port cities temporarily. Perhaps they eluded census takers and city directory enrollers because of this. Or, perhaps as odd jobbers, men who William J. Brown would see on city bridges waiting for work, they rented homes or rooms only temporarily, going where there was work.[49] Each of these scenarios might seem unlikely for a committee of such stature, but in Providence's Black community, they might have had stronger connections to each other, their church, or white benefactors than their homes or jobs. Perhaps they exist somewhere in the historical record not yet mined.

A Social and Political Space

The construction of the African Union Meeting House began to bear fruit for Providence's Black community even before the roof was laid over its top. Most of the committee that planned the building of the meetinghouse were signers of a February 1820 petition to the state's General Assembly for incorporation of the "African Society in the Town of Providence." Incorporation would grant them official recognition as a "body politic" unto itself and bestow to the society the right to bring suit (and be sued) and defend itself under Rhode Island's court system—recognition that they were a part of the larger republican body politic.

This document can also be read as an assertion of racial consciousness: using "African" in their society's title signified both a separation from white institutions and a recognition of common ancestral roots, a notion that would be contested in the years after as "colored" came to signify a more common Americanness among the country's Black citizens. The fact that the document's authors referred to themselves as "people of colour" despite the moniker "African Society" may show that this was still a formative period of American racial ideology.

The reason for the African Society's proposed existence is telling of what community leaders saw as the clearest path to citizenship. They were forming the society, they said, "in order so that the people of colour in said Town [Providence], Should be duly educated in such branches of knowledge as may qualify them to become useful members of Society when they should have received that Christian instruction and Education that your petitioners have in view, to give them."[50] The two main premises on which their case for inclusion would be built were religion and education. An understanding of the social and political context surrounding Black leaders' choosing of this tactic elucidates what they were up against, what they saw as their collective strengths, and why they saw commitment to religion and education as qualifications for citizenship.

Historian Mark Schantz has identified a "revival of extraordinary power" of Christianity that saw Providence ablaze in religious enthusiasm in the spring of 1820, an outgrowth of the Second Great Awakening, which led many converts to newly founded and more democratically organized denominations around the country. Schantz writes that this movement provided the "flame" that led to the building of the meetinghouse.[51] This may be partially true, but the African Society was aiming toward a different strand of the state's religiosity—that of its conservative elites. The state's political and social establishment saw itself in religious terms, as Schantz convincingly argues, and alluding to its religious bent served the purposes both of appealing to the General Assembly's sensibilities and of the need to push back on persistent claims of Black neighborhoods as dens of vice.[52] The petition's explicit thanking of Henry Jackson, a white Brown University graduate and up-and-coming minister in Providence's revered First Baptist Church (who also wrote the definitive account of the African Meeting House's construction), and Quaker merchant elites like Moses Brown, his son Obadiah, and George Benson, show that they were more interested in playing up traditional connections than allying with other offshoot churches of the 1820 revival. This was perhaps to be expected, especially because Moses Brown was one of Providence's Black community's most stalwart allies. George Benson was too; the latter was a cofounder of the Providence Abolition Society with Brown in 1789, and his family became early proponents of immediatist abolition, with white abolitionist William Lloyd Garrison marrying into the family.[53]

Black leaders saw education, and especially publicizing their desire for it, as essential for their case for citizenship largely for the same reasons—that educated Black children and adults would combat whites' ideas about Black intellect. Since passage of the gradual emancipation law, Black children's education had largely been limited to "apprenticeships," which, because these arrangements often just meant temporary servitude, simultaneously reinforced ideas about Black inferiority and attempted to keep those notions alive for future generations.[54] The leaders' call also reflected the reality that formal public education had long been reserved for white children, codified briefly in the 1800 "Act to Establish Free Schools." The act stated that "each and every town in the State shall annually cause to be established and kept, at the expense of such town, one or more free schools, for the instruction of all the white inhabitants of said town, between the ages of six and twenty years." In order to make the "white" provision seem fair, Providence proceeded to drop African Americans from their tax rolls—an action that may have provided temporary relief for some struggling families but one that placed them further outside the bounds of citizenship. Most towns in the state immediately pushed back against the law and it was repealed three years later, but the "white" provision in education made clear the General Assembly's view. Despite the state's repeal, Providence had eagerly begun to implement the act and established a public school system, with Black children barred from attending and their parents exempt from the taxation required to fund it. One further addition Providence's school department made to its instruction was "endeavor[ing] to impress the minds of their pupils with the sense of the Being and Providence of God," which perhaps also explains the Black leaders' concentration on "Christian instruction" in tandem with other "such branches of knowledge." Should the time come when their children would be included in the town's public education system, they wanted to be prepared.[55]

A few private schools appear to have opened briefly in the first two decades of the nineteenth century, one by a benevolent Baptist group named the "Female Society for the Education of Coloured Children" and another by Lucy Townsend, a Black woman who was paid periodically by the town for her school.[56] Robert Cottrol has also pointed out that a few children of color may have been able to attend Quaker or other religious schools, but the costs were so prohibitive that their admittance was usually dependent on connections with prominent white families.[57] William J. Brown, a young boy in the early 1820s, at times used connections to whites he knew but also discussed the hardships he and his schoolmates who badly wanted an education faced while trying to pay tuition. In return for white sponsorship to attend a school for children of color held in the basement of a white public school, Brown had to saw wood for his teacher, and after still falling seventy dollars into debt, he was only able to continue after winning a lottery.[58] Black children would have to work much harder than their white counterparts to gain the knowledge and skills necessary for citizenship while also facing uncertain futures.

While the building of the meetinghouse included a school and so necessarily put education on the agenda for Providence's Black leaders, the move to incorporate the African Society based on its commitment to education was clearly meant to protect what was seen as a boon to the community and a way to promote opportunity for future generations. The school opened in 1821, getting off to a precarious start. The General Assembly had received the African Society's petition on February 22, 1820, but referred it to a committee four days later where nothing happened to it for the rest of the session; it was then "continued" in the assembly's June session, never to be revived.[59] The school's tuition was set at $1.50, an attainable sum for much of Providence's Black community, now numbering almost 1,000 strong and nearly 10 percent of the town's total population. Within a very short amount of time there were 125 students enrolled in the day school, from ages four to almost seventy, and 200 enrolled in the Sabbath school. However, without consistent revenue from the state, and with an economically unstable student body, the school had a hard time funding its upkeep and hiring teachers. The "Lancasterian plan," which involved older students helping teach younger ones, was employed, possibly to offset this. William J. Brown remembered that when teachers were to be found, they were often ridiculed by white citizens of Providence. He remembered a white teacher named Mr. Anthony who, after a student of color respectfully tipped his cap to him when he saw him outside of school, threatened to flog students if they acknowledged him on the street. John Ormsbee, a white Baptist minister, ran the day school in its first year, and despite high praise from the Black leaders' ally Henry Jackson, Brown remembered him as a severe authoritarian who "used the cowhide very freely." With nearly 20 percent of the population mobilized, however, Providence's Black community achieved skyrocketing literacy rates, keeping pace with their white neighbors and making it harder for whites to claim inherent inferiority as a reason for continuing discrimination.[60]

* * *

In discussing the first permanent class of Providence's leaders of color, we can come to several further conclusions. First, despite connections to white elites and despite the narrative offered by Henry Jackson's history of the African Union Meeting House, Providence's Black community more than likely came together themselves with the idea of building their own meetinghouse—a space that would serve as more of a community center than just a house for worship. William J. Brown's narrative, when looked at in the context of Black community organizational history, is clearly more plausible. It was on land owned by a wealthy Black man that the community built the meetinghouse. It was mostly independent Black householders—many of whom had found success in jobs that were not typically lucrative, and despite white prejudice designed to keep them economically oppressed—who made up the committee and surely did not need white elites to tell them how to improve their own community. They were laborers, ministers, real estate investors, war veterans, mariners, odd jobbers, and may have filled other roles that were not picked up by the records of history. It appears to be the connections they were able to forge—with each other, their community, churches, and elite whites—that allowed them to lay the physical and cultural foundation from which they were able to build community and further connections that would pay off in the movement for citizenship rights in the ensuing decades. Some of them—George Willis and George McCarty in particular—played major roles themselves, while the rest paved the way for future leaders in the struggle like barber Alfred Niger, minister John W. Lewis, laborer Ichabod Northup, and educator Ransom Parker, all of whom are discussed in the following chapters.

Second, though they clearly came together on their own accord, connections to elite whites were important to several of the members of the committee. While the political winds were blowing against both elite white Federalists and the Black community just as the meetinghouse was being built, and disfranchisement had met with little fanfare, Providence's wealthy remained powerful allies. Black leaders stood ready and willing to put that alliance to work for their benefit. This dynamic would play out in complicated ways over the next two decades, as elites faced challenges to their power and Black neighborhoods twice became sites of violence and destruction—all at the hands of angry white men eager for their own citizenship rights and the right to police the color line.

CHAPTER 4

"The Clouds of Evil"
SURVIVAL AND ORGANIZATION, 1820–1831

When Christopher Hall died in January 1830, the *Providence Journal* ran a lengthy obituary—unusual for a Black Providence resident. Hall had worked as a boatman on the Potomac and may have been a servant to George Washington in his early years. He then moved to Providence where he made his living by toiling as a wood sawyer. By 1824, he was a widower with three children and owned several homes, including his own and three others that he rented to other Black Providence residents like Revolutionary War veteran Britton Saltonstall. Writing five decades later, Black community leader William J. Brown remembered him as a "pious man." He was also fiercely protective of his independence and his family. The *Journal* writer mentioned that he was the victim of a vicious attack on October 18, 1824, in which a mob of white men entered his neighborhood, known colloquially as "Hard-Scrabble," tore down his house, and beat him. After the attack, he attached the roof of his house to the foundation to shield himself and his children from the cold of the upcoming winter, refusing to give up custody of his children to a group of well-meaning white women who offered to take them in. The *Journal* writer lamented caustically that "though he loved the world ... this world to him, was worse than ten thousand purgatories."[1]

His life was remembered in print similarly to that of Robert Vorhis, the formerly enslaved man who lost his wife and children to the institution, lived just outside the city limits, and had been profiled as "Robert the Hermit" in the *Providence Literary Cadet* a few years earlier. "Old Kit," as Christopher Hall was known, was caricatured in his obituary as an outsider, a "King Lear" who had money but "could not and would not brook an insult," and supposedly made enemies among people both Black and white. If Vorhis symbolized the physical distance white Providence readers hoped African Americans would keep from the body politic, Hall's obituary portrayed the ridiculousness—even dangerousness—of African Americans' fitness for citizenship. Although he met the financial and real estate qualifications of a freeholder, he was "pregnant with vile passions;—easily excited to wrath and vengeance," and was almost always seen about town with a "bloody nose and broken head." The editor went on to spew line after hackneyed line of insults, calling Hall a "negro terror" and a "constitutionally bad negro."[2] Like Vorhis, Hall's life was reduced to a passing curiosity, a stranger among citizens, his candidacy for fellowship in the body politic undone by his Blackness and its associated attributes. Perhaps his anger stemmed not from his "constitution" but from the fact that all he received in return for living as any republican citizen was expected to live was a mob of white men—many of whom were not citizens themselves—attempting to raze his claim to a place in the body politic.[3]

Hall's defiant reaction to the mob and the overtures for outside help can be seen as an illustrative example of how Providence's Black community responded to the rising tide of white supremacy in Providence, a trend that was taking hold across all northern cities. Elsewhere, as Federalism was dying out and industrialization creating an expansive—and restless—working class, property requirements for voting were falling. White elites, still feeling the need to protect the sanctity of the franchise, began a rhetorical campaign extolling the supposed virtues of their newly enfranchised voting blocs, transforming the idea of hard-working white manhood into republican virtue. Potential rivals for industrial jobs in cities, Black men faced the simultaneous loss of their old Federalist allies and a poor white and European immigrant population keen on exploiting its only tie to power—white manhood.[4] While Democratic-Republican Andrew Jackson's three runs for president (1824, 1828, and 1832) galvanized poor and artisan white men everywhere, Rhode Island's stubborn conservative establishment continued waving off calls for relaxing the property requirement. Increasingly frustrated with their own lack of access to citizenship rights, white Rhode Islanders twice in seven years vented their anger on Black communities in an effort to replicate the new racial order that the state's elites were denying them. Despite earning only a passing mention from Hall's obituary writer, the Hard-Scrabble riot, like the more violent one in "Snow Town" seven years later, was significant not for victimizing Providence's Black men and women but for the way it spurred organizing aimed at accessing the benefits of citizenship.

Like Christopher Hall did with his family, Providence's Black community turned inward, shielding itself from the insults that rained down on them on the town's streets and the uptick in stinging newspaper distortions of its members' dress, speech, and behavior. Hall himself never joined the ranks of the leaders; perhaps his supposed abrasiveness precluded his involvement with the community writ large. Those who did endeavor to lead used their new community space, the African Union Meeting House, to reincarnate mutual benefit societies and turned outward when necessary to engage their traditional, if highly unreliable, white allies in powerful circles. In an era when petitioning was seen as an accepted form of communication between ordinary citizens and government, they used this power to show their fitness for citizenship, putting their arguments on the General Assembly's agenda. In these petitions, they detailed their adherence to republican norms of Christianity, sobriety, industry, and independence, pointing out that the only difference between themselves and freemen was often the color of their skin. This strategy of resistance to white supremacy but accommodation to republican ideals and processes earned them little to celebrate in the 1820s and 1830s but helped them work out strategies for future activism.

Hard-Scrabble

The years that followed the building of the meetinghouse and the opening of its school were turbulent for both whites and people of color in Providence. The Black community saw its population skyrocket: there were 1,414 people of color listed on the town's 1825 census, which represented an increase of over 50 percent from 1820, outpacing the also rapid rise in the white population. As the Black community became more visible, more independent, and more literate, the town's white population swelled with wage-working families, most of whom were disfranchised by the state's freemanship requirement and many of whom were frustrated with the lack of progress in the "general suffrage" campaign.[5] It appears also that, while there had been several clusters of Black homes around the East Side, developers were buying up lots in those neighborhoods for low prices and attracting impoverished whites, sailors who only needed temporary lodgings, and families of color who were either poor themselves or wished to live in previously established Black neighborhoods near family and friends. Some residents of color—like those of Addison Hollow near the northern periphery of the town—long barred from skilled trades and used to waiting for day labor on the nearby bridges, saw opportunity. Opening and running boardinghouses in these neighborhoods was one way to make a living for Black men and women. In Addison Hollow, an underground economy appeared to take shape, with some whites and African Americans running taverns, dance halls, and brothels out of their homes. These spaces of racial mixing, by necessity functioning outside of respectable republican norms, were tinderboxes for racially charged conflict and obvious sites for surveillance, and these locales earned plenty of scorn from the surrounding community. Elite whites decried the "vice" that these places seemed to bring, and Black Providence residents who lived both inside and outside of these neighborhoods combated the growing association with Blackness and "vice" often by reinforcing "respectable" behavior in their children. William J. Brown, who grew up on the East Side, was taught always to retain a polite demeanor, even though when he was a child he could not understand the angry insults he was forced to endure from his white neighbors.[6]

The frustrations of white Providence men with the General Assembly's continuous rejection of measures to widen the voting pool were briefly mitigated when, in its January 1824 session, the legislative body passed provisions for a constitutional convention to be held in the summer. After witnessing the admission of six new states, all with constitutions, and constitutional reform conventions in neighboring Connecticut, Massachusetts, and New York, Rhode Island's freemen finally agreed to at least entertain the idea of abolishing the colonial charter in favor of a constitution. The convention met in June of that year, and though a proposal to enfranchise all white taxpaying men was badly defeated (garnering a mere three votes), "One of the People" editorialized in the Democratic-Republican *Providence Patriot* that he hoped the debates had uncovered at least a moderate lean toward an expansion of the voting population.[7] The constitution generated considerable support in Providence because it allotted the city representation in the legislature more proportionate to its rapidly increasing population. Landless white men there had even more reason to hope that this could be a step forward toward enfranchisement: in addition to state politics being more heavily influenced by Providence, its freemen leaning hard toward reform in general meant that the landless certainly had the elites' ears. In fact, on October 11, the date of the official statewide referendum on the constitution, Providence freemen voted in its favor 653–26; it fared poorly elsewhere and went down to defeat, the rest of the state voting against it by more than a 3–1 margin.[8]

The growing Black population, increasing frustration of disfranchised whites, and both groups living, working, and moving in the same crowded waterfront made Providence a tinderbox. The bitter observations of whites in other northern cities were reprinted in the Providence newspapers, notably the *Providence Patriot*, seemingly warning Providence readers of the dangers the growing Black community posed. From the *Boston Gazette* came an 1820 story about dozens of armed Black men extrajudicially attempting to free an alleged fugitive slave from a Boston jail. In the wake of Denmark Vesey's planned slave rebellion in Charleston, South Carolina, in the summer of 1822, a Morristown, New Jersey, committee of "citizens" had met and empowered themselves to ensure free Black people had good references for employment and gave themselves the authority to break up African Americans' "riotous and disorderly meetings." The Morristown committee, like the Providence Town Council that year, was charged with taking a census and, using stronger language than the Providence body, removing "worthless free people of color" who were not residents.[9] Even the Federalist and National Republican-leaning *Rhode Island American* commented that Black children in Providence were growing up without morals, and that "this solitary fact imports a state of things warranting serious apprehensions on the part of our inhabitants, and requiring the adoption of some plan, commensurate to the nature and extent of the evil." Correspondent "R.A.C.," while cautiously dissenting from some of the prevailing racial pseudoscience by affirming "Hottentots'" humanity, also urged a special evangelism of the Black race, which he claimed had been corrupted in Africa by Islam.[10] As seems clear, white disdain for the expanding Black community was bipartisan.

Exactly one week after the defeat of the 1824 proposed constitution, the fuse was lit and violence exploded in the Addison Hollow neighborhood in the northern part of town. Its immediate cause seems to have been an altercation on Providence's streets between a group of Black and white people over who was entitled to the "inside walk." The middle of unpaved roads in early nineteenth-century cities and towns was often thick with a mixture of mud and the droppings from horses drawing carts, and the areas closest to the buildings—the "inside walks"—were drier and easier to walk on. Gender custom dictated that men would cede the walk to women, and racial custom apparently dictated that people of color would defer to whites.[11] However, on October 17, 1824, in their "peregrinations through the town," one group of Black people decided to defy that convention, precipitating a "battle royal" on the street and prompting devastating rioting on the part of white Providence the next night. The meaning of the riot, and the actions of both Black residents and white participants, were highly significant and foreshadowed the social and political struggles involving nonelite whites and African Americans over the next few decades. It helped to set the parameters in which the fight for inclusion in the body politic would be conditioned.[12]

Providence's Black community in the early decades of the nineteenth century had to face affronts and taunts from their white neighbors. William J. Brown recalled this especially being true on Sundays, remembering that, as he walked to and from church on the main thoroughfares, "if you were well dressed, they [white bystanders] would insult you for that, and if you were ragged, you would surely be insulted for being so." Further, these "white gentlemen" would physically harass churchgoers of color, "knocking off men's hats and pulling off ladies' shawls." He remembered a time in which he and a friend got into a fight with two white men over the "inside walk." While on their way to the evening school, they were confronted by the white men, who had just ordered two "colored ladies" off the "inside walk." Brown and his friend refused to be intimidated, fighting back and nearly being carried to jail before white druggist Joseph Balch intervened. After insulting one of the white men for being beaten up by two children, Balch angrily announced that they "had no business troubling" Brown and his friend, as he was "well acquainted" with them and knew them to be "nice boys." Brown's assertiveness in his right to occupy the sidewalk, his fighting back when the old racial order reared its ugly head, and his connection with a white man of influence were just one person's story. But perhaps these factors in countless undocumented incidents like this over the course of the 1810s and 1820s all signaled that Providence residents of color would know how best to handle the pogroms that were to come.[13]

The incident that led to the destruction on October 18, 1824, was apparently not worth mentioning in the transcripts of the trials of four white men who were arrested in its aftermath, which stand as the official record of the riot.[14] They were charged under the state law against riotous assembly, and as such charges were brought by the state attorney general. The facts the prosecution laid out against Oliver Cummins, the first rioter tried, were corroborated by several white witnesses, most prominently Jesse B. Sweet, a grocer who kept a store on North Main Street near Addison Hollow. Sweet claimed that he saw Oliver Cummins and several other white men tearing down the houses of Henry T. Wheeler and Christopher ("Old Kit") Hall, saw them "engaged in chopping off the studs of Wheeler's House with an axe and afterward assisting in pushing it over" sometime after 9 o'clock that evening, and later saw them "at work pulling down" Hall's. Although only a few were charged, the mob that night destroyed about twenty buildings in the neighborhood. The town watchman, Samuel V. Allen, stood by idly, thinking that "he was doing his duty by keeping still as possible" as he "did not think it prudent to interfere." The matter had not "*imperiously* called him" to intervene. Several of the witnesses testified that Cummins was shot in the mouth by someone from inside Wheeler's house as he approached it with an axe. They only stopped when, apparently tiring themselves out, the whole group did what they had been denied the right to do for years—they took a vote, and the majority decided to cease.[15] With Wheeler's house destroyed and Hall's nearly so—save for the roof pulled over the foundation—and a parade of witnesses putting axes in the four white men's hands, there was little doubt that they had done what they were accused of doing.

Nonetheless, the men's defense attorney, Joseph L. Tillinghast, had an ingenious strategy to keep his clients out of jail. He began his closing argument in Cummins's trial with a salaciously racist diatribe. He claimed that Wheeler's and Hall's residences were not houses but places of dance, drinking, and revelry. He even tried to suggest that Wheeler did not own the home, and it took the presentation of the home's deed and the testimony of the man whom Tillinghast asserted owned the home to put that matter to rest. During this process, he suggestively said that the jury had the right to know whether the structure was a "home or a pig sty," because the attorney general "would not contend the prisoner could be indicted for tearing down a pig sty." This was all part of his attempt to play to the old assumptions of Black inferiority—and the new equation of free African Americans with the susceptibility to drink, dance, and crime. "Like the ancient Babylon," Tillinghast thundered sarcastically, Addison's Hollow "has fallen with all its graven images, its tables of impure oblation, its idolatrous rights and sacrifices." He referred to it by its other name, "Hard-Scrabble," claiming that he could not determine whether the moniker derived from the fact that "you have to scrabble hard to get there or to scrabble hard to get safe away." "Perhaps," he added, "after all it is only meant to be descriptive of the *shuffling*, which there is practiced in the graceful evolutions of the dance, or the zig zag movements of Pomp and Phillis," the latter of whom were well-known proto-minstrel characters of bobalition broadsides circulating in New England newspapers. "Phillis" was most likely a caricature evolved from whites' knowledge of African American poet Phillis Wheatley. He then doubled down, saying, "We must all agree the destruction of this place is a benefit to the morals of the community." The equating of Blackness with vice had been increasing in print media, but the physical destruction of a largely Black neighborhood and then this defense of the perpetrators of the pogrom certainly raised the stakes of racial animosity.[16]

Rhode Island attorney general Duttee J. Pearce closed for the state, claiming that "he had nothing to do with whites or blacks in this prosecution," and argued that the behavior of the tenants did not matter. If "the blacks" were riotous themselves, then the law "was open to punish them. . . . If they live here and are not outlawed they have a right to be protected by the law in their persons and property." An official statement of African Americans' right to protection—even if it was hedged by the disdainful assumption that they just "live[d] here"—was a significant acknowledgment during a time of advancing white supremacy. Further, maligning the white rioters pushed back against the growing bombast of white men, who throughout the North had been emboldened by the demagoguery and rough-and-tumble politics of that year's presidential campaign. While it is tempting to lump all poor whites together, at least four of the men indicted were of the middling or artisan ranks: these included masons Gilbert Humes and Arthur Farrier, jeweler Ezra Hubbard, and future town crier Nathaniel Metcalf.[17] Conceivably, their exclusion from participating in such a heated election after years of promising steps toward suffrage—and most likely reading that other states had relaxed suffrage enough to include most white men—added to the rage they felt when their right to the "inside walk" was challenged.[18] The riot had, after all, culminated in a vote. Regardless, Pearce's admonition of the rioters proclaimed that the elites' order, and perhaps its tenuous alliance with the Black community, appeared to have withstood the first outburst of Jacksonian-style democracy.[19]

The trials of the rioters ended anticlimactically: Oliver Cummins, tried first, was found "not guilty." The second trial found Nathaniel Metcalf guilty of rioting, but the jury recommended the "most lenient and merciful consideration of the court" in his sentencing. After one more "not guilty" verdict, a fourth trial ended when the five judges who benched the Court of Common Pleas, which had been hearing the trials, entertained a motion by defense attorney

Tillinghast that claimed the prosecution had not sufficiently proved that what happened on the night of the 18th was a riot according to Rhode Island law. Rather, it had been an "affray," which carried a misdemeanor charge and not the weight of a "riot." The judges voted three-to-two in favor of this argument and released Metcalf and all future defendants on the grounds that they had been indicted under the wrong charge. No one would be held accountable for the destruction in Addison Hollow.[20]

The events of October 17–18 and their aftermath revealed two major developments for Providence's Black community, themes that would reappear as undercurrents in the larger riot of 1831 and the more extensive push for voting rights in the early 1840s. The first was that African Americans would not be bullied by disfranchised whites into a continuation of the pre-emancipation social or political order. Those whose names are lost to history, who refused to cede the inside walk, sent that message perhaps the most explicitly. Henry T. Wheeler, or whomever it was in his house who shot at Oliver Cummins, also boldly risked inflaming the approaching mob by fighting back. Christopher Hall, whose run-ins with others became fodder for the local opinion page after his death, refused to let the mob—or even white Providence—win, as in the days and weeks after the riot he pulled the roof over his cellar to shelter from the winter and refused the overtures of a white benevolent women's society that offered to take his children. He was teaching the upcoming generation of Providence African Americans a valuable lesson about the self-sufficiency required for a group of outsiders to make inroads into the republican body politic.

The second development was a tacit reaffirmation of the Black community's ties to elite whites. An oddity in terms of antebellum rioting, apparently no attempt to arrest the shooter from inside Wheeler's house was made—just the white perpetrators of the destruction, all of whom were identified by the *Hard-Scrabble Calendar* as "labourers and traders," and some of whom were either sailors or transient residents. Only William Taylor, one of the men who had his case dismissed before trial, was listed in the 1824 *Providence City Directory*, indicating that the rest had no established profession or home the directory creators deemed worth mentioning.[21] The class dimensions are thus clear, as is the crosscurrent of the failure to shake up the state's entrenched political elite through the implementation of a new constitution just the week prior—the latter emblemized by the rioters' stopping to take a vote on whether to retire for the night. The Black community, largely undeterred save for a few leaving on a venture to Liberia two years later, using the African

Union Meeting House as a base, organized for a more nuanced approach to survival and citizenship. The white working class and the few elites who rallied to their cause would try to use might in an effort to force their way into the body politic. In an interesting coda, the two young lawyers who squared off in the case would seemingly change sides: Joseph L. Tillinghast later joined the elite Whig establishment, served in Congress, and argued against the proslavery "gag rule." Duttee J. Pearce, the attorney general who appealed to calm reason during the trial, later was accused of inciting an anti-abolitionist mob in Newport, in particular shouting down abolitionist Parker Pillsbury's advocacy of voting rights for Black men.[22]

Organizing after Hard-Scrabble

The three years after the pogrom were a period of relative calm in Providence. The aftermath of the riot saw the Black community maintain its precarious place in the social order of the town, and white hostility simmered but did not explode like it did in October 1824. On July 4, 1826, in a parade commemorating the fiftieth anniversary of the country's founding, elderly soldiers of color marched beside white soldiers without any distinction being made on account of race. In fact, the whole set of marchers formed a "peculiar race" all to themselves, according to the *Rhode Island American*. Patriotism, at least for a moment, subsumed racial distinction—a theme that African Americans had employed in the 1770s and that would be brought up repeatedly in the struggles to come.

The year 1828 saw a renewed activism on the part of the Black community, as its leaders formed the Providence African Society for Mutual Relief and sponsored a rousing speech in their meetinghouse by prominent Black minister Hosea Easton—events that invigorated their fight for citizenship rights. Easton's address was a major turning point as the abolitionist minister's implorations reflected the shifting contours of American citizenship. He, like the petitioners of 1820, added the tenets of education and Christian devotion to more fully round out the older requirements of property ownership and independence, both of which were becoming harder for many, whites or people of color, to attain in rapidly industrializing New England. If the African Union Meeting House had provided the physical space from which African Americans could make their case for citizenship, Easton injected the ideological framework.

Before that happened, colonization reappeared on Rhode Island's agenda in 1825, possibly as a reaction to the riot in Addison Hollow, though it seems that Newport was this groundswell's epicenter. Since the failed movements of the 1770s and 1790s, renewed interest in colonization had infiltrated the highest reaches of white elite circles, with the American Colonization Society's founding in 1816 in Washington. Its leaders included president-elect James Monroe, future president Andrew Jackson, and George Washington's nephew and Supreme Court justice Bushrod Washington. A Rhode Island branch was established in 1820, itself a microcosm of the parent organization with leadership including current governor Nehemiah R. Knight, former governor William Jones, and leading industrialist Zachariah Allen.[23] Support for colonization never seemed to take firm root in the state, though, as it did elsewhere. Still, while inspiring revulsion among some African Americans, it also may have inspired others to consider emigration.[24] By 1825, the aging Newport emigrationists of the past Newport Gardner and Salmar Nubia finally saw their opportunity to return to the land of their birth on the brig *Vine*, albeit under the auspices of the American Colonization Society and its agent Horace Sessions. They were elected deacons for a mission to both start a settlement and proselytize among people native to the land claimed for Liberia, but both died within six months of their arrival, which occurred to some fanfare among other colonists in February 1826.[25] This mission, though it went a step farther than that of 1794–1795, met a similar fate. Along with its elderly leaders, about half of the party had succumbed to "fever" within six months.

Further, the *Newport Mercury* claimed, the mission had taken some of the most prominent Black leaders from the city—a fact that undercut the American Colonization Society's appeal to northern whites. As most recent scholarship on the American Colonization Society has shown, the society's mission was mainly an attempt to secure the dual goals of strengthening slavery in the South by ridding the region of free African Americans, while creating an all-white North and West. Northern whites, many of whom were skeptical of the project's feasibility and affordability, could argue, like the *Newport Mercury* did, that taking Black leaders out of their home communities made those communities more susceptible to the vices they were supposed to have been more prone to—an argument that, peculiarly perhaps, employed racism to supposedly benefit Black communities.[26] Few, if any, Providence residents were on this particular ship.[27] Christopher Hall was rumored to have gone, though he is not found on official manifests; if he did go, he was back in Providence soon after.[28]

Then, in 1826, Providence's defunct Prince Hall mason lodge was resuscitated and officially incorporated in December. It was led by George C. Wyllis, a sexton, laborer, and member of the African Union Meeting House building committee; Alfred Niger; Ichabod Northup; and Peter Browning. Although very few records exist of its activism during this period, this event marked the introduction of post-riot organizing and two important community leaders in the 1830s and 1840s. Connecticut-born Niger was a barber by trade and would go on to have a career in activism that ran from the colored convention movement to antislavery to Black suffrage, as would laborer Ichabod Northup, who would also factor prominently in the 1850s movement to integrate public schools. Niger's occupation especially situated him in a position of prominence in Black public culture: he could be relatively independent from white management, relatively wealthy, and ownership of one's own shop meant it could become a community meeting space or a repository for print materials so crucial to the social movements of the 1830s. Northup represented perhaps a more enterprising path to wealth and prominence—he was listed in the 1830s and 1840s as a "laborer" in city directories, but later worked as a clerk and a porter, by 1860 owning $3,200 of real estate.[29]

On January 2, 1828, some of Providence's other Black leaders—George J. Smith, from the building committee of the African Union Meeting House, among them—met and formed the African Society for Mutual Relief. It was seemingly modeled after the Free African Union Society of the late eighteenth century, assuring a "respectable" membership by having a committee conduct background checks on applicants to join the society. The African Society's twenty-five-cents-per-month fee was similar to the Union Society's eighteen shillings quarterly fee. Ichabod Northup was also a member of this society, as were several other laborers, but the conspicuous absence of Alfred Niger and George C. Wyllis may have meant that the leadership of Providence's Black community had undergone something of a bifurcation, at least by 1833. That year, the African Society for Mutual Relief applied to the General Assembly for incorporation (which was denied) without Niger and Wyllis. By that point, they were representing Providence in the colored convention movement and at regional abolitionist meetings. Northup's lasting association with Wyllis and Niger and later popular leader George T. Downing, however, suggests cohesion was the norm among potential leadership factions.[30]

Also in 1828, the presidential election brought with it perhaps the strongest questioning of citizenship in Rhode Island since the Revolution. White propertyless workers and artisans began clamoring for greater access to citizenship after seeing another election go by in which they were the prime target for messaging. By this point, the only other state that had a freemanship requirement similar to Rhode Island's was Virginia; whites in the surrounding states were voting at much higher rates. In the deeply polarizing election, Andrew Jackson's campaign employed outreach to the "freemen" who could now vote in most states—and by this time, as historian David Roediger has shown, the term "freemen" was gaining political currency as an empowering moniker for white men, affirming their status as republican citizens and differentiating them from the enslaved. The anger at being white, male, and unable to access freemanship in such an animated political season certainly seemed to factor into the resurgence of Rhode Island's suffrage movement the following March, in which protesters in Pawtucket called specifically for the extension of the vote to all free white men over the age of twenty-one.[31]

Before the whites of Providence County moved, however, Providence's Black community was roused to action by a powerful speech delivered on Thanksgiving day, just a few weeks after Jackson's election to the presidency. Hosea Easton had most likely just completed his training as a Congregationalist minister and was already making an impact in the Black leadership circles of Boston. In March 1828, he had addressed a large Boston crowd and urged them to support *Freedom's Journal*, the first African American newspaper in the country, founded by New Yorker Samuel Cornish.[32] Although he owned a home in Boston, Easton also operated a store on South Main Street in Providence from which he later advertised the sale of David Walker's seminal tract *Appeal . . . to the Colored Citizens of the World*—a document whose language reflected much of Easton's dire warnings to whites.[33] He would later ascend to the pastorate of Hartford's Talcott Street Church and then that city's Colored Methodist Episcopal Church. His activism was channeled toward abolitionism, racial uplift in the colored convention movement, and arguing strenuously against the pseudoscience that attempted to prove people of African descent were inherently inferior.[34] He is perhaps most famous for his 1837 *Treatise on the Intellectual Character, and the Civil and Political Condition of the Colored People of the U. States*. In it he argued—as many Black intellectuals of the antebellum era did—that the problem of race lay in the minds of whites, that it existed independently of whether African Americans were able to "uplift" themselves. He died shortly after the treatise's publication, and while the trajectory of his activism and his having lived through some of the most violent backlash to the abolitionist movement seemed to have changed his stance on uplift, his Thanksgiving address to the African Union Meeting House in 1828 gave direction and breathed inspiration to a new leadership class. The speech was so powerful that Providence's Black community commissioned a Boston printer to publish it for wider distribution.[35]

In the address, Easton first stated that the problem facing African Americans, the barriers to liberty, had become multifaceted. The political nature of oppression was clear: those in the audience were unable to hold political office and were not even considered "subjects of the government." Those facts, along with being barred from "initiat[ion] into free schools" and not being "patronised as salary men in any public business . . . sufficiently lucrative to raise us to any material state of honour and respectability," meant that African Americans were not signatories to the "social compact with Society at large." They were outside the bounds of the bedrock of American republicanism.[36] While he repeatedly acknowledged that responsibility for this injustice lay with the white power structure of the state, the speech is remarkable for its appeal to "respectability," a "master value," according to historian Patrick Rael, meaning that "one had, through dint of individual industry and perseverance, cultivated one's inner character sufficiently to harvest the rewards of material success. Most importantly, this potential was available to all." While the politics of respectability have a fraught history in the Black freedom struggle, antebellum Black intellectuals like Easton employed this type of language to, as Rael's last sentence suggests, universalize Black Americans' capacity for citizenship and expose the barrier of color as artificially constructed, at least in the North, in order to both excuse the country's compromise with slavery and appease struggling white artisans and laborers by removing them as economic competitors.[37] Easton was not giving Black Providence residents new information. He was giving them a language to state their case for citizenship and a voice to make the case heard, simultaneously perhaps beseeching the state's white elites, steeped as they were in their republican conservatism.

He proceeded to describe three essential and interconnected "improvements" African Americans had made in the "ordinary course since American Independence": their "march in religious improvement," their commitment to education, and their industriousness despite economic restrictions. Reinforcing the principles Providence's Black leaders had put forth in their petition to incorporate the African Society eight years earlier, Easton lauded the fact that

"God has caused his light to shine through [Black church leaders], to the great shame of our oppressors." He added that where Black children were afforded education, they took advantage of "the means of acquiring literary information." However, he decried the circumstances in which a Black minister was kicked out of his seat on a stagecoach to Fall River in favor of a white sailor "of low grade" and a white factory girl. He also pointed out that, when educated, Black children were imbued with all the knowledge and values that made them "well qualified for the common business of life," but because they were not hired as mechanics, lawyers, and clerks, they "know enough only to feel sensible of their misery." These sentiments, he said, proved that it was not inherent inferiority preventing African Americans from "do[ing] business like other people" but *custom*. Custom is mutable; however, he despaired, the more rapid the "growth" of people of color in their Christian devotion and intellectual pursuits, the more "alarmed" the white population became. "Clouds of evil," he lamented, were "thickening over this Republic," perhaps alluding to Jackson's victory earlier that month. There was much work to be done.[38]

The first thing Easton implored Providence's Black community to do was unite. In what was perhaps an early manifestation of Black nationalism that left room for salvation within the American republic, he urged Black Americans to reject the "*Colonization Craft*"—which he determined to be an entrapment scheme meant only to preserve slavery—and turn their collective attention to "moral improvement." Unity among the Black population of the country, he claimed, would entail aiding each other in times of need, ensuring the education of subsequent generations so they could "give a character to our community, and take away our reproach." He urged inculcating "industry and virtue" so that they could benefit from the fruits of their collective labor and control their future. This part of the speech may read as circular or illogically ordered, and clearly young Easton was wrestling with articulating an ethos in which African Americans would maintain a separate, perhaps higher moral plane than their white counterparts while also recognizing the need to reconcile with the republican body politic that surrounded them. However, we can also see this as reflective of a major difference between disfranchised whites and African Americans. Whereas white Rhode Islanders argued that they were entitled to citizenship because the founding philosophy meant to include them, Black Rhode Islanders (and those in other northern communities) grudgingly recognized that they had to prove themselves worthy. "Distinguish yourselves as pious, industrious, and intelligent men and women," Easton summarized in his closing remarks to attendees at the meetinghouse. "This will demand respect from those who exalt themselves above you."[39]

He was quite explicit about adhering to one element of American citizenship: that of the "spheres" of gender. "You, that are the fathers of our community," he said, "ought to use your feeble efforts to the establishment of the temple of Liberty," and "mothers, . . . your virtuous council to your daughters, will qualify them to become useful in their circles." The project of Black citizenship would necessarily make political engagement the province of men. Black women were charged by Easton to, as Rachel and Leah "did build the house of Israel," bear children and instill in them the virtues of the republic. He also posited that "the haunt of the dance-hall will be broken" should mothers keep their daughters in their "circles"—a statement loaded with concessionary contradiction.[40] On the one hand, he was reproducing the language and stereotypes employed by the white power structure as a tool of oppression—"eating from the ideological table" of his oppressor as one historian put it, and a "serious limitation" of "Black spokespersons' manipulation of the values and public discourse of the America they helped fabricate."[41] Was this a blind spot in Easton's activism? To make ends meet, many women ran boardinghouses and taverns, which were occupations that took them outside of the "sphere" of the home and conflicted with the ideal power structure of the nuclear family. Perhaps Easton could have recognized this as part of the economic barriers people of color faced and called for its rectification. On the other hand, having to contend with the dehumanizing racial pseudoscience of the day, as another historian rationalized Black activists' use of gender spheres, Easton might have been imploring the Black community to adhere to republican gender norms as proof of their very humanity.[42] This was not the first and certainly not the last time that Black women would be asked to sacrifice their autonomy on the altar of republican ideology.

Suffrage and the First Petitions

Because of further developments in 1828 and in the three years after Easton's rousing address, Black residents of Providence and Rhode Island as a whole faced a new series of setbacks and opportunities. In its June 1828 session, the state's General Assembly passed new provisions for establishing public schools throughout the state, and Providence, which had been operating public schools for white children since 1800, decided to reform its own system. In order to "place the schools in a condition of greater usefulness to all classes of the community," a committee headed by Brown University president Francis Wayland proposed and implemented a primary and grammar school system. The committee designated that teachers would be female and paid $175 per year out of the public coffers. A school for children of color was also to be established, albeit with only one teacher making $400 per year—a higher sum than teachers at the white schools perhaps because the committee foresaw difficulty in obtaining a teacher, and that teacher alone would be responsible for a class much larger than those at white schools. No provision was made to separate Black primary and grammar students either. It was hardly ideal but still a small positive step for the Black community, whose leaders had shown a commitment to their children's education in the preceding years. People of color were also added back to the tax rolls in order to pay for the school—and this was an opening that stirred Black leaders to act affirmatively beginning in 1829.[43]

That year also brought renewed activism on the part of white suffragists, with one Rhode Island historian attributing it to having been largely left out of the raucous 1828 presidential election. It began in the mill village of Pawtucket (then part of North Providence) and spread into Providence, where on March 28 a rally of between 1,200 and 1,500 people prepared a petition for the General Assembly asking to remove the freemanship requirement for voting, determining that at least 60 percent of white men in the state were disfranchised by it.[44] Specifically, the petitioners—who, by the time of its presentation to the May session of the General Assembly claimed over two thousand signatures—asked for an extension of the suffrage at least "to embrace a majority of the free white male citizens of the state." This would include all those whose permanent residence was Rhode Island, who paid taxes, who owned property, who performed military service, or whose circumstances were "consistent with the fundamental principle, that the sovereignty of a republican government resides in the people at large." Whiteness, according to these suffragists, was a prerequisite to citizenship, but education and religious devotion were not.[45]

In response to the petition, state assemblyman Benjamin Hazard, a twenty-year veteran of Rhode Island politics and a man deeply read in classical republican philosophy, was appointed chair of a committee to consider the petition's merits.[46] In a blistering critique of the liberal suffrage movement, Hazard's report, issued in June, denounced the suffragists as lacking "wholesome qualifications"—namely, significant property—required of good republican citizens. In a reiteration of the country's founding philosophy, Hazard assumed that people who did not own property must not have the intellectual or moral sense necessary to acquire it, and as government existed largely to protect that, the propertyless should not expect to share in the duty of fashioning that government. Rhode Island's government existed to cater to "a virtuous race of people," and though other people, "conversant in all the scenes of depravity," may reside within the geographical limits of the state, the latter were to be dictated to, not made part of a society's decision-making process. He acknowledged that he risked lumping virtuous non-property-owners in, but that it was better to disfranchise them "as a class" than potentially allow people with no attachment to the land or virtuous ideas about justice access to the levers of political power.[47] Hazard, whose constituents included old Newport aristocrats keen on maintaining freemanship as a mechanism of retaining their own power, thus grievously alienated white suffragists in the Providence County industrial towns.

While most of his allusions to a "virtuous race" early in the polemic were directed at immigrants, both Europeans and transient Americans, he took an equally powerful axe to any pretensions African Americans might have had toward enfranchisement. Black voting was admitted, or at least not legally excluded, he said, in eleven other states: Maine, New Hampshire, Massachusetts, Vermont, New York, New Jersey, Pennsylvania, Maryland, North Carolina, Georgia, and Tennessee. He was incorrect to include Maryland and New Jersey, as they had excluded Black voters by inserting "white" into their voter requirements in 1801 and 1807, respectively, and while Georgia had no specific statute related to race and voting, it had apparently confirmed in 1789 that the vote was the province of white taxpayers.[48] He also made the point that New York restricted suffrage to African Americans who owned significant property. Thirteen other states—including all states admitted after 1803—barred African Americans from voting. No states allowed women to vote. Why was this? Because, he claimed, in those states that allowed Black voting, men of inferior mind had fallen victim to their "visionary and baseless . . . theories" and blinded themselves to the inherent inferiority of people of color, as "nothing short of such a propensity" could have brought about such a thing. He then went on to list four reasons that Black people should never be granted the right to vote. The first was that Black people were indelibly marked as perhaps belonging to a different species, "whether justly or not." Second, using the same logic Supreme Court Chief Justice Roger Taney would employ three decades later in his *Dred Scott* decision, because African Americans were descended from people brought to the United States as captives, they were never intended by the founders to be part of the country's political community. Third, because of their or their ancestors' enslavement, they could never be trusted to use their vote for anything but vengeance. They would seek only to gain "undisputed ascendancy," not equality; the experiment of emancipation taught Hazard that Black people would act either as subservient or hostile—not considerate republicans. Finally, he said—with some actual foresight—the political advancement of African Americans would bring American slavery in the South nearer to demise. However evil the institution was, he saw general emancipation as only ending in the horrors of amalgamation and extermination of the white race. In sum, one would have to suspend the "laws of nature," so important to the survival of republics, in order to implement Black—or non-freeman white—voting.[49]

While Hazard's harangue was not binding legislation, his stature in the General Assembly gave it an air of authority, and indeed that was the stance of the state legislature as it absorbed wave after wave of voter activism in the coming years. Dominated as it was by the Newport aristocracy and agrarian former plantation country, and maintained that way through an antiquated system of representative apportionment, the challenges that reformers of any stripe faced were formidable. Nonetheless, in naming the establishment's parameters for voting rights, Hazard gave reformers ideas about how potentially to direct their activism. For disfranchised whites, the property requirement seemed to be the major impediment, despite Hazard's condescending "virtuous race of people" commentary. They would have to find a rationale for men of little or no real estate to become voters—something that, when looking around the country, particularly to other state legislatures and the Democratic-Republican Party (in the process of becoming just "Democrats"), seemed doable if not inevitable. Property restrictions had fallen elsewhere, and Virginia's abolishing of its freehold requirement in 1830 left Rhode Island with one of the least democratic systems of voting in the country as it pertained to white men.[50]

For African Americans, the main obstacle was race. They would have to find a rationale for citizenship that downplayed the importance of skin color and push back against the notion of inherent inferiority. Doing this would take a multifaceted approach, as they would have to first contend with the perception of poverty and vice, convincing authorities that their supposed susceptibility to, as Hazard put it, "subserviency or hostility" stemmed not from innate behavior but from their lack of access to avenues for financial success. Also keeping ideas about racial inferiority alive, as we can glean from Hazard's tract, was the recent history of slavery in the state and the persistence of it in the South. They were severely handicapped by the latter: "King Cotton" was quickly becoming the bedrock of the nation's economy, and as such slavery showed no signs of slowing down where it was presently contained. Despite decrying the evils of slavery for their own respectability's sake, Rhode Island politicians on both sides of the aisle had little inclination to favor its abolition. The state's Democrats, though aristocratic, were "rabid" Jackson adherents and could hardly be counted on to hold moderate views on race. But now, the entrenched mercantile elites of old Federalist persuasions, dominant in state politics but without a coherent party structure, had business ties to the national cottonocracy and a reason to ally with Democrats: to tamp down the white voter reform movement.[51] Further, although whites and African Americans had the conservative elite as a common enemy, the millstone of race meant there existed little possibility for an alliance among the disfranchised. As whiteness (and of course maleness) in other states was the main dividing line between voters and nonvoters, citizens and noncitizens, disfranchised whites most likely saw potential Black allies as hurting their cause rather than helping. Although this thinking on the part of whites would prove a significant miscalculation in the future, in 1829 Black leaders knew that they had to approach this problem with few friends outside of their community, and with caution and clarity.

Beginning that fall, they decided to petition the General Assembly. While they had been re-added to the tax rolls, the free public school they had been promised—and for which their tax dollars were supposed to pay—had apparently not yet opened. In their petition, whose text has not been found but which the *Rhode Island American* reported on, the Black leaders asked to be reexempted from taxation based on four factors: they could not vote, they could not take out licenses for the sale of goods, they could not "keep houses of entertainment," and they could not educate their children in the free schools.[52] The former congressman and longtime assemblyman Elisha R. Potter, a Federalist lawyer representing South County farmers' interests, received the petition favorably and referred it to the committee on finance, where it died.[53] This early effort, like the efforts of disfranchised whites of the prior two decades, went down in defeat. However, whereas their white counterparts were building their case based on numerical strength and trying to ride the ideological currents around them, the Black community regrouped to take a more nuanced, philosophical approach that adhered more closely to founding republican theory.

Still without a free school for children of color in 1830, the old Federalist and anti-Democratic Party press publicly took up the debate about Black people being taxed for a school that did not exist. In June, the *Rhode Island American* lauded the sixty "neat and well behaved" children from the "interesting" African Union Meeting House school who took part in a celebration of the town's Sunday schools.[54] "Interesting" may have seemed patronizing, but it was a far cry from overt degradation. By September, an editorial appeared in the newly formed *Providence Journal* that decried the lack of access to free education and the fact that people of color had to pay taxes without the suffrage. The writer urged not an expansion of the franchise or the building of a school necessarily but removal from the tax rolls. The *Rhode Island American* in October then ran an editorial in which it declined to take a stance on either a free school for Black children or integration of the town's public schools—not out of principle but because of expediency. The *Providence Journal*, which would become staunchly Whig in the coming years, was apparently peeling off subscribers, and the *American* writer frankly feared that support for Black children's education could be self-destructive should it be linked with the collapse of Federalism. This suggests that at least one of the holdups with public support for the free school may have been the slow death of Federalism as a Black-white bridge and the uncertainty accompanying the realignment intendant with (future) Whiggism. The *American* then quickly published an outside communication favoring education for Black children as fair given the tax burden, but also because it assumed that the denial of education to Black parents bred ignorance which could be replicated in the future generation. The tone was again suspect, but allies were few—and thus welcome.[55]

On the night of January 6, 1831, Providence's Black community leaders met at the African Union Meeting House and devised a new petition strategy. The meeting was chaired by George Waterman, a laborer and future temperance advocate, and James E. Ellis, a barber and future Providence agent for the influential abolitionist newspaper the *Liberator*. After some discussion, Ellis recorded that a resolution passed, stating that "this meeting consider the tax upon the Coloured people of this town to be a burthen upon them which the

Law and Spirit of this government do not tolerate, or, if tolerated, the coloured people who are liable to these taxes, have a right to vote for town and state officers, and ought to have the privilege of sending their children to the free schools." They then voted to petition the General Assembly, scheduled to begin their session the following Monday, "praying for relief against said taxes, or that if they are compelled to pay them, they may have the right of suffrage & the privilege of schooling their children, in proportion to the amount of taxes which they pay." Tasked with writing the petition were veteran leaders George C. Wyllis and George McCarty, along with Alfred Niger, a relative newcomer but dedicated activist.[56] Since the prior petition had been disposed of fairly quickly, and Black people were still paying taxes without other privileges of citizenship, some adjustments in their approach were necessary.

The most obvious change from the first petition was that they would now be offering the state an alternative to removal from the tax rolls: enfranchisement and public schooling. The second was the dropping of the complaint against being able to "keep houses of entertainment" and being barred from acquiring licenses to sell goods. The latter, though perhaps subtle, signaled a change in tactic from the centering of the practical financial hardship attendant to taxation and economic exclusion to a more advanced critique of the state's commitment to republican values. They were in reality only formally barred from selling liquor, and the dropping of this and the malleable notion of "houses of entertainment" from their complaint may have suggested they wanted to concentrate on the more "respectable" elements of their argument. Or, as Easton had complained, because they were barred from obtaining other licenses to sell goods by custom rather than law, they might have foreseen a dead end in seeking a *de jure* solution to a *de facto* problem.

The decision to ask for *either* relief from taxes *or* access to the franchise and public education had potentially dramatic consequences—of course, only if the legislature decided to take up the petition. They hoped for better results than an attempt half a century earlier in Massachusetts: that state rejected a similar petition from shipping business owner Paul Cuffe and other free men of color.[57] If it were decided to remove Black people from the tax rolls, they would be back to where they started the decade, without schools and further removed from the rights of citizenship they were striving for. Access to public schooling would also conceivably knock down one of the barriers to prosperity and respectability. If they were granted the franchise, they might only have a few votes due to the freehold requirement, but those votes would be considered the property of the community and—especially in local contests, as evidenced by the Primus Bailey controversy in Little Compton—their votes could sway elections (and thus might have appealed to certain city and state authorities).[58] This could also open possibilities for white suffragists, for expansion of the right to vote to Black people while *not* including more whites was probably not politically viable. This factor could also prove fatal to the petition if it were to be debated in the assembly.

The petition at first glance used overtly deferential language, marking a sharp turn away from Easton's speech of 1828 but also from David Walker's *Appeal*, which had been published just three months before the meeting of Providence's Black leaders. The *Appeal* had been circulating in Providence since shortly after its publication and had exploded in the country's political discourse three weeks prior, with Georgia's governor George Gilmer alerting the nation after sixty copies were seized in Savannah, setting off a firestorm of anti-abolition fulmination, North and South.[59] Providence's Black leaders knew that this was a sensitive time and that Rhode Island's conservative regime was more likely to respond positively to flattery, calm, and maintenance of order than anything else, so they began their petition quite tepidly. In fact, Niger's title read simply, "Petition for Relief against Taxes," perhaps belying the leaders' true intent in order that it might break through and be discussed. The first paragraph sought to "respectfully sheweth that, being blessed by Divine Providence with health, they have, by the course of industrious and economical habits, acquired for themselves, freehold or real estate in said town." Having been taxed as such for the past few years, they "most respectfully represent[ed]" that, though they held these attributes of republican citizenship and were performing its duties, they were "denied the privileges and immunities common to all other freeholders in the state." Essentially, Black freeholders were no different than white freeholders.

Having carefully established the basic problem, they moved on to an intellectual rationale behind the problem:

> They would further respectfully represent, that so far as they have been able to ascertain & understand the great and permanent principles of government, under which they live, they have arrived at the conclusion, that the right to impose taxes, either upon persons or their property necessarily includes the corresponding rights of suffrage & representation; Any law, therefore, that authorizes the one and denies the exercise of the others, it is respectfully suggested, must be deemed adverse to the policy

and principles of the Government, which they have we understood was based upon the equal rights of all.

Harkening back to the revolutionary period, one in which their own forebearers had fought side by side with the forebearers of the assemblymen, recalled not only the pride in the establishment of the great republican experiment—the principled reasoning behind suffrage of, by, and for property-holding men—but also the logic with which the state had abolished slavery. The leaders then "conceived, and do now conceive that, if their property be liable to taxation, or that, if the municipal authorities of the Town have the legal right to levy & collect taxes of them, they in justice, are entitled to participate in the benevolent purposes, intended to be secured by the free school system, which your Honors have wisely established." They still, conspicuously and despite the title of their petition, had not yet asked for an exemption from taxation.

In the third and final paragraph, they zoomed in on the school issue as the main catalyst for the petition. They first affirmed that they were appealing to the state instead of the town of Providence because the tax allocation was state law, school funding would come out of state coffers (at least for Providence), and though they paid their taxes to the town, they understood that their money was ultimately funneled upward to the state to be redistributed. For suffrage, they would also need state approval, as the "white" provision in the state code would supersede should the town approve an appeal for Black men to become freemen of Providence. They closed by saying,

> Therefore they pray that this Honble Assembly would take into their wise consideration the subject matter of their grievances and relieve them from the payment of taxes; or, if they and their freeholds are to remain subject to taxation, they may be permitted to exercise the right of suffrage in common with other sufficient freeholders, and be permitted to participate in the benefits of said schools for the maintenance of which, these taxes are made—or grant them such other relief in the promises(?), as your honours, may in your wisdom deem proper. They also further respectfully pray they may be heard by counsel in such manner as may be deemed the most proper.

This last passage seems to suggest, with only the brief allusion to the idea of being removed from tax rolls, that the central hope of the petitioners was inclusion in the right to vote—which they saw as necessary to enact, at the very least, the establishment of the public school for children of color. They may have recognized that the petition would have little chance of success, but they certainly created a strong case for their inclusion in the body politic.[60]

The petition was received on January 11, 1831, and referred to the Committee on the Judiciary, meaning that unlike the 1829 petition, the General Assembly recognized this was not merely a financial problem but that Black leaders had raised questions with broader implications. The committee decided to "not recommend" it, but it was given a full reading on January 15, after which it was dismissed by the legislature. It seems as though the assembly might have been leaning toward exemption from taxation. Two weeks later, in reporting on the General Assembly's January session, the *Providence Journal* reported that there was no action on the petition because old Federalist Elisha Potter speculated that, if people of color were exempted from taxation, there would be a problem determining who exactly was Black, and that there were varying "degrees of color."[61] Inadvertently, he was making their point—that in a society in which citizenship was predicated on property ownership, and in which people of color accumulated more than the minimum property requirement for freemanship, skin color was an arbitrary barrier. If the problem was not with property ownership but with skin color, the whole philosophy behind the "white" clause in Rhode Island's suffrage statute was flawed. The battle was lost but the point was gained.

By January 1831, Providence's Black leaders had begun crafting a strategy for citizenship that reflected their position both in Black intellectual circles and a conservative, Federalist-dominated society. Their self-determination that brought about the African Union Meeting House; the defiance of Henry T. Wheeler and Christopher Hall during the 1824 pogrom and its aftermath; and their invitation of Hosea Easton, an unapologetic abolitionist and colleague of David Walker, to address them placed them firmly—if not conspicuously—in the regional trend of Black speakers and writers, many of whom combined expressions of respectability with a hardened resolve to end slavery and discrimination. Leaders' determination to work with white ministers and educators, along with the deferential tone of their 1831 petition, meant that they felt a careful approach afforded them the best chance for tangible remediation. Their plan also won approval from influential abolitionist William Lloyd Garrison, who in an early edition of the *Liberator* said Providence's Black leaders, through their petition, would "not only redeem the character of the State, but furnish an example worthy to be followed by every member of the Union."[62] Alfred Niger, George C. Wyllis, and their colleagues had placed themselves in high conversations about the future of race and citizenship in the country and were simultaneously mapping out the practical liberation of themselves and their children.

Escalation toward Violence in Snow Town

The evening of Wednesday, September 21, 1831, brought an eruption of violence to a largely Black neighborhood called "Snow Town," not far from where the Hard-Scrabble pogrom had taken place. This one, however, lasted four nights and dwarfed the riot from seven years earlier. By the time rocks and brickbats lay harmlessly strewn about Olney's Lane, five white men had been killed by gunfire and at least seventeen houses, homes to many of Providence's Black residents, sat windowless, "much injured," or "mostly destroyed."[63] Black residents once again had defended themselves from their hostile white neighbors and emerged from it prepared to face a decade of organizing, both inside the state and among their peers across the North, for their rights as citizens.

Central to the renewed spirit of activism was the bottom-line recognition that it was the minds of whites—particularly the freemen—that had to change in order for the fortunes of the Black community to improve. Providence's Black leaders made the choice to portray republican respectability (however complicated its effects would be) and find pressure points in the state's ideology, so protective as it was of traditional republicanism. Always understanding that the abolition of slavery would be crucial in transforming ideas about race, Black community leaders contributed to and were bolstered themselves by the massive "Second Wave" of abolitionist activity as the 1820s turned into the 1830s—along with the satellite movements it generated, like temperance and self-improvement. The violence in Snow Town, however, perhaps foreshadowed what they would be up against from poor and artisan whites, who themselves stepped up their suffrage activism on their own terms. It set the tone for the continuation of previous hostilities among Black and white workers but also, judging by the government's response, proved again that the always-tenuous alliance between Black people and elite whites was still alive and potentially exploitable under the right circumstances.

In some ways, the prelude to the outbreak of violence was similar to that of 1824. Before the prior rioting, poor and artisan whites had faced a political setback—the constitution proposed to the freemen, which seemed to promise positive change for white suffragists, had been soundly defeated. A few months prior to the violence of 1831, Democratic-Republican governor James Fenner had lost his bid for a twelfth term (it would have been his eight consecutive reelection), which the Democratic press tied to the freemen's rejection of his affiliation with Andrew Jackson. It was a particularly bitter election, rife with personal accusations and innuendo. The Fenner-Arnold spat, which had begun the year prior in a similarly acrimonious election between Fenner and Asa Messer, in fact also exposed a class divide in white Providence, as the *Providence Patriot* decried that the old Federalist aristocrats of the town, "almost to a man," voted for the National Republican Lemuel Arnold against the man they felt stood in favor of the "yeomanry" and people of Providence.[64] The white "yeomanry" of Providence would show its disdain for Arnold explicitly during the riot, refusing to stop their destruction of Snow Town despite the governor's orders.

Unlike the years and months prior to the 1824 riot, the Black population had according to the official census decreased since 1825: by 1830, there were 1,213 Black residents of Providence. From 1820 to 1830, they had fallen from 8.3 to 7.2 percent of the population of the city as a whole, while the white population rose dramatically—now numbering 15,620 compared with 10,788 ten years earlier.[65] That, however, did not stop newspapers from printing sensationalist stories speculating that the population of color was growing out of control. Perhaps most disheartening was the fact that much of this was coming from the *Providence Journal*, by 1830 the main opposition newspaper to the Democratic *Patriot*. The *Journal*'s inclination to criticize Black Providence was probably tied to its support for colonization, which in turn was tied to the paper's pro–Henry Clay bent. Clay, the Kentuckian and Andrew Jackson's nemesis, was a leader in the American Colonization Society.[66] In 1830, the paper ran editorials like one decrying the town's large and "promiscuous" population, growing more insolent because relations between servants and employers were not as good as they were in places like New York. "WEST SIDE" claimed that travelers from out of state called Providence "Negro Town" because Black people were so numerous. "A.T." warned that within twenty years, the town would be entirely Black because of the supposedly spiraling population. It was not only the numbers but the supposed behavior of Black people that was out of control and needed policing from white neighbors—a problem that seemed to stem from a renewed acceptance of the racial pseudoscience buttressing both the colonization movement and slavery. The Providence Theater gallery in February 1830 was allegedly full of "negroes, drunken sailors, and 'Black white folks'"—the latter suggesting not only a connection between appearance and behavior but that whites were perhaps susceptible to losing their race entirely by behaving like African Americans, or even by their close proximity.[67]

Also beginning in the year prior to the rioting, a series of articles appeared in the formerly Federalist *Rhode Island American* decrying the ways Black domestic workers were pushing back on antiquated ideas about racial deference and social hierarchy. Black behavior was again taken simultaneously as ingrained but also in need of white control. Black domestic workers had the audacity, according to one writer, to demand higher pay and to slack off on Mondays; housekeepers and supervisors needed to take back control by forming the "Providence Society for the Encouragement of Faithful Servants." "A Housekeeper," editorializing shortly thereafter, honed in on the fact that "domestics passed from one house to another with the greatest ease," signaling that African American workers understood that their labor was in high demand and used the value they brought to the labor market to wrest control of their lives, potentially bettering their own situations in the process. They were now "the masters and mistresses of those who hired them." The solution, the writer said, was a society similar to the one suggested earlier, which would reinforce in Black domestics their obligations and "duties," ideas that directly refuted what Black community leaders were trying to gain through education and the right to vote. In April 1831, a correspondent used blunter language, referring to Black Providence as a "race of domestics" that needed to be persuaded back into subservience through rewards for faithfulness. When the Society for the Encouragement of Faithful Servants was officially established, it numbered among its members Moses Brown, governors James Fenner and Lemuel Arnold, and congressman Tristam Burges—thus forcing African Americans to navigate the racial chauvinism of their allies, a theme that has persisted throughout the Black freedom struggle.[68]

It may have been the independence of women like Elleanor Eldridge who provoked such paranoia from the white elite. Eldridge had been a domestic worker in Warwick and Providence beginning when she was ten years old but also went into business for herself, whitewashing, paperhanging, and running a boardinghouse. She would return to domestic service from time to time, but only on her terms. She later became moderately famous by the sale of her "memoir," which was more of a biography written by abolitionist Frances Whipple Green. Green dramatized the events surrounding Eldridge's years of speculating in real estate and earning positive credit, the legal action she took when her loans were called in while she was out of town, and how her house was auctioned off and then razed. In the 1820s and early 1830s, Eldridge's independence may have also inspired other women of color to save their earnings: more than 10 percent (52 out of 507) of 1830's female depositors in the Providence Institute for Savings (the "Old Stone Bank") were women of color—a number that outpaced the percentage of people of color in Providence's population, and a development that occurred despite the economic discrimination they faced. Combined with the New England textile industry taking many white women out of domestic service and into factories, women of color who worked as domestics and who either knew, were employed by, or just happened to find themselves in similar situations in their working lives as Eldridge, appeared to be taking control of their own labor. They used their savings and circumstances to issue their own demands, pushing back against the ideas about Black dependence and independence held over from slavery.[69]

Reports from outside of Providence also warned about the potential consequences of Black assertions of independence and citizenship rights, and these derisions were likewise tied to race pseudoscience. In January 1830, reporting on a meeting in which African Americans in New York claimed the natural rights of citizenship by birth, the *Providence Journal*'s editor gruffly stated that contemporary people of color had "outgrown" their natural rights because of the multigenerational experience of slavery and recent failed "mutinies." Quite circularly he argued, possibly anticipating objections by those with longer memories, Black people who fought in the American Revolution would have fought for their rights in a more respectable way had they been alive in 1830. From Boston came the claim that a riot had started after Black men held a rally to lay claim to citizenship rights.[70] Reports of race riots from other cities also may have heightened anxieties in Providence. From Cincinnati in 1829 came tales of horrific violence, which the *Rhode Island American*'s editor blamed on the city's lax enforcement of Ohio's law stating that Black immigrants to the state had to post a five-hundred-dollar bond to ensure their good behavior. In an aftermath that may have tantalized colonizationists, white suffragists, and white artisans competing with African Americans for jobs, the riot caused between 1,100 and 1,500 Black people to leave Cincinnati.[71] A brawl much closer to home the next year took place at the state fair in Warwick's Pawtuxet village, resulting in the death of John Proffitt, a man of color, and injuries to numerous other "inoffensive" people of color. In addition to incessant reports of Black criminality from the presses on both sides of the political aisle, these stories of violence that seemed to accompany Black presence in northern communities certainly inflamed the town's white readership.[72]

The *Providence Patriot* similarly made political hay out of the potentiality of Black voting specifically; it strengthened its commitment to expansion of the suffrage to more white men by ridiculing African Americans. The clearest example of this came in 1830 as a response to the first major challenge to Democrat James Fenner's grip on the governor's seat in five years. A minstrelesque correspondence from "SOLON" presented a fake conversation with an "illiterate colored man" named Cuffe about the upcoming election, imagining Cuffe playing trickster to Fenner's opposition. Cuffe accused Anti-Masonic candidate Asa Messer, an old Federalist manufacturer and president of Brown University, of "bending to circumstance" by abandoning his views on the extension of suffrage to African Americans, in favor of the conservative opposition to Democratic attempts to extend it to white men. The author made a point that Black Rhode Islanders, and later their abolitionist allies, would also make—that in opposing extension of the suffrage in all cases, the Federalists, then National Republicans and Anti-Masons, then Whigs (all evolving iterations of Democratic opposition) were also forsaking the "principle" of propertied citizenship by adhering to the racial proscription. Of course, the author was simultaneously denigrating Fenner's opposition (even the "illiterate colored man" knew not to vote for Messer) and Black people (having Cuffe speaking in plantation dialect and suggesting the ridiculousness of Black men voting), positing his candidate as unencumbered by the tenuous alliance with African Americans and implicitly exposing the "principle" requirement of suffrage—property—as fluid and changeable. If even the anti-Democratic parties would not support African American suffrage due to "circumstance," then the true dividing line between citizen and noncitizen, the "principle" on which citizenship lay, was whiteness, not property. This was where the white suffrage extension movement stood by 1830.[73]

In April 1831, just after Fenner's humiliating defeat, the *Patriot* reported on a "gathering together of the Clay people"—that is, anti-Jacksonites—which included both white and Black men. The meeting, after attempting to settle "some old quarrel," then "fell to blows," with "the Cuffes" winning by severely beating many of the white men. This article seems partly an allegorical tale about the alliance between Black Providence and the evolving anti-Jackson faction of elite whites, and partly a warning to disfranchised whites as to what that alliance could produce and what Benjamin Hazard had warned about a few years prior should Black men gain the vote: Black superiority.[74]

This kind of story, when read in context with everything else surrounding the prelude to the violence in Snow Town, produced a sense of imminent danger among disfranchised whites. This was particularly true of white artisans whose positions of power were increasingly compromised by, first, the industrial manufacturing order's replacing their individual labor with factory production and, second, the supposed threat that a newly empowered Black community, capable of producing its own artisans and professionals, posed. In New York and Philadelphia, where white artisans could vote, they responded to the factory menace by forming the Workingmen's Party and sought to disrupt the bourgeois elements of both the Democratic and anti-Jackson parties.[75] In Rhode Island, there were fleeting attempts to form a Workingmen's Party, but without the franchise, white artisans had little recourse from either of the aforementioned threats. The fact that seven of the nine listed as dead or wounded from the final night's melee were white artisans suggests that these "gentlemen of property and standing" may have been, in addition to asserting control over what little they felt they could, responding to their political anxieties as the whites of 1824 had been. Men like this—white, disfranchised, and restless—would be the target of the political messaging from white suffrage leaders like Seth Luther over the next decade.

Of course, the riot took place within a wider context of race and the major events that kicked off the rise of the immediatist, or second-wave, abolitionist movement. The first of these was the publication and distribution of David Walker's *Appeal*. Like other northern cities, Providence was fertile ground for the fiery pamphlet's cultivation. Long connected to Boston, New York, and Philadelphia through mutual benefit society correspondence, Providence's Black community also had an agent for *Freedom's Journal*, the first African American newspaper. George C. Wyllis was listed as the paper's liaison almost from the beginning of its publication in 1827, and Providence's readers would have imbibed its program for racial uplift through education and enfranchisement and its advocacy of immediate abolition.[76] The African Union Meeting House had from its beginning a valuable connection in Nathaniel Paul, an antislavery crusader who traveled not only the American North but later Ireland and Great Britain, speaking and fundraising in an attempt to build a "moral cordon" around the institution. The positive reception of Hosea

Easton's Thanksgiving 1828 address also predicted interest in the *Appeal* among Providence's Black leaders. Easton's continued advertisements in the *Providence Journal* certainly helped drum up support, and a copy of the *Appeal* was found in the possessions of Jane Congdon, wife of African Union Meeting House planner Hodge Congdon.[77]

Just a month prior to the riot, in August 1831, the nation was shocked as a slave insurrection in Southampton, Virginia, claimed the lives of about sixty whites, and then in retaliation, whites killed more than double that number of enslaved and free Black people across the South.[78] While it was later found to have been started by Nat Turner, an enslaved preacher, the immediate aftermath of the rebellion saw an ideological tussle over the meaning of the *Appeal* and the abolitionist movement that was proliferating around the Atlantic world. Great Britain, the empire built in the eighteenth century on slavery and the slave trade, seemed on the verge of emancipating its Caribbean captives after decades of violent rebellions.[79] By September, with abolitionism, "King Cotton," and Jacksonian white supremacy (linked to the president's persistence in ridding the Southeast of Native people) all ascendant, violent confrontation rooted in race seemed inevitable around the country. In fact, the decade of the 1830s, and particularly the summer of 1835, saw a sharp rise in mob violence, with white artisans seeking to quash abolitionism and force Black communities all across the North into subservience.[80]

The Snow Town rioting had its start in ambiguous circumstances, similar to that of "Hard-Scrabble" seven years earlier. According to William J. Brown, a Black man who called himself "the Rattler" had shown up at the Power Street home of James Axum, a former mariner who ran a lucrative boardinghouse that often doubled as a brothel, tavern, and dance hall when sailors were in town. When Axum told him that there was nothing going on there and that he should travel the mile or so northward to Olney's Lane if he wished to dance, the Rattler did so. The Rattler, dancing wildly in one of the halls, "running against one man and pushing against another," then caught the attention of James Treadwell, another Black man "known to be a great fighter," and a struggle ensued. It spilled into the street where a group of white sailors and a group of Black sailors entered the fray, and the fight quickly became white versus Black. During the mayhem, "the blacks were the conquerors, and drove the whites out of the street," causing the latter to "double their forces" and return to destroy the neighborhood.[81]

According to trial transcripts of two of the Black men who were tried in the riot's aftermath, the struggle either began at or at least had absorbed another underground establishment in a building known as the "Red House." In the basement of the Red House, a Black man named Richard Johnson operated a "cooky" stand—defined by William J. Brown as a "bar-room, where liquors were dealt out," that also "sold cakes, pies, doughnuts, &c." By definition, this would have been illegal, owing to Rhode Island's law preventing people of color from being licensed to sell liquor. In the upper part of the Red House resided sailors William Jordan and Augustus Williams, laborer Cato Coggeshall, and two women who supposedly lived as "wives" of several Black and white sailors, whoever was in town at a given time. The Red House was well known to both sailors and the town watch, as frequent brawls there had resulted in Johnson's cooky stand being shut down just the week before the riot.[82] On the night of the 21st, Johnson claimed he was selling off the last of his merchandise before closing in accordance with his order when his housemate William Jordan beat a white sailor who refused to pay the fiddler entertaining the Red House's clients. The white sailor then rounded up more whites, many of whom had come in on the Swedish ship *Lion*, China trader *New Jersey*, and East Indies trader *Ann and Hope*. Perhaps this group had been beaten in the brawl described by William J. Brown and were thus looking for trouble.[83]

Richard Johnson then saw "six or seven" men outside his cellar, armed with sticks and clubs, commence "stoning" the house, and after being hit with a rock while trying to secure his belongings, joined Richard Jordan and Augustus Williams upstairs. The mob was growing outside, and the destruction was intensifying and spreading to nearby buildings. A Black man from one of the other buildings shot into the crowd, injuring a white sailor and stoking the intensity of the mob. The Black men in the Red House grabbed two guns—Johnson claimed Jordan and Williams were armed, and Jordan claimed Johnson and Williams were armed. One of the white sailors recognized Jordan; they might have sailed together on the *Ann and Hope*, and at least one account claimed the men were looking for that ship's cook. From the front step, Williams warned the whites to "clear out," to which one sailor replied, "Fire and be damned." Williams then, perhaps echoing decades of collective frustration with their living condition, cried out, "Is this the way the blacks are to live, to be obliged to defend themselves from stones?" No one seemed to agree as to who fired, but after at least two shots rang out, Swedish sailor George Erickson lay mortally wounded. Further incensed, the mob tore down two more houses and the three Black men fled.[84]

The next night, after news spread that a white man had been killed by a Black man, the mob reconvened. By seven o'clock, the sheriff, constables, and town watchmen had also assembled and succeeded in arresting seven whites in the waning daylight. Governor Lemuel Arnold, an anti-Jackson statesman, lawyer, and manufacturing magnate—and thus probably no friend to the class of whites he was addressing—was also there and "frequently and repeatedly" ordered the crowd to disperse. By the time darkness arrived, the mob quite clearly had the upper hand, and the governor called in a twenty-five-man militia unit, Captain James Shaw's First Light Infantry. They were no match, however, for this mob was intent on destroying Snow Town's property, most of which was owned by either the Black men and women who lived there or elite whites who owned the homes wherein Black people and Black peoples' property resided. The mob beat back the watchmen and soldiers, attacking them with stones and brickbats. At least one soldier received a "considerably" bleeding wound to his head, and Captain Shaw himself was hit repeatedly by projectiles. "No personal injury or insult was offered to the Governor," an investigative committee later reported, "other than a total disregard of his orders." Defeated, the law watched while the lawless tore down seven more houses before retiring for the evening.[85]

The next day, Friday, September 23, the Providence town council, the town's sheriff, and Governor Lemuel Arnold all met, with the governor agreeing to call in four additional militia units to supplement the watch and Shaw's infantry. That night, the mob assembled near the jail ostensibly to free the prisoners taken the night before. However, the prisoners had already been released, and outgunned, the best the mob could muster was "some bullying language" before dispersing. Saturday the 24th threatened all-out war as the mob reappeared and began destroying houses near Smith's Bridge despite a militia unit training its firepower on the rioters. When more militia units showed up, numbering 130 armed men, the crowd temporarily halted their activities. After a brief struggle between a mobster and a militiaman, the justice of the peace read the riot act to the crowd, and the governor warned that the muskets were loaded with live ammunition. The crowd repeated the refrain they had given the armed Black men three nights earlier: "Fire and be damned." They continued tearing down houses and advanced on the militia. Seeing no other alternative, Captain Shaw ordered his infantrymen to fire. In one volley, four of the mob were killed and five others wounded. Significantly, three of the dead and four of the wounded were artisans—killed were a shoemaker, a paperhanger, and a bookbinder; wounded were a carpenter, a blacksmith, a blacksmith's apprentice, and a man who worked in a furnace on Eddy's Point. The mob dispersed almost immediately, ending the most violent series of events Rhode Island had seen since the American Revolution.[86]

The result of the riot was the formation of a city government, whose charter of October 22, 1831, the General Assembly agreed to and Providence voters ratified the next month. Finding that the town council system was too weak to handle both its supposedly vice-ridden Black and "riotous" white populations, the new charter empowered the mayor to inspect any "houses inhabited by persons of ill fame" and jail "any dissolute persons who may be detected reveling in the streets, committing any mischief, quarrelling, or otherwise behaving in a disorderly manner, to the disturbance or annoyance of the peaceable inhabitance of said City [Providence]." While clearly using racial overtones in the idea of "houses of ill fame," the city government also displayed a level of contempt for the rowdy white mob that few other municipal authorities around the North would in the 1830s—a position consistent with Rhode Island's centering of property rights above all and meant to protect its elite residents. This can be interpreted as a way, like historian John Wood Sweet says, to regulate the interactions of nonelite groups of people and "to uphold order with a supervening authority of surveillance, discipline, and police." Providence's Black leaders, however, seemed to detect that they could break that paradigm and show themselves to be more like the elite "peaceable citizens," separate from and even superior to the whites "committing mischief." The elite white-Black alliance, however shaky, still offered an avenue for Black leaders to exploit.[87]

The rest of the 1830s would be a period marked by intense organizing spirit around the country as the abolitionist movement electrified reformers and conservatives alike. While the beginnings of the abolitionist movement have traditionally been traced to David Walker's *Appeal*, the publication of William Lloyd Garrison's *Liberator*, and Nat Turner's rebellion, historian Manisha Sinha has shown that the seeds of the movement—actually its second wave—were largely sewn by the African American associational activism of the 1820s and earlier. Black leadership in Providence beginning with the planning of the African Union Meeting House and the community's weathering of the pogrom of 1831 helped make the city fertile ground for abolitionism and its attendant causes like temperance, women's rights, and evangelism. In turn, the spread of those causes and the abolitionists' focus on implementing an interracial democracy helped leaders like Alfred Niger, George Wyllis, George McCarty, and others establish themselves as regional players in Black intellectual/activist circles, thereby strengthening their resolve in local matters.[88] Compared to white suffrage activists whose movement would continue to gather steam throughout the decade but who blundered at nearly every turn, Black leaders were building a case for citizenship based on respectability and adherence to republican norms. Out of the darkest of days, the way forward for a savvy, energetic, and a carefully constructed movement was clear.

CHAPTER 5

"How Long Will the Lord Suffer Us to Remain as We Now Are?"

ACTIVISTS AND CITIZENSHIP IN THE 1830S

George C. Wyllis always seemed to be in the middle of the push for citizenship by Providence's Black community. Like many of the leaders of this study, however, he is not the focus of a biographical study. He left behind few of his own words for scholars to analyze: his speeches were not recorded, and he did not write a diary or amass a pile of correspondence that we know of. Much of what we can piece together comes from what was written *about* him. National abolitionists who attended meetings in Providence wrote of his speaking prowess. Black leader and autobiographer William J. Brown noted Wyllis's membership in almost all the mutual benefit societies and his deaconship in the Freewill Baptist Church formed in the African Union Meeting House in the mid-1830s. He was even eulogized in the *Providence Journal* upon his death in 1858 as "humble and meritorious" and "one of our [Providence's] best known colored citizens."[1]

We may never know whether he was humble, but he was certainly "meritorious," and perhaps the leader most directly responsible for organizational development in the 1830s, when Providence's Black community positioned itself ever more advantageously in its fight for its members to become citizens. Wyllis joined Alfred Niger in the national convention movement of people of color in the early part of the decade and allied himself with the abolitionist movement radiating out of Boston. Wyllis's affiliation with the African Union Meeting House's religious life and moral suasion abolitionism led him to take the reins in organizing a temperance society in the city. In joining these causes, he placed himself at the forefront of the most important step taken by Providence's Black leaders during the 1830s: turning outward in order to portray a respectability steeped in republican values.

Joining these movements had the twofold effect of bolstering the case for citizenship for Black Rhode Islanders and combating the racism that propped up the color provision in the first place. Black leaders across the North, Providence included, understood that though slavery had been eradicated in their part of the country, the stain of southern slavery perpetuated the myth of Black inferiority. The Conventions of People of Color in the 1830s, discussed below, along with the other movements attendant to abolition—temperance and education especially—helped combat the racist ideas of Black people's supposed lack of independence and tendency toward vice, harmful stereotypes that placed them outside the bounds of republican citizenship. The road toward winning back the right to vote was long, but Wyllis helped pave it, and on it would travel leaders like James Hazard, John W. Lewis, Ichabod Northup, and Ransom Parker, to name a few. If not for the new public discourse of the 1830s, enfranchisement in 1842 would almost certainly not have been possible.

Rise of Abolitionism in Providence

The spread of the abolitionist movement to Providence, perhaps more than anything, gave Black leaders a platform from which they could articulate their critique of the color line. The founding of the abolitionist newspaper the *Liberator* in Boston gave them a voice. William Lloyd Garrison, who created the *Liberator*, was heavily influenced by Black abolitionists during his time in Baltimore coediting Benjamin Lundy's *Genius of Universal Emancipation*, and the *Liberator* would give voice during the 1830s to Black abolitionists around the North. The publishing of articles and speeches by Black intellectuals helped articulate the paper's stance that, in addition to advocating immediate emancipation, it was anti-colonizationist and staunchly in favor of abolishing the color line in all aspects of citizenship, including education and voting. Almost immediately after its first issue in January 1831, Garrison praised David Walker's *Appeal* and championed the petition Providence's Black leaders had sent to the General Assembly earlier that month, encouraging Black residents to refuse to pay the taxes levied on them and turn to the courts to solve the issue of taxation without representation. Providence's Black community early on recognized an ally.[2]

Garrison's connection to Providence's Black community was stronger than the fact that the two cities were the principal ones of New England and geographically close. George Benson, a Providence Quaker and business associate of Moses Brown, one of "the most respectable men of the state," was a founding member of the Providence Society for Abolishing the Slave Trade in 1789. Benson's daughters Mary, Sarah, Anna, Charlotte, and Helen were all members of a Connecticut-based female antislavery society, and Garrison would marry Helen in 1834. Charlotte and her brother George W. held antislavery meetings in Providence. George's other son Henry became an early correspondent with Garrison and introduced him to barber Alfred Niger, who had rapidly ascended to the top of the Providence Black community's leadership during its petition campaign for suffrage and education funding. Niger and Benson became Providence's agents for the *Liberator* beginning in August 1831 and continued in that role over the next few years. Niger was actually the second Black man—and second barber—to serve as a Providence agent: James E. Ellis was listed as the Providence agent in its first few months of publication. Garrison, the Bensons, and Providence's Black community went on to have a close relationship over the next few decades, with Garrison addressing the African Union Meeting House many times over the next thirty years.[3]

The *Liberator* was crucial during the 1830s in supporting the activism of Providence's Black leaders, publishing their calls for action and editorializing on their struggles for citizenship rights. In November 1831, the newspaper published the resolutions from a meeting in the African Union Meeting House chaired by Wyllis and at which Niger served as secretary.[4] The two men seemed to be taking the reins of community leadership, as they had been the delegates from Providence at both the first and second meetings, in 1830 and 1831, of the Conventions of People of Color. These conventions denounced the American Colonization Society as not representative of the will of African American leaders around the North and sought discussion on ways to improve Black people's "situation" in the United States.[5] The October 31, 1831, meeting at the African Union Meeting House reflected much of the dialogue Wyllis and Niger had been involved in during the national conventions. First, the meeting was called to "consider the objects and motives of the American Colonization Society," and after a speech by Wyllis, it was unanimously resolved that the meeting was in full agreement with their "brethren in different parts of the United States" to "express their disapprobation" with the scheme. It was fitting that the reemergence of Providence's Black community on the national scene represented a major reversal of the previous leadership classes of the late eighteenth century, whose fundraising goals included emigration to Africa.

They went a step further in their opposition to the American Colonization Society, claiming that it perpetuated not only southern slavery but the prejudices of northern whites. The leaders resented the fact that the prevailing ideology held that Black people were inherently inferior in "natural abilities," when in fact perceptions about African Americans' supposed "ignorance and degradation" had their roots in "oppressive treatment . . . from the whites in general." Then came a sharp critique of the racial views of the anti-Jacksonian elites, potential allies. They "*Resolved*, That we view, with unfeigned astonishment, the anti-christian and inconsistent conduct of those who strenuously advocate our removal from this our native country to the burning shores of Liberia, and who with the same breath contend against the cruelty and injustice of Georgia in her attempt to remove the Cherokee Indians west of the Mississippi."[6]

It is possible that many members of Providence's Black leadership class had Native ancestry themselves, for, as William J. Brown remembered from his own family's past, intermarriage among people of African and Narragansett descent was quite common, especially in the eighteenth century. The many Spywoods, Prophets (including other homophonic spellings of the name), and Browns in Providence's community of color had Native, African, and European ancestry—a common feature among communities of color across New England that either developed around land populated by Native people or attracted Native and Black laborers and mariners.[7] The resolution was also indicative of the wider world of immediate abolitionists' understanding that behind Andrew Jackson's Indian removal policy lay a dangerous escalation of white supremacy that bonded people of Native and African ancestry in a common struggle.[8]

The next resolution fit in with Black leaders' linking of education with liberation, not only on the tax issue but also to combat racism that lay at the root of the colonization movement. They approved of nearby New Haven's preliminary approval of a manual labor college for people of color, declaring hopefully, "It will deprive [colonizationists] of one of their principle arguments for our removal." They then hit on two more themes in another resolution that would come into play later in their suffrage movement: they declared that their "fathers participated with the whites in their struggle for liberty and independence, and believing with the declaration of that independence, 'that all men are created free and equal; that they are endowed by their Creator with certain unalienable rights, among which are life, liberty, and the pursuit of happiness.'"[9] The use of the Declaration of Independence was the centerpiece of their taxation-without-representation argument for the vote, and the particular passage they quoted was often used by Black abolitionists and their allies to prove that race had artificially emerged as a citizenship qualification. Revolutionary war service, and remembering the First Rhode Island Regiment and others that were racially integrated, was not only an abstract idea; the "fathers" they alluded to were often their actual fathers. For instance, Ichabod Northup, who might have been present at this particular meeting in light of his relationships with Niger and Wyllis through freemasonry and 1828's African Society for Mutual Relief, had served in the First Rhode Island.[10] The meeting ended with a vow to recommend the *Liberator* to their "friends throughout the country" and a lesson in how dual sparks of vehement anti-colonization sentiment and an outlet for Black leaders' voices could ignite a passionate critique of race and citizenship in America.[11]

The colonization movement, however, roared back into the spotlight in 1832, especially as pro-colonization politician Henry Clay emerged as the front-runner to challenge Jackson's reelection bid. Further bolstered by sensational reports of a vessel in the Providence River with a "cargo" of free Black people, and an influx of five hundred African Americans from Southampton, Virginia, rippling northward after Nat Turner's rebellion, the lapsed-Federalist-proto-Whig *Rhode Island American* provided Providence with a public forum for both sides of the colonization debate. On May 23, the paper printed an editorial from "A Friend of Humanity" in which the author condemned a speech given recently by American Colonization Society agent Joshua Danforth. Echoing the city's Black leaders, the author claimed that the "evils" that would supposedly accompany emancipation were exaggerated, that the movement excused slaveholders, and that it was supported by nothing other than the prejudices of whites. Turning a potent argument against colonizationists, the author asked how, if people of African descent were so ignorant as they said, could a colony in Africa possibly thrive? "A Friend" was willing to accede to gradual, or "ameliorative," emancipation but nothing further. In June, the paper printed two editorials by "A Member of the Society of Friends," which decried the Colonization Society's professions of "humaneness" as a sham and sarcastically suggested that if Liberia was improved so vastly by African Americans, perhaps they should be *re*-colonized in America to improve it. While claiming their identities as Quakers necessitated their objections to colonization, these Friends were also simply reflecting arguments first put forth by Black intellectuals in the 1820s.[12]

As if to prove the anti-colonizationist author's point about prejudice, the paper printed pro-colonization articles that used nothing but race pseudoscience to bolster their claims. One uncredited editorial suggested that Black people in the North were worse off than they were a generation ago; that they inherited a status of "political nothingness," natural subordination; and that "what incites the white is no stimulus to the black." Ignorant—either willfully or actually—of the operations of the city's Black leaders, this author also suggested that African Americans did not care to participate in government. A later editorial averred, with no supporting information, that Black political rights would take five hundred years to enact and at a cost substantially greater than shipping all Black Americans to Africa. Answering one of the Friends' critiques, the pro-colonizationist also said that all-Black states like Haiti and Liberia could thrive because there was no one superior to them; because whites in the United States would never consent to ceding their superiority by working side by side with African Americans, removing Black people from the United States would be the only way to ensure no racial conflict held either race back. Perhaps unwilling to drag the debate out and damage the unity of the anti-Jackson coalition, the paper halted the debate by the end of the summer of 1832.[13]

One Black leader in Providence appeared to have been at one time sympathetic to colonization, but after hearing Danforth and reading the May–June debate in the city newspapers, he formally came out against it. Wyllis had given money to the American Colonization Society but said he attended a Danforth speech interested to see how the American Colonization Society planned to affect the "final emancipation of the *colored* slaves of our country." Instead, he heard a plan "to depress still lower the free people of color, and to fix more permanently the chains of slavery on those who are now groaning under the pressure of involuntary servitude." Anxious, Wyllis then read Garrison's *Thoughts on African Colonization* and said, had the tract been read by Providence residents prior to Danforth's visit to Providence, Danforth "would not have found an individual in Providence who could have been so completely lost to every principle of common honesty as to have aided him in his designs." Wyllis published his apology for aiding the Colonization Society and his vow to fight it in the *Liberator*.[14]

In cities and towns across the country, the colonization movement of the early 1830s provoked a backlash of abolitionist activity. Earlier in 1832, Garrison had formed the New England Anti-Slavery Society, whose anti-colonization professions built on the Black-led Massachusetts General Colored Association and whose members included Hosea Easton, David Walker, and other Black Boston leaders. In Rhode Island, Providence women were the first to organize, forming the Providence Female Anti-Slavery Society on July 1, 1832, with a preamble that permitted the admittance of "any member or members who may feel the necessity of joining." This implied that women of color were eligible to join but they apparently had some hesitation; as white Quaker Elizabeth Brewer wrote to Garrison, Providence women of color "manifest a diffidence in meeting with us," and so the white members sought to aid women of color in starting their own society.[15] With or without white support (the record does not say), by the end of the summer Providence women of color had formed the Providence Colored Ladies Society. In September, Garrison published a series of their essays that give us insights into their activism, writings that may tell us why they eschewed cooperation with white women in Providence.

The brief essays dripped with references to religious respectability. The "beautiful and sublime precepts of Christianity" suggest that people should "be friendly to each other, and live in harmony, and yet how few of us practice on this principle!" fifteen-year-old "Almira" wrote, a message that could be heard and contemplated by anyone—white or Black, man or woman. But "how long will the Lord suffer us to remain as we now are?" she asked, a question that could be interpreted either as an indictment of the condition of people of color in Providence or an affirmation of solidarity with the enslaved. Therein lay one of the main differences with the white women of the Providence Female Anti-Slavery Society; the women of color recognized that abolitionism meant not just the abolition of slavery as an *institution*, which was the sole goal of the white society, according to its preamble and founding resolutions, but also of the racism that gripped the minds of whites long after the institution's death. Perhaps Providence's women of color held back their cooperation until this aspect of abolitionism was acknowledged. The city's Colored Ladies' Literary Society (which may have been the same group to which the aforementioned essayists belonged, under a different name) and the Colored Female Tract Society continued to operate independently, helping to secure funding for Garrison's visit to Great Britain in 1833. Later, there was an interracial sewing circle in Providence that earned Garrison's praise, and the Rhode Island

Anti-Slavery Society, which was founded later in the decade, declared itself more fully committed to Black civil and political rights.[16]

"Lauretta," another young essayist, adhered more to the traditional republican "circle" reserved for women when she urged "the acquisition of knowledge and virtue," reflection on the advantages they possessed, and "the source from whence they are all derived," meaning "the great Omnipotent." "Margaretta" similarly expressed the hope that the proliferation of women's literary societies would aid their diligence in giving "gratitude to the God of all grace," so that "the present and future generations will reap the benefit." Like teacher, orator, and David Walker's compatriot Maria Stewart had argued in Boston just the day before these essays were published, these were not calls to "retreat to a separate female realm." Rather, as historian Martha S. Jones has postulated in her study of women's public culture in the nineteenth century, these paeans to Christian respectability and virtue absent of political overtones were "intended to distance themselves [African American women] from the degradations that slavery had imposed on their lives." These statements were protests against the ideological lenses of vice and disrepute through which Black women were seen by their white neighbors—even some white abolitionists.[17]

"Destouches" and "Paulina" took a decidedly different track. Destouches warned abolitionists to "heed not the tongue of the slanderer," as they would have to bear "the many unnecessary and unfriendly remarks that will be made upon our feeble efforts." Bravely, she proclaimed that "our enemies can only hurt the body," while only God can "destroy both body and soul." Paulina used an overtly political approach, recognizing the historical moment in which she and her fellow abolitionists found themselves in a stirring essay titled "Think of the Slave." "Lady," she began, "when the page of history is spread before thee and thou holdest communion with the great and good of departed ages, and from their example catchest the glow of liberty and patriotism—when thy heart exults in the thought that thy country is the 'freest on earth,' then think that she is so celebrated throughout the world for her love of liberty, is pressing to the earth two millions of her own children, and while thou mournest her cruelty, her inconstancy, Think of the slave."[18] Combining a clear Quaker sensibility with a strong political message about the detrimental effects slavery had on American professions of liberty, Paulina's message, when read alongside the others, showed how masterfully the women of the Providence Colored Ladies Society were able to leverage gender convention—women being the bearers of Christian virtue—into roles as activists. While much has been written about white women abolitionists in greater Providence, these essays certainly foreshadowed, if not influenced, the later writings of Black men like Alfred Niger, George C. Wyllis, Ichabod Northup, and those of the Rhode Island Anti-Slavery Society, which would be organized four years later.

Abolitionism and Black Leadership

The abolitionist revival that accompanied the colonization fight also boosted prospects for those engaged in the struggle for political rights. Attendant to this was Black leaders' desire to portray republican respectability, which manifested in a campaign to rise above hostile whites' tactics and prove readiness for citizenship. A visit from William Lloyd Garrison to Providence, where he addressed people of color in the African Union Meeting House on three successive nights, spawned the formation of a temperance society and also a bond with the leadership of the national abolitionist movement—a connection that breathed inspiration into Providence Black people's struggle, and one that allowed them to contribute to the reform campaigns of the 1830s. Garrison's brief stay, which took place from September 9–11, 1832, may have connected him with the Colored Ladies Society, whose essays he published a few weeks later.

While not an explicit contour of citizenship, temperance involved a measure of self-control that placed the self above the passions and vice supposedly inherent to those beneath citizens, and kept the mind stable enough to make independent decisions. On a practical level, a movement for temperance had begun in Providence middle-class circles in the 1820s, a development that threatened the underground economy to which many Black residents were relegated. After the Snow Town riot, which influential minister and president of Brown University Francis Wayland publicly blamed on rum, temperance became a way for Black leaders to disassociate themselves both from the imagery of vice-ridden Black neighborhoods and from the lawless white mob.[19] Therefore, when Garrison held his third address in the African Union Meeting House, this one "for the purpose of forming a Temperance Society," he found an audience ready to organize. George C. Wyllis chaired the meeting, which consisted of both Black and white men and women. After Wyllis, a few other men of color and a few white men all made speeches, and "nearly all who were present" (forty or fifty people) signed up to become members of the new temperance society, which refused to adopt even the "except as a medicine" clause that some societies permitted. Providence's Black leaders, with their vow of temperance and society to proclaim it, now had "a weapon, with which to beat down the enemies of their race."[20]

On October 24, 1832, the Colored Association of Providence for the Promotion of Temperance was inaugurated with the formation of its executive committee and constitution, which was sent to the *Liberator* for circulation among abolitionists nationwide. White men Arnold Buffum, a hatter turned antislavery crusader from nearby Smithfield, and New Haven minister Simeon Jocelyn were both on hand to witness and address the founding meeting in the African Union Meeting House. Buffum was an ally, a Quaker who routinely harbored fugitive slaves and who had recently decried the racism of his "colonizationist friends" and abhorred their "slanders" against free people of color. He also claimed knowledge of a group of forty African Americans from North Carolina in a "village near Providence"—most likely at the home of his daughter Elizabeth Buffum Chace in Valley Falls (present-day Cumberland, Rhode Island). Jocelyn was the minister of a Black church in New Haven, a guest at the national Conventions of People of Color, a main proponent of the aforementioned manual labor college for people of color in New Haven, and an advocate for Black equality.[21]

At the temperance association's inaugural meeting, Buffum reported that he and Jocelyn's addresses were "succeeded" by that of one man of color who urged strict abstinence from alcohol, even as medicine, as "he had known some of the members, who were very apt to be sick about eleven and four o'clock." This was most likely nineteen-year-old William J. Brown, who wrote extensively about his associational life as a young man in his autobiography. While initially made up primarily of Black men in their thirties, such as Cato Northup (Ichabod's brother) and George Waterman, "respectable young people who were anxious to sustain a good reputation" were also added to the committee.[22] According to Brown, this was not the first association he helped to found—he and some of his teenaged peers had formed the Young Men's Union Friendly Association in 1828. That association started as a small mutual benefit society for young men anxious about the precariousness of their economic outlook and eager to portray respectability; it grew steadily and then was incorporated in 1844 as the first Black-run association to be chartered by the General Assembly. While Brown's timeline is often fuzzy and he sometimes mixed up details about certain events, his claim that his speech "was said to be the best" would seem to be corroborated by Buffum's report in the *Liberator*. Additionally, Brown often wrote about his aversion to alcohol because of the abuse it seemed to engender from white dockworkers (who famously took their "medicine" at eleven and four o'clock) and the drain he could see on the faces of older men of color who were alcoholics.[23]

Wyllis was the temperance association's first president, a post he held through the 1830s. Other members included a cadre of laborers who lived and worked on or near Benevolent Street—Robert Jones (vice president), James Hazard (secretary), and Charles Gorham (committee member). Although his occupation was listed as a laborer in the 1830s, Hazard later became a clothing dealer. Brown begrudgingly claimed that Hazard was "the richest colored man in the city," for he also considered Hazard "a man who liked to have people think he was worth twice as much as he really was." Brown, Hazard, and Gorham would also later play a role in the armed stage of the Dorr Rebellion, and after winning enfranchisement they became Whig Party operatives, turning out votes from people of color for the party in their ward. For now, the young men were getting their first experiences in institutional activism. The constitution ratified on the night of October 24, 1832, promised that each member would "entirely abstain" from "the use of ardent spirits"—notably, unless recommended by a physician—and as respectable leaders, would "discountenance the use of them throughout the community."[24]

The antislavery activism originating in Boston also radiated southward into Providence. Given Boston and Providence's long—and recent—history, and the taste of national activism a few of the leaders had gotten in the National Conventions of People of Color, it was perhaps natural that Providence played an early role in the second wave of abolitionism. The founding of the New England Anti-Slavery Society in the "hub" of the region, sourcing its strength from Boston's Black community and having its philosophy articulated by allies like Garrison, also motivated the Providence leadership. In November 1832, a passionate call for the formation of an antislavery society in Providence, one aimed not only at the abolition of southern slavery but at the rights of free African Americans nationwide, appeared in the *Liberator*. In March 1833, Wyllis was listed as a member of the board of managers for the New England Anti-Slavery Society during its first annual meeting and may have been a factor in the proposal to create a "manual school" for people of color in Newport. In May of that year, "abolitionist friends" in Providence helped secure the freedom of John Williams, a freeborn man who was enslaved while looking for work in New Orleans. He stowed away on the *Benjamin Franklin*, whose captain, once Williams was discovered, could find no one to take him ashore and so brought him to Newport and then Providence. There, the abolitionist community took him in and helped secure for him a writ of *habeas corpus*. Black men and women in the city were also integral fundraisers for Garrison's 1833 trip to tour the British Isles. "Colored Friends in Providence" donated thirty dollars, a "colored" mutual relief society (most likely the African Union Society) donated thirteen, the Colored Female Literary Society donated six, and the Colored Female Tract Society contributed four dollars.[25]

The Providence Anti-Slavery Society was organized on June 7, 1833. Wishing to ally itself with nine other like-minded societies in Massachusetts, Maine, Connecticut, New York, Pennsylvania, and Ohio, the Providence society was remarkably egalitarian. Its members professed the belief that there were no inherent differences between races, and that African Americans were entitled to the same political rights, privileges, and immunities as all American citizens. The initial founders being all white men, they proclaimed that Black people were "no more Africans, than we are Europeans."[26] In Providence, as elsewhere, organized antislavery started from the grassroots—and a perhaps unlikely alliance between the white artisan and Black laboring classes. The society's president, Josiah Cady, was a shoemaker, treasurer John Prentice a tailor, and corresponding secretary Gilbert Richmond a hatter. Storekeepers Martin Robinson and John Edwin Brown, as well as temperance activist Wyllys Ames and Brown University student Wilbor Tillinghast, were "counsellors." Henry E. Benson provided the Garrisonian connection. Ray Potter, a Pawtucket working-class activist, Freewill Baptist minister, and "fanatic" abolitionist cofounder of the American Anti-Slavery Society (AASS) later in the year, became the society's vice president.[27]

Despite the society's founding document being written from an entirely white point of view and listing all white men as members of its executive committee, there was a "committee of the colored people" in the society's ranks. Laborers and temperance society members Charles Gorham, Robert Jones, and James Hazard teamed up with Henry Martin and Nathan Gilbert (also laborers) to form this committee. In June, they held a meeting in the African Union Meeting House and penned an extraordinary rebuke of Andrew Jackson's proslavery stance that was published in the new, more overtly political, wealthy abolitionist Arthur Tappan–backed newspaper *The Emancipator*. After the members of the Black committee asserted the egalitarian, now common abolitionist belief in the "brotherhood of man," they selflessly dedicated their efforts to those enslaved, particularly in the territories of Arkansas, Florida, and the District of Columbia, claiming that the federal government had the power to abolish slavery in the last. This was because, first, Congress controlled the governance of the territories, an assertion that foreshadowed the dramatic battles in the 1850s over Congress's power to regulate slavery. Second, free-state votes in Congress vastly outnumbered slave-state votes—despite there being twenty-five "slave votes," referring to the number of congressional seats awarded to slave states by the three-fifths clause. This shows how politically minded the Providence Anti-Slavery Society was, despite its connections with the Garrisonian faction, whose moral suasionism led many to eschew the realm of politics. The year 1832 had seen the issue of representation battled over in Congress after the 1830 census showed that the North was far outpacing the South in terms of population growth and therefore representation in Congress—despite slave-seat augmentation.[28]

In much stronger language than other petitions that had come out of the African Union Meeting House over the previous thirteen years, this committee of the Providence Anti-Slavery Society issued a stark warning regarding the consequences attendant to abrogation of the "precious doctrines" of the Declaration of Independence, those being natural rights and equal creation. Reminding Andrew Jackson of the millions in bondage where it existed legally, they proclaimed,

> The God of heaven and earth, the God of truth and justice and mercy will pity their sorrows and avenge their wrongs. Their tears, their wounds and their blood are before his eyes and on his heart. Can a people be honored and prospered under his holy and supreme government, while they traffic in slaves and souls of men?
>
> As you fear God and regard man, as you love your country and would be a blessing to this great people, as you would live in honor, die in peace and find rest in heaven, despise not the woes and sorrows of our injured and afflicted brethren and sisters, who are holden in slavery in the United States of America.

They signed it "on behalf of twelve hundred colored people in the city of Providence." This leadership group, which had splintered from the Niger and Wyllis faction—at least for the moment—most likely represented the sentiments of most of Providence's residents of color, but it is conceivable that Niger and Wyllis were left out of the meeting, or at least out of the signing, because of the tone. Although steeped in the divine retribution language of David

Walker and Hosea Easton, Niger and Wyllis had so far preferred to portray a gentler, perhaps more traditionally republican sense of respectability. They seemingly were poking and prodding the elites in Rhode Island's government, massaging their unwilling allies' egos when they had to, keeping their concerns on the General Assembly's agenda, and searching for an opening to exploit. The laborers were not afraid to take their remonstrance to the highest seats of power and ally with the radically political abolitionist faction. While this bifurcation of leadership strategy might have seemed uneven at this point, rhetorical bludgeons and olive branches would have their times and places in the fight for citizenship rights.[29]

The decidedly interracial Providence Anti-Slavery Society, despite its leadership being mostly white, became the city's leading organization for Black civil rights over the next few years. In its first annual meeting in November 1833, white Presbyterian minister George Bourne, a veteran of abolitionism from before its national resurgence in the early 1830s and now based in New York, offered up a resolution declaring the improvement in the condition of people of color a "debt of vast magnitude, which is owing by us to that class of American citizens, full and prompt payment of which is enforced by all the claims of justice and the Christian religion." While calling African Americans a "class of American citizens" might seem alienating, it was quite an empowering reflection of the status for which Black leaders had been clamoring. The resolution, after Bourne's "energetic and able" address, was passed unanimously and sealed yet another bond among Providence abolitionists, New York activists, and the national movement. Bourne would play an important role at the founding meeting of the AASS the next month, helping direct the society's clerical outreach.[30]

Members of the Providence society quickly put action behind their words. On their way to the AASS organizational meeting, Prentice and Potter met James Barbadoes, a Boston delegate to the meeting and an African American man who was denied a cabin ticket and forced onto the deck of the steamer they had all boarded. With freedom to travel being a "cog to geographic mobility," according to one historian, and as such a "pillar" of republican citizenship rights, this infringement was a heinous affront to Barbadoes and the other abolitionists traveling with him. Although ultimately unsuccessful, the white delegates on board, including Prentice and Potter, signed a remonstrance that appealed to Barbadoes's respectability and the fact that he was the son of a revolutionary veteran.[31] The following February, the society sent a donation to

Susanna Peterson of New York, a woman of color whose son drowned saving a group of white boys from their own "watery grave." With the dual goal of recognizing the heroism of the young man of color and the interracial aspect of the calamitous event, the society publicized its own interracial nature by making sure Peterson (and the readers of the *Emancipator*) knew that the contribution came from "persons of both colors." Clearly meant for public consumption, the letter lauded the plethora of antislavery societies being organized around the North—"little rivulets, swelling the tides of that mighty river which is to sweep away" not only slavery but also the "despotism and prejudice" that it fostered. Peterson's son's bravery in saving his fellow citizens, regardless of color, seemed to the Providence Anti-Slavery Society to vindicate its interracial character, a fact, as understood by its members, to be a novelty that would potentially have to weather a stormy backlash.[32]

They had good reason to fear the ire of whites. Their close association with the New York faction of abolitionists made them acutely aware that the struggling colonizationist movement seemed to be devolving into mob rule. In October 1833, following a series of racist editorials published to a wide readership in New York by James Watson Webb in the *Courier and Enquirer* and Solomon Lang in the New York *Gazette*, colonizationists attacked a meeting of abolitionist "amalgamationists" and "fanatics," calling for the blood of Garrison and Tappan, the leading philanthropist of New York abolitionism. The next July, anti-abolitionists struck again.[33] In Rhode Island, white Providence residents were again agitating for an extension of the right to vote, but for now their efforts were confined to lobbing their sharpest rhetorical barbs at the General Assembly via the Democratic press. There were several articles published in the *Providence Patriot* that contained racist, bobalition-type portrayals of African Americans but no veiled calls for violence as there were in New York. Colonizationism was the official policy of what was now the main elite-backed Federalist-Whig organ, the *Providence Journal*, though its attendant antislavery leanings meant that it was not fully committed on that subject and it continued often to pair pro-colonization articles with those arguing against it.[34] Partly because artisans "of property and standing" were preoccupied with suffrage and elites were lukewarm on colonization, no mob violence threatened Providence's Black community during the "red hot summers" of the 1830s quite like it did in almost every other city around the North. Another reason for Providence's relative calm during this turbulent period, as writers in both *Zion's Herald* and the *Boston Times* later pointed out, was probably the

Providence authorities' decisive response in Snow Town, while in other cities mobs were permitted—or even joined by—white lawmen.[35]

The Providence Anti-Slavery Society continued in 1834 to promote Black citizenship alongside its crusade to end slavery. On March 6, they held a meeting that resolved, during a renewed call to expand the right to vote among white Rhode Islanders, not to endorse "any Constitution for this State which should exclude colored men from the right of suffrage, whose qualifications are equal to those to whom that right is extended." It would be "highly inconsistent in any member of any Anti-Slavery Society, or friend of Abolition and the rights of man, to give his vote" in its favor.[36] Then, inspired by the July anti-abolitionist rioting in New York, the society's corresponding secretary and Quaker educator James Scott emphasized the respectability of members of interracial abolitionist societies relative to the white mobs who were attacking them.[37] Claiming for abolitionists the status of true exercisers of constitutional rights, they were using their free speech to transform American democracy for the better while mobs sought to unlawfully and artificially quash these natural and prescribed rights. "Our only objects are," Scott wrote for the society, "to enforce the fundamental principles of our own government and of all righteous government, in regard to a sixth part of our depressed population—and our only means, the moral force of truth and love." He also noted that the day of his writing, August 1, was the jubilee for the 800,000 enslaved people in the British Caribbean who would on that day "rise to the dignity" of free people. The cause for the slave was not only respectable but also a marker for national progress and a blow for Black citizenship—for those already nominally free and those still to be freed.[38]

Other efforts at antislavery organization were taking root in the city amid the turmoil of 1834–1835 mob violence. Two large abolitionist meetings occurred on Independence Day 1834 in the city, and then in November British abolitionist George Thompson visited, rousing crowds for three straight nights and attracting between 1,200 and 1,500 people in his final speech. Garrison praised Henry Benson and Alfred Niger for their efforts in cultivating the *Liberator* in Providence, with the high readership and consistently punctual payments indicating a fertile ideological landscape for abolitionism. It was a "sign of the times" that antislavery was being discussed openly on steamships. In one such occasion, aboard the Providence-bound *President*, a two-hundred-person canvass found unanimous support for immediate emancipation. The

Providence Ladies' Anti-Slavery Society was founded in the wake of Thompson's sojourn in the city, though the problem of race that plagued its antecedent apparently continued. Founded by elite women, they reached out to women of color and found them welcoming, but the white women's chauvinistic language bemoaning the work that needed to be done to "improve" their Black sisters, and commentary on their "peculiar" Sunday schools, probably cut off much opportunity for interracial cooperation. More promising, perhaps, was the next generation: the Providence Female Juvenile Anti-Slavery Society was interracial. They were able to raise ninety dollars for the cause, though attendance at their weekly meeting dropped due largely to intimidation from a large group of men who watched through the windows of one of their meetings.[39] A year later, both abolition and Black citizenship rights received a massive boost when the Rhode Island Anti-Slavery Society, discussed in the next chapter, was inaugurated in Providence.

The Convention Movement and John W. Lewis

Black community leader Alfred Niger took a more decidedly holistic approach to his activism, including antislavery in a cornucopia of ideological weapons he wielded in his fight for citizenship rights. He, along with George C. Wyllis, William J. Brown, and Nathan Gilbert, attended the fifth Convention for the Improvement of the Free People of Colour in Philadelphia in June 1835. On his way to the convention, he, Gilbert, and New Bedford Black leader William Powell all signed a "card" commending the captain of the steamer *Lexington* for his kind treatment toward passengers of color. The ship made daily runs between Providence and New York, and they recommended it highly for patronage by people of color. Once in Philadelphia, Niger, Gilbert, and another young Rhode Islander, a Newport resident recently arrived from Salem, Massachusetts, Charles Lenox Remond, lodged with William Whipper, the staunch Philadelphia abolitionist and temperance advocate who within two years would be leading the charge against disfranchisement of Black Pennsylvanians. Whipper was a well-established leader in Philadelphia and Columbia, Pennsylvania, a businessman who owned a lumber company and small railroad, and so was well-suited to argue in favor of republican citizenship for people of color. He was also situated geographically in a prime location for escaped slaves, Columbia being about twenty miles from the

Mason-Dixon line, close to Philadelphia, and on the way to Rochester and Buffalo, New York. Niger's connection to Whipper helped propel him into the most elite of abolitionist and Black intellectual circles.[40]

In fact, Niger would be tapped to coauthor with Whipper the most significant publication to come out of the convention that year, its untitled address "to the American people." Also coauthored with Augustus Price, an aide to none other than President Andrew Jackson, the document spelled out the ideology behind what would become the American Moral Reform Society, an apt reflection of Niger's multipronged approach to civic activism. "We have selected four valuable subjects for rallying points," the authors asserted, "viz: Education, Temperance, Economy, and Universal Liberty." These were the core tenets they saw as crucial for advancement within the bounds of republicanism, a public affirmation of respectability to be used as a shield against mobs calling them "fanatics," and an activism that recalled the sentiments of the country's very founders:

> We plead for the extension of those principles on which our government was formed, that it in turn may become purified from those iniquitous inconsistencies into which she has fallen by her aberration from first principles; that the laws of our country may cease to conflict with the spirit of that sacred instrument, the Declaration of American Independence. We believe in a pure, unmixed republicanism, as a form of government best suited to the condition of man, by its promoting equality, virtue, and happiness to all within its jurisdiction. We love our country, and pray for the perpetuation of its government, that it may yet stand illustrious before the nations of the earth, both for the purity of its precepts, and the mildness and equableness of its laws.

Seeking to downplay race as a separating factor between citizen and noncitizen, and aiming to show that the barrier of color was an artificially constructed one, Providence's Black leaders over the next few years heeded this call to focus their activism into the four aforementioned channels, especially those of education and temperance.[41]

In these two realms, a new leader briefly came to the forefront. John W. Lewis was originally ordained as a minister in the African Methodist Episcopal Zion church alongside Hosea Easton in 1832, and when he came to Providence in early 1835 he guided a series of revivals that led to the creation of a Freewill Baptist congregation in the African Union Meeting House. As part of this revivalist spirit, Lewis initiated a private school for children of color called the Providence English School for Colored Youth. By December of that year, the Providence Female Juvenile Anti-Slavery Society reported that Lewis's school had forty scholars. Reflecting his "benevolent efforts and untiring zeal," the following April Lewis began advertising in the pages of the *Liberator*. His school was co-run by Ransom Parker, then a student at the Wesleyan Academy in Wilbraham, Massachusetts, and later a school integration crusader. Lewis's vision was apparently to train future Black intellectual leaders, as he advertised to Black parents "throughout the country" that students would be taught "Reading, Writing, Arithmetic, History, Geography, Botany, English Grammar, Algebra, Book keeping, Double and Single Entry, Natural Philosophy, and Astronomy." Tuition was set at a considerable $3 per quarter, with a boarding fee of $1.50 per week. Later in 1836, perhaps amid growing conversations in Black intellectual circles around adjoining "African" or "Colored" to their national "American" identity, he dropped "colored youth" from the title of his school, renaming it the New-England Union Academy. He was able to raise $388 during the school's first year, mostly from churches around New England after a brief antislavery lecturing tour of northern Massachusetts, New Hampshire, and Maine. That only covered part of his $600 operating budget; the difference was made up by donors in Providence. He exhorted readers of the *Liberator* and members of antislavery societies around the country to support his efforts, the import of which was changing "the public mind . . . in behalf of the oppressed, for whom the friends of humanity are so pleading."[42]

The petition campaign following the public school reorganization of 1828 also appeared to have paid off somewhat, with an "African School" opening in 1832 in the Meeting Street schoolhouse. While records showed that one hundred students enrolled in the school's first year, attendance had dropped dramatically between by early 1836, when only between fifteen and twenty students were enrolled. The city council's School Committee determined that the drop in attendance was due primarily to the "prejudices" of people of color against the white teacher and because the school's location on the east side of the Providence River cut off easy access for those in the growing west-side neighborhoods. Nonetheless, the committee recognized that Providence's Black children wanted to learn and proposed firing the current teacher, and opening two schools for children of color—one on each side of the city—to be taught by female teachers. The Pond Street School opened as the second school for children of color, and instead of a female, Lewis's associate Ransom

Parker was hired as the "preceptor" of the Meeting Street School, replacing the white teacher. The hiring of an African American teacher precipitated quite a rebound; Parker's school alone by September 1837 had at least eighty children of color in attendance.[43]

Although Lewis's school only stayed open for a short time (it disappears from the records after 1836), further opportunity seemed to emerge in the spring of 1838 as the city's rapidly growing population burdened the system set up ten years earlier. In a dramatic overhaul, the city council increased the number of schools, raised teacher pay, and made formal provisions for the education of Black children. This recognition, however, came with a further entrenchment of segregation and it legally promulgated inequality in an important contour of citizenship. The two schools, Meeting Street and Pond Street, were formally set aside to teach Black children "in the ordinary branches of English education." However, these would exist without the distinction between the tiers of primary (ages four to seven), grammar (ages seven to twelve), or high (ages twelve and up) schools, as white schools would now be differentiated. Further, the pay would be $500 for a male principal or $200 for a female principal in each school, and $250 per male or $150 per female "assistant teacher." These salaries were above what educators could expect to make in a white primary school but below what they could make at a white grammar school, an indication of what the city council thought would be the educational attainment of most Black children. As usual, progress—in this case, legal recognition of the right of education for people of color—came with a catch: Black children could be educated but neither alongside white children nor with many of the benefits granted to white children.[44]

John W. Lewis also took the reins on the second proposed avenue to respectability put forward by Whipper, Niger, and Price—temperance. On May 7, 1836, Lewis and others in Providence called a "Temperance Convention for People of Color in New England" to meet ten days later in the city. The bulk of the convention would be made up of leaders from Providence and New Bedford. Aside from Lewis, the Providence delegation consisted of men of note like Ransom Parker; William J. Brown; African Union Meeting House leader Winsor Gardner, "the oldest Deacon and oldest man in the church"; and stevedore, future Christ Church trustee, and first Black officeholder in the state Thomas Howland. From New Bedford came Richard P. Johnson, a former sailor who had become a prosperous coastal trader; Nathan Johnson, a confectioner and active Underground Railroad "conductor" who sheltered

Frederick Douglass when he first came to the city; and William P. Powell, who ran a boardinghouse for sailors. All were recognized as the most prominent Black leaders in the city, staunch abolitionists, and active in the convention movement. Interestingly, from Mashpee, Massachusetts, came William Apess, a Methodist minister from the Pequot tribe, an eloquent speaker who had recently helped the Mashpee Wampanoag tribe restore their autonomous government and control of their natural resources. The delegates recognized, as Niger, Whipper, and Price did, that "the connexion between temperance, intelligence, virtue, self-control and true freedom is close and undeniable," and that all were in "the best interests" of "every portion of the people." The political reckoning of temperance, therefore, was central to the cause of the "Temperance Reformation."[45]

The result of the meeting on May 17 was the call for a more widely regional temperance convention, proposed for Boston that October. This was to be led by Lewis, Deacon Winsor Gardiner, and James W. Johnson, the latter a laborer or drayman from Providence who had also just attended the New England Anti-Slavery convention with Niger and Wyllis, and New Bedford leader Charles Cook. Lewis most likely authored the meeting's address "to the People of Color throughout New-England." Perfectly connecting the political connotations of the temperance movement among leaders of color, he declared that "we long to stand among the men of our country, as fellow-citizens, worthy of our country and the human race. Our first step is to put far away from vice and every immorality."[46]

At the October meeting in Boston, the New England Temperance Society of Colored Persons was formed, with Lewis elected president and J. T. Hilton, the Boston barber and activist, secretary. In this meeting's address, once again most likely composed by Lewis, the society warned Black America that "all eyes are upon us," that because white prejudice only served to "magnify our faults and justify their [whites'] unkindness toward us," it was imperative not to give ammunition to white supremacy. However, the author was careful to acknowledge that "we neither suppose nor believe, that the sin of intemperance prevails among our people, as a class, to a greater extent than the white people." Temperance, he said, would not only help the case for Black citizenship but would assist the abolitionist cause by removing the notion of racial inferiority. "Let every colored person no sooner put the intoxicating cup to his lips, than he would give his back to the lash of the slave driver," he concluded. "And to the God of the oppressed, we look for guidance and success; and while ours shall be the rich reward of righteousness, his shall be all the glory and renown." If the respectability campaign undertaken by the temperance movement would not change white minds in the short term, Black Americans could at least control their own righteousness—in front of both the power structure that oppressed them and a God that drew no racial distinction.[47]

For the next few years, Lewis continued his presidency of the New England Temperance Society, continually linking it to the causes of abolition and citizenship. In the call for its 1838 convention, he proclaimed that "Temperance, Religion, Virtue, Patriotism, and true Philanthropy are the only principles which can elevate our people."[48] In 1837, he began his abolitionist crusade in earnest, offering the opening prayer to Garrison's Independence Day address to the High Street Meeting House in Providence. That summer, Lewis also linked abolitionism to his earlier passion for educating the rising generation, publishing a series of letters in New Hampshire's abolitionist newspaper the *Herald of Freedom* praising the Concord Juvenile Anti-Slavery Society and mixing in some political commentary. Because children only knew how to love, their "tender hearts" were well-suited for cultivating the righteousness that would win the country over to the side of abolition. Children could be true inheritors of the sentiments of the Declaration of Independence, a document that, though corrupted by the perpetuation of bondage and discrimination in the North, deserved the minister's exaltation because its message of equality served to dignify the oppressed.[49] Lewis left Providence for New Hampshire in 1839, handing the reins of temperance in the city back to Wyllis, who had appeared after an extended absence from temperance leadership as the vice president for the New England Temperance Society the year before. However, an editorial in the abolitionist newspaper *Pennsylvania Freeman* describing an August 1, 1839, address by Lewis perhaps best summed up his brief leadership tenure in Providence: "Nobody thinks of colored *inferiority* when they hear brother Lewis."[50]

Rhode Island Anti-Slavery Society

Parallel to the organizing spirit of Providence's Black leaders in the mid-1830s, the American Anti-Slavery Society, of which the Providence Anti-Slavery Society was an affiliate, was rapidly forming state and local chapters around the country. Around Rhode Island, other societies were forming as well. The mill villages radiating around Providence in particular provided fertile ground for fundraising fairs, as they often already had benevolent Quaker and Baptist religious ideology woven into their fabric and a taste for activism among operatives and artisans who felt they were being exploited like the enslaved. In the summer of 1835, amid the national petitioning campaign and a rising tide of violence elsewhere in the country, young men and women of Kent County formed gender-separated antislavery societies in Coventry and the Pawtuxet mill village. Societies were also created during and after visits from Lane Seminary rebel Henry B. Stanton and English abolitionist George Thompson.[51] The Kent County Female Anti-Slavery Society, which was founded in August 1835 and was the largest of nine total societies in the county with 273 initial subscribers, professed the will not only to break the chains of the enslaved but also to "obtain for them, their unalienable rights, as men and women, as guaranteed to the citizens of this Country." The Pawtucket Anti-Slavery Society was another mill village group formed by a Providence Anti-Slavery Society member, minister Ray Potter, and so the egalitarian sentiment was carried out of the city itself.[52]

Seeking to more formally unite the local societies into a state chapter auxiliary to the AASS, Rhode Island's abolitionist leaders held a convention at the High Street Congregational Meeting House in February 1836, at which the Rhode Island Anti-Slavery Society (RIASS) was born. Niger and African Union Meeting House deacon Winsor Gardner were in attendance from Providence, but it was otherwise an all-white gathering. The delegates drew up a constitution that reflected that reality, and while professing a belief in equality among the human race and that the sacred "inalienable rights" of life, liberty, and pursuit of happiness were God-given, they also vowed to "raise them [people of color] to a rank befitting rational, accountable, and immortal beings."[53] It might seem odd that white abolitionists felt the need to "raise" people of color, as the latter had been publicly organizing and petitioning for the better part of the past decade, but the diverse strands of activism by and for people of color would soon be tied more closely together. For instance, at the first annual meeting of the RIASS that November, Lewis Tappan addressed the duty of white abolitionists to prove to the rest of the country their commitment to the cause by living out the equality they abstractly professed. According to the recording secretary,

> Be assured, said Mr. T., that on the question of treating men irrespective of color, the great battle is to be decided between the friends of liberty and the supporters of slavery. That will prove the Thermopolae in the Anti-Slavery cause. Abolitionists must enter into this conflict; the question

must be decided, or slavery will be perpetual. We must eat, walk, travel and worship with people of color, and show to slaveholders, and their abettors at the north, that we will recognize them as brethren. I do not mean, said Mr. T., that we ought to associate intimately with those colored persons, whom we should not thus associate with, if they were white, but I do mean that we ought to conduct towards colored persons as all would do if they were white. This is practical abolitionism; and until we adopt it heartily, we shall be considered as hypocrites by slaveholders, and throw the weight of our example on the side of prejudice and oppression.[54]

The RIASS and Rhode Island's Black community strengthened their ties over the next few years. William Drown, a highly educated farmer from the western town of Foster and the society's recording secretary, was commissioned to write a report on the free people of color in Rhode Island with a view toward strengthening the interracial abolitionist movement. This was to be done by, first, showing how dedicated Black people were to the movement, and second, to prove that ideas of inherent inferiority proposed by anti-abolitionists were false. He showed this through interviews with teachers who said that Black children progressed as fast as white children when given the chance, that people of color were as temperate or more so than whites, and that nearly all favored the destruction of slavery. They were also perhaps more attuned to Christianity than their white counterparts—numbers observed in church ceremonies demonstrated this in Newport. Further, to counter the idea put forward by Benjamin Hazard that African Americans would seek only to rule over whites, Drown claimed that, while white churches still segregated Black parishioners in inferior accommodations, Black churches invited white guests into the "best seats below." All barriers to upward economic and social mobility were artificial, and most importantly, were reinforced by the racism of white parents and by ministers who neglected abolitionism as part of their preaching.[55]

In terms of economic mobility, Drown wrote that the main issue facing Black Rhode Islanders was that they were barred from valuable apprenticeships at a time when skilled trades were still common avenues toward economic independence—a central virtue of republican citizenship. A clear plurality of African Americans listed in the 1836 Providence city directory were laborers—43 percent. Just over three-quarters were either a laborer, mariner, or had no steady occupation listed. The city's eleven barbers represented one of the clearest pathways toward prosperity in northern Black communities, as men like Niger and James Scott had the cultural space and knew the community well enough to become leaders in the fight for respectability and also act as clearinghouses for Black and abolitionist publications. The whole city had only one Black shoemaker—an occupation, for example, with lucrative potential that relied on an apprentice system—and one baker, a job that required not only an apprenticeship but also a municipal license to open a shop. Tellingly, there were no African Americans listed as employed in the city's bourgeoning jewelry or silversmithing industries, no shopkeepers or grocers, and no lawyers. There were also no teachers listed in what may be an indication that this survey drastically undercounted people of color (perhaps intentionally), or that the occupation was so tenuous that no one could claim to be a teacher consistently enough for it to be their primary income source.[56]

As the RIASS met for the second "anniversary" gathering in November 1837, a young "Colored American" now residing in Newport addressed the meeting in favor of its resolutions promoting citizenship rights for African Americans—in the process, cementing this fight as part of the society's foundational ideology. Twenty-seven-year-old Charles Lenox Remond was already on his way to prominence in antislavery circles: he had helped organize the New England Anti-Slavery Society and the AASS, along with other state branches, and was an accomplished speaker on the abolitionist circuit. Originally from Salem, Massachusetts, he was the son of John Remond, an early associate of Garrison and that town's agent for the *Liberator*, and brother of Sarah Parker Remond, later prominent in the transatlantic abolitionist movement. The activist family had just moved to Newport that year after the Remond sisters were denied a high school education in Salem. Charles Lenox Remond would later be one of the representatives of the AASS to fundraise in the British Isles, famously, along with Garrison and the other AASS delegates, sitting with the women in protest of the gender exclusivity of the 1840 World Anti-Slavery Convention in London. He also formed an instructive alliance with Irish civil rights activists like Daniel O'Connell, hoping that Irish Americans would follow the lead of their former countrymen in supporting the abolition of slavery, as the Irish were oppressed by forces similar to those oppressing Black Americans. However, as events soon showed, most Irish Americans in Rhode Island were too busy seeking out alliances with the conservative elite and white artisans to see the commonalities between themselves and African Americans.[57]

While Remond's address was given to a primarily white audience in the RIASS, his words were a clarion call for Black Rhode Islanders—and Black northerners in general—to recognize that the fight against slavery and the fight for Black citizenship were inextricably linked. Slavery had marked Americans of African descent with a common identity, and now, as a class, they must "rise or fall together." Partly as a performative act to draw Black and white activists together, he claimed a particular disdain for African Americans who did not join abolitionist groups and employed the ever-common defense against the charge of "amalgamation," saying that if slaveholders wanted to see amalgamationists, all they had to do was look in the mirror—an allusion to the open secret of sexual aggression often exhibited by white men toward enslaved women. He returned to citizenship rights in his closing crescendo, saying, "Upon our conduct as men, we ask our birthright, LIBERTY. Upon our merits as citizens, we ask our RIGHTS and PRIVILEGES. And believing the resolution asks nothing more than a practical demonstration of our professed principles, I hope it may prevail." With Remond making a strong impression that was commended in the *Colored American* and the *Emancipator*, and the delegates reacting "with perfect unanimity of sentiment," the resolution to fight the color line in the ostensibly free North passed.[58]

Remond's speech was an important reminder that equality of citizenship rights stretched beyond the ballot box, as the color line was being increasingly policed elsewhere. By 1838, the railroad boom and growing use of steamships had drastically reduced the time it took to travel among northern cities, linking the business and political interests of Boston, Providence, New York, and Philadelphia, and "lubricat[ing] the cogs of citizenship," according to historian Elizabeth Stordeur Pryor.[59] Aboard steamships, captains often made passengers of color remain on decks to face the harsh New England weather. Thomas Van Rensselaer, formerly enslaved man, restaurateur, Sabbath School teacher, and now an active abolitionist, was physically assaulted by a white captain and forced to spend a chilly November night on the decks of a steamer between New York and Providence. Black waiters and other sympathetic passengers kept him company. Such was nearly the experience of three unnamed women of color from Massachusetts traveling between Point Judith and Providence after leaving the third annual Anti-Slavery Convention of American Women. While it had not been an issue between New York and Point Judith, the women were told to leave the cabin if they were not servants, per the company's policy. AASS agent Arnold Buffum attempted to secure the women's right to remain by asking the captain if he would do the same for southern white women on their way to Newport. Seeking validation, the captain polled the rest of the passengers, and more than three-quarters agreed that Buffum had pulled a stunt; the stalemate was ended only by the ship's arrival in Providence shortly after the canvass. In a particularly dangerous instance, a kidnapper who had previously sold three Black boys in New Orleans was found to be "hiding" or possibly working on a revenue cutter between New Bedford and Providence. He was found by Black abolitionist David Ruggles and pursued from Providence to Newport to New Bedford before being arrested.[60]

The railroads also became a major arena for the battle over the color line. In August 1838, Ruggles, most famously a purveyor of escaped slaves to the Underground Railroad networks around the North, wrote to the *Providence Courier*, outraged at being "defrauded and lynched" and escorted to the "jim crow car" on the railroad from Stonington, Connecticut, to Providence. As such, Rhode Island may have been the scene where the minstrel character "Jim Crow," a popular device for whites to ridicule the behavior supposedly inherent to African Americans, made the jump from the stage to the real world in a devastating way. A few months later, Reverend Noah Caldwell Cannon, an AME minister from Boston, was denied a seat inside a stagecoach in Providence, proving that the color line in this new contour of citizenship was inflexible enough to bar even the most "respectable" of African American leaders. Black activists like Ruggles, Frederick Douglass, Charles Ray, and Samuel Cornish all urged African Americans to fight more openly for their rights as American citizens, recognizing, as Providence's Black leaders did, that that fight would necessarily be multipronged. In its November 1838 meeting, after another "eloquent" and stirring address from Charles Remond, the RIASS passed a resolution "rebuking the foul spirit of prejudice . . . and promising to give preference, support, and countenance, to such steam-boats, rail-roads, and stages as will give to persons of color their privileges, rights, and conveniences as American citizens." The RIASS, taking its cues from men like Niger and Remond, was now the most powerful force for equal rights in the state.[61]

* * *

The Black leadership class that emerged in Providence during the petitioning campaign over taxation, education, and representation had endured rejection from Rhode Island's elite—and firmly entrenched—power structure and a pogrom that backfired on the white mob. Given a boost by the convention movement of people of color and the rise of support for immediatist abolitionism, people like Alfred Niger, George C. Wyllis, and John W. Lewis, along with those in the Providence Anti-Slavery Society, moved forward with the vision laid out by the African Union Meeting House founders—inclusion in the republic as a powerful body politic. Efforts at fostering a projection of respectability, such as through participation in the temperance movement and those aimed at removing the stigma of the color line like antislavery and the push for inclusion in public schooling, helped set the stage for Providence's Black leadership to enter the simmering contest for the extension of voting rights in the early 1840s. The Rhode Island Anti-Slavery Society—a powerful organization that would replace the Providence society as the city's premier interracial activist group—would build on leadership and tactics that had emerged in the 1830s to force the state once and for all to confront the dilemma of race when it came to suffrage, the foremost contour of republican citizenship.

CHAPTER 6

"The Mustard Seed," Part I

BLACK LEADERS, ALLIES, AND ESCALATION
OF THE SUFFRAGE MOVEMENT

Alfred Niger was used to rubbing elbows with national antislavery figures. In the early 1830s, he had been a regular delegate from Providence to the Conventions of People of Color in Philadelphia and New York, and in 1835 had teamed with abolitionist William Whipper to draft that meeting's important address to the American people. Therefore, at the 1837 general meeting of the Rhode Island Anti-Slavery Society (RIASS), the barber and only Black member of the society's executive committee was probably well within his comfort zone sitting alongside antislavery politician and future Liberty Party presidential candidate James G. Birney and Lewis Tappan, one of the premier financial backers of interracial, immediatist abolitionism. A veteran of citizenship rights activism, Niger likely had a hand in drafting that meeting's fifteenth and sixteenth resolutions, the first of which declared that "all legislation which is based on distinctions of color among the people, is an infringement of the declaration, that 'all men are created equal,' and a gross insult to the Father of mankind." The sixteenth claimed that it was the "duty" of all Rhode Island abolitionists to draw up and support petitions to the General Assembly "to restore to the people of color all the rights of which they are now deprived." Composed of Black and white men, laborers, philanthropists, and politicians, the RIASS clearly provided the state's residents of color with a powerful ally in their fight for equal citizenship rights.[1]

Also on the RIASS executive committee was a lawyer, recent convert from colonizationism, staunch advocate of free speech for abolitionists, and member of the General Assembly named Thomas Dorr. Born into the white Providence aristocracy, Dorr would come to be remembered as a folk hero for leading the "Dorr Rebellion" or "Dorr War" in the early 1840s. In this conflict, white non-freeholders, along with Dorr and some elite allies, brazenly attempted to overthrow the official state government. It might have been hard for him to imagine at the time, but he was sitting on this committee with the very man who would almost single-handedly ensure his movement's failure. Niger, in his attempt to unite Black and white non-freeholders in the fight for the right to vote, became the "mustard seed," the creeping bugbear of race that constantly followed and eventually overtook the white Suffrage Association. In 1837, Dorr had no idea about the infamy that was destined to burden him. Niger was biding his time.[2]

When the dust settled at the end of the rebellion by white suffragists, the victors were Providence's Black community, who won in resounding fashion the right to vote for all Black Rhode Island men. The previous historical scholarship on the rebellion has included studies of white class issues, radicalism, and the place of majority rule in a democratic republic. The first deep historical dive into the conflict blamed hyper-partisanship as the reason for the suffragists' failures.[3] To other historians, the white suffragists could not translate republican theory into practice, largely due to the entrenched notion that land—or "real property"—bound one to the community above all else.[4] The most recent, by Erik Chaput, is a scholarly biography on Thomas Dorr that refreshingly examines the prominent role Black Providence and abolitionist leaders played in a more realistic light.[5] A new look at the evidence shows that, first, the white suffrage leaders' unwillingness to incorporate Black suffrage into their platform—despite warnings that they could not square their purist republican ideology with an arbitrary delineation between freemen— led to their downfall. Second, and most importantly, after two decades of organization, Providence's Black leadership was able to force the hands of the state's Whig elites and convince the voting population generally to drop the "white" provision in the voting qualification. In the process, African American leaders proved the merits of their vision of republicanism, one without a racial distinction in the most fundamental right of citizenship despite what the founding philosophers said about nonwhites' place in civilized society. Removing the "white" provision was the only way Rhode Island could adhere to the principles of the Declaration of Independence and the U.S. Constitution in an ideologically sustainable way. This was what Black intellectuals had been writing and speaking about throughout the antebellum period—and the next two chapters shed light on what a victory (with all its necessary conditions and complications) in that vein looked like.

Black and White Suffrage in the 1830s

While Providence's Black community was organizing around abolition, education, temperance, and segregation, the 1830s saw sustained suffrage activism from disfranchised groups around the North—namely, whites in Rhode Island and African Americans in Pennsylvania and New York. These movements, as they had in 1820, 1824, and 1828, seemed to coalesce in the leadup and aftermath of presidential election years. This was borne out by the increase in activity by Rhode Island whites in 1832–1834 and African Americans in New York and Pennsylvania in 1836–1837. Coinciding with the turbulent beginning of the Second Party System—the Jacksonian Democrats and their opposition, which had by 1836 mostly gathered under the Whig banner—the disfranchised sought new allies in shifting race, class, and political dynamics. Generally speaking, the Democrats, beholden to their southern wing, opposed all efforts to extend the suffrage to African Americans and supported its expansion to poorer whites and European immigrants. Black voters in Massachusetts, Pennsylvania, and New York (where the property requirement enacted in 1821 meant that there were only about three thousand Black people eligible to vote) shifted their allegiance from the Federalists to the Whigs. Their new allies, however, were tepid and only supported Black rights when Black voters could swing elections. In Rhode Island, which by this time still disfranchised both African Americans and white non-freeholders, a different dynamic had begun to take hold, and with neither major party showing much interest in expansion, it was up to the people to get the extension of suffrage on the state's agenda.[6]

After the election of 1832, in which freeman turnout—as well as the proportion of white men disfranchised—ticked upward, rumblings of suffrage agitation began anew. The renewed movement started in January of that year in the Democratic press and was then boosted by house carpenter Seth Luther's *Address on the Right of Free Suffrage*, which he presented twice in April to groups of artisans. Almost immediately, race was playing a major factor. In Luther's declaration that Rhode Island's population consisted of only freemen and slaves, and claiming for themselves the rights of freemen, the artisans were drawing a distinction that could only be understood to have racial implications. It was not a far ideological leap from the freeman/slave metaphor, increasingly popular among white working men in many northern cities, to the white/Black reality in a country in which all enslaved people were Black and all Black people, whether free or not, were assumed to have been descendants of slaves. This connection was made more clear as the movement picked up steam that summer, when one editorialist in the Democratic press claimed that Rhode Island white men were the only people outside of "Negro slaves" who did not vote—purposefully or not, identifying the approximately seven hundred free Black men of voting age with the status of slave.[7] Finally cementing the connection was conservative universalist minister Jacob Frieze, when he addressed a gathering at Providence's Old Town House in October. After listing all of the redresses the artisans had *because* they were not slaves—the court system, petitions, and armed self-defense—he said, "All these, and many others that might be named, are not the prerogatives of slaves—none of these are enjoyed by that degraded race of men."[8]

On their march toward another constitution—watered down to consist of "amendments" to the state charter—that would go down in defeat in November 1834, white artisans did leave a potential opening for Black men, despite the clearly racializing language of slavery. They pushed back on Benjamin Hazard and the conservative establishment's notion of the Rhode Island republic as a "great land bank," which centered ostensibly on tying interest in the soil (real estate holding) with the right to a voice in government. By claiming that real estate ownership was an arbitrary distinction dividing voters and nonvoters, that all men had an interest in governance in a social contract, they would then open themselves up to charges of ideological impurity should they attempt to codify the distinction of race. The Providence Anti-Slavery Society signaled that they were watching these developments closely, publishing in the Democratic press their resolution opposing "any constitution for this state which should exclude colored men from the right of suffrage, whose qualifications are equal with those to whose that right is extended." The society would certainly not let one of the central tenets of the new movement, their claim as heirs to the principles of the American Revolution—of which there were still elderly, disfranchised survivors—go unchallenged. In several editorials in the *Providence Patriot*, writers like "Shiloni" advocated abolishing all distinctions, incorrectly remembering their forefathers conferring rights on all, slave and free, when they abolished slavery. The suffragists had also heard back favorably from John Quincy Adams when they inquired about the practicability of adopting Massachusetts's electoral qualifications, which enfranchised all taxpayers without racial distinction. Further, Thomas Dorr, a member of the newly minted "Constitutionalist" Party and assemblyman, an abolitionist who helped ally the Constitutionalists with the reform wing of the new Whig Party, sat on the committee tasked with drafting a potential constitution. His first political tract, an address in favor of a new constitution in March 1834, suggested that extension of suffrage might be based on a voter's "substance" or intelligence—though he also claimed that exclusive qualifications could be employed by a majority of the voters as a matter of expediency. Dorr's conflicting ideas on extension were reflected by other editorialists and speakers who clearly sought to extend the franchise to whites by limiting it to those who performed military duties or excluding those prone to "ignorance and vice," words usually reserved for harangues against people of color. By the fall of 1834, Dorr seemed to have caved to "expediency," for the suffrage amendment he helped author extended the vote to white men who paid taxes. It did not matter; Hazard and his wing of the Whig Party combined with conservative Democrats to defeat all amendments so offered.[9]

After the defeat of suffragists, the conservative General Assembly turned their attention to the other surging movement in the state—abolition. Along with the bourgeoning textile industry, located in the same mill villages organizing for the antislavery cause, came strong economic ties to slavery through the demand for cotton. Elites in the General Assembly, many of whom were textile capitalists or Newport aristocrats, and the latter of whom often spent their summers alongside southern slaveholders, pushed back against the rising tide of abolitionism by proposing a gag rule on the antislavery petitions that were trickling in from the societies. Just as the House of Representatives in Washington was implementing its gag, the General Assembly's May 1836 session responded to the February antislavery convention by appointing sworn enemies Benjamin Hazard and Thomas Dorr, among others, to a committee tasked with hearing a public debate on the matter. The nascent RIASS fired the first shot in this battle, petitioning the legislature seeking recognition that their "remonstrances" against slavery constituted free speech. Before the first antislavery petitioners could make their case, Hazard denounced abolitionists as being part of an English plot determined to implement "amalgamation," or intermarriage between whites and Blacks, a charge that abolitionists had and would continue to have to answer. Dorr denounced Hazard's hypothesis, saying that such invective was only a tool to stigmatize abolitionists. Hazard then moved to table the petition, which was sustained by a vote of thirty-eight to twenty-eight. Fellow Whig Richard K. Randolph—a native of Virginia, nephew of prominent Whig William Henry Harrison, adopted member of the Newport aristocracy, and Hazard's law partner—also led the charge to gag the abolitionists. This move again confirmed to Rhode Islanders of color that, while the Democrats were beyond the pale because of their ties to slavery and their stoking of anti-abolitionism elsewhere, they could scarcely count on the Whigs as allies either.[10]

Elsewhere, especially where Black men could vote, the Whig Party offered more of an opening for Black political participation and abolitionists' voices. In Massachusetts, former president John Quincy Adams, leader of the antislavery Whig faction, was perhaps the most dominant political figure in the state. The popularity of *Liberator* founder William Lloyd Garrison, the spread of abolitionism, and a small but important bloc of Black voters helped foster an antislavery spirit in the state's Democratic Party as well. However, the unsteady Whig coalition of abolitionists and wealthy manufacturers with ties to the South, who downplayed federal power to end the institution, dominated the state all the way through the party's demise in the 1850s. On the national level, Adams fought the congressional gag rule, which automatically tabled petitions related to slavery and was passed after abolitionists launched a vigorous petition campaign against the domestic slave trade and annexation of Texas, and in favor of abolishing slavery in the District of Columbia and the recognition of Haiti. In the Senate, Whig leader Henry Clay—a slaveholder and colonizationist—equivocated somewhat but ultimately helped prevent a similar gag rule in the upper chamber. Democrats were much more united in favor of the gag when it was passed in 1836. Although southern Whigs persisted in keeping the party as a whole from making any united stand against slavery, the election in 1838 of a handful of vociferously antislavery Whigs to Congress, and more who followed, gave abolition—and thus Black activism—its first foothold in national politics.[11]

The turbulent end of Jackson's administration in 1837, after his "Specie Circular" sparked an economic panic that threatened Democratic supremacy, brought new opportunities for its opponents, now unified under the Whig banner. Samuel Cornish, a minister and one of the editors of the short-lived *Freedom's Journal* at the end of the 1820s, started *Colored American* in New York. One of the new publication's first actions was to encourage a petition campaign already underway to abolish the property requirement for men of color to vote in that state. This first major challenge to the Democratic stranglehold on state politics since the days of the Federalist Party may have spurred Cornish and the state's Black activists. The Bucktail Republicans, predecessors to the Democrats and led by Martin Van Buren, had taken over the state legislature and dominated the 1821 convention that passed the "odious" requirement that a $250 freehold be placed on Black men in order for them to vote, while property requirements were abolished for white men. Now, in March 1837 Cornish declared, "We live in a brighter day than our fathers did." He printed extracts from speeches of the Federalists who had denounced the proposed distinction of color at the convention of 1821, showing how the law was based on the absurdity of prejudice and answering the central objection the Democrats had to Black voting—namely, the circular logic that they did not perform traditional republican citizenship duties like militia service and seeking quality education (they were outlawed from participating in militia exercises and barred from many public schools). While this petition campaign bore no immediate fruit, African Americans in New York continued their crusade throughout the antebellum era, inspiring one young minister named Alexander Crummell, who would in a few years play a leading role in the Black Rhode Islanders' movement.[12]

Also in 1837, in Pennsylvania, an event occurred that was reminiscent of developments in Rhode Island in the 1810s and 1820s. That May, a constitutional convention met and as part of its proceedings discussed amending the language in the state's voting qualification statute. After a Democratic delegate suggested adding "white" to the requirement, the convention decided to postpone debate on the motion until it reconvened in October. Simultaneously, a lawsuit was making its way through the state's court system. In 1835, William Fogg, a Black man, claimed he was denied the right to vote in Luzerne County on account of his race. A local judge ruled in his favor, citing Pennsylvania's gradual abolition act of 1780, which the judge interpreted to mean that the state had intended to make former slaves and their descendants "freemen." The white county official who barred Fogg from voting appealed to the Pennsylvania Supreme Court in 1837, but the court delayed its ruling, waiting to hear how the convention would reword the suffrage statute. In the meantime, the *Colored American* and the *Liberator* kept Black readers and their allies well informed about the proceedings in Pennsylvania, urging them to organize and push for their rights as free citizens. Black Pennsylvanians petitioned the convention but were rebuffed when it was determined that their plea "traveled over" slavery and abolition and used "disrespectful language," a position that perhaps turned up the noses of elitist Whigs.[13]

Just before the convention reconvened in October, Democrats from Bucks County claimed that some had lost their races that fall because Black men had "illegally" voted and tipped the election to their Whig opponents—a similar argument that Rhode Island Democratic-Republicans had attempted after Primus Bailey's supposed election-changing vote for a Federalist twenty years earlier in Little Compton. Debates about Black voting exploded onto the pages of Pennsylvania's newspapers, many of which blamed abolitionists for encouraging Black men to vote and condemning Black voting with the traditional racist ideas of supposed Black inferiority and tendency toward vice and violence. Unlike the Pennsylvania Supreme Court, the local judge in Bucks County ruled quickly in favor of the Democrats, claiming that Black people were never intended to be citizens by the state's founders—language that, like Benjamin Hazard had used in 1829, presaged the Roger Taney ruling two decades later in *Dred Scott* and echoed the philosophers who had inspired the country's founders. Armed with this opinion, the convention then ruled decisively in favor of adding "white" to the voting requirement but only after an impassioned defense of Black suffrage from abolitionist (and later Liberty Party vice presidential candidate) Thomas Earle and Whig delegate William Forward. Thaddeus Stevens, an abolitionist Anti-Mason delegate, may have been able to hold the pro-Black-voting bloc together to stop the motion had he been present, but he was in Harrisburg attending to other business. Forty-two allied Whigs and Anti-Masons along with three Democrats voted against the insertion of "white," while nineteen of the Whig-Anti-Masonic bloc and fifty-eight Democrats voted in its favor. The vote reflected the Whigs' palpable, yet unsteady, support for Black rights.[14]

The agitation surrounding Black voting in the two largest northern states, and disfranchisement generally over the past two decades, prompted the publication of the first major political treatise written in favor of African American citizenship rights. A white man, William H. Yates was an agent for the *Liberator* in Troy, New York, and in 1836 had been appointed to a committee of four AASS members to seek avenues for racial uplift from Black communities themselves. Although this enterprise ran out of funding due to the Panic of 1837, Yates had amassed studies of Black communities in Delaware and on Long Island, and used his knowledge of the law and Black history to write his seminal *Rights of Colored Men to Suffrage, Citizenship, and Trial by Jury*. It was published in 1838, just after Pennsylvania's constitutional convention wrote Black people out of the voting statute—though it had not yet been approved by a referendum of voters—whose proceedings Yates followed and reported on for the *Colored American*. In it, like Cornish the year before, Yates reproduced speeches from the New York constitutional convention of 1821 to prove that the color line in voting rights was entirely arbitrary. The constitution, he said, in its "privileges and immunities clause" makes no distinction about race, implied or otherwise. "The colored man is not an intermediate class—his relations to society are the same as others; his absolute and relative rights; his rights of person and to things; his acquisitions of property by contract . . . every favor or right conferred on the citizens by general legislation, reaches *him*." Although the author saw no reason why distinctions of color should be made among people who were free, he broke with his abolitionist contemporaries by allowing that enslaved people were property and as such not citizens. It was a curious concession and most likely made because Yates was formulating an argument based on accepted constitutional interpretation of property rights and slavery, not the abolitionists' interpretation of natural rights. Perhaps he thought it would be better received by fellow legal scholars or the people of Pennsylvania (who would be voting on the new constitution later in the year) if he distanced himself from abolitionist doctrine and made an airtight legal case. Undercut by the judge in Bucks County and voters of the state who approved the constitution and its "white" provision for voting, the treatise nevertheless was widely advertised in the Black and abolitionist press, with Cornish praising its use of historical fact to prove that ideas about race were malleable and subject to political expediency.[15]

Perhaps the most forceful document yet published in defense of Black citizenship came from Philadelphia's Black leadership. A committee chaired by Robert Purvis, the wealthy son of a free woman of color and a white merchant from South Carolina, drafted an *Appeal of Forty Thousand Citizens Threatened with Disfranchisement, to the People of Pennsylvania*, which both reflected and presaged many of the arguments Providence's Black leaders would make in the coming years. The committee dissected the Declaration of Independence and the U.S. Constitution, and especially the revolutionary notion of taxation without representation, claiming that Black people had paid over $1 million in taxes on real and personal estate. The authors reprinted the quotes of many powerful government officials, among them Tristam Burges of Rhode Island, who praised the heroism and commitment of Black troops in the American Revolution and the War of 1812. Despite all this, they understood that the tide was against them shortly before the state was to vote on the new constitution. Purvis and his colleagues blasted the "tyrannical usurpation" of the "just powers from the consent of the governed," and shared the committee's "amazement and grief" at the "apathy of white Pennsylvanians" at the addition of "this outrage upon the good old principles of Pennsylvania freedom." They warned that the state would struggle mightily to vindicate the wrongs done in "the conversion into enemies of 40,000 friends." Cornish wrote from New York that Black leaders now "must respect our own rights, before we expect others to do so, and we must show to the world that we know our rights, and have keen sensibilities, when they are invaded, or we shall always be subject to unlawful encroachments." Providence's Black leaders knew this all too well.[16]

Inside Rhode Island, conditions were ripening for crisis. Disfranchised white men were watching from the sidelines as another, protracted presidential election took shape, this one amid the backdrop of economic depression and the first in twelve years in which the opposition seemed poised to break Democratic dominance of national politics. As such, passions were inflamed all over the country. With the enactment of the "white" provision in Pennsylvania, the equal suffrage crusade in New York, and the Black and abolitionist press urging action on citizenship, Black Rhode Islanders were just as eager as whites to fight for their rights. They had spent the previous two decades organizing, fostering an image of respectability, and probing the General Assembly for openings. When white suffragists fumbled their chance, Providence's Black community was ready to seize the initiative.

Race, Politics, and Suffrage, 1839–1840

Black Rhode Islanders received a boost in 1839 when abolitionism returned to state politics, this time into an environment seemingly more open to its tenets. In January, the RIASS published a letter they had received from John Quincy Adams, the originator of political abolitionism on the national scene. Stretching the truth about as far as he could, Adams claimed that both George Washington and Thomas Jefferson were abolitionists, and that anyone interested in carrying forward the revolutionary principle of liberty should be too, affording the state's abolitionists much needed political respectability. The Whig Party in Rhode Island also softened from Hazard's overt racism. With its elder statesman on the verge of retirement, the Providence faction was in the process of replacing the old, Hazard-led landed aristocracy of Newport. The former traced its political ancestry to the Federalists of old, who had a much better (however fraught) relationship with Black Rhode Islanders than the Newporters, who summered with slaveholders. This shift was first evinced in the General Assembly's January 1839 session. After a long petition campaign by abolitionist women, notably from the Kent County Female Anti-Slavery Society, a committee appointed by the Whig-dominated General Assembly sat to consider the resolutions of the campaign's five thousand signers. James F. Simmons, a Whig from Johnston and future U.S. senator as both a Whig and Republican, recommended on behalf of the committee that the legislature immediately emancipate the thirteen enslaved people still living in Rhode Island, repeal the laws against interfering with enslavers who brought their human property into the state, and provide for a jury trial in which an accused slave's liberty was at stake. The committee also favored passage of a resolution instructing the governor to publicly denounce the congressional gag rule against receiving antislavery petitions, an action the national Black and antislavery press strenuously argued for.[17]

However, Whigs were still untrustworthy allies. Influential party man John Whipple, who represented the conservative faction of the Whigs, threw cold water on the anti-gag resolutions, claiming that the gag was not only constitutional but expedient. The state party anticipated another presidential run by slaveowner Henry Clay in 1840 and did not want to sully his candidacy by associating it with abolitionism. Further, abolitionist Thomas Dorr, impatient with the Whigs' lethargy in reforming the state's outdated charter, abandoned the party to run for Congress in 1837 on a fusion Constitutionalist-Whig Party ticket, a move that failed dramatically (winning just 72 out of 7,615 statewide votes). Dorr decided to run for Congress a second time in 1839, this time as a Democrat, and earned from the *Liberator* both a full-throated endorsement and that publication's admonishment of Whiggery. Abolitionists could not support most Democrats because of their affiliation with Van Buren, Texas annexation, and the prominence of its southern wing, but Whigs earned rebuke for continuing to follow Clay and slow-walking the Rhode Island abolitionist petitions (they had died after being moved from committee). As long as Clay headed the party, the *Colored American* proclaimed, the Whigs could not claim moral superiority over the Democrats on the issue of slavery. The *Emancipator* also endorsed Dorr, claiming that abolitionism transcended political party, and that the result of the election would depend not on Whig or Democrat strength in the state but on the strength of abolitionist sentiment. Dorr lost again, but this time by only two hundred votes—still a decisive defeat given the state's low number of eligible voters. Abolitionist excitement about Dorr's candidacy may have been misplaced. Other reform interests had taken over his mind, and by January 1840 he had resigned from the RIASS.[18]

Sparked by the passage of an onerous militia law that month, and encouraged by New York's Locofoco Democrats (descended from that city's Workingmen's Party), suffrage agitation in favor of the "unenfranchised white people" returned to Rhode Island. In the spring of 1840, white artisans and workers of Providence and the northern towns formed the Suffrage Association, whose principal aim was extending the right to vote. From the start, however, it was hampered by divisions over who to extend the franchise to and how they would get the General Assembly to act. The alignment of white suffragists with the Locofocos removed them one step further from their Black counterparts, as it injected a language of white manhood into the movement perhaps more strongly than Seth Luther and Jacob Frieze had in 1833. Orestes Brownson and George Henry Evans, leading Locofoco ideologues, proclaimed "white slavery" a greater evil than the one abolitionists complained about, and argued that white class issues should be fixed before any interference with southern slavery, and by extension northern Black rights. The Suffrage Association members garnered their strength from Irish immigrants eager to prove their respectability by shaking off charges of inherent inferiority, ideas that harkened back to British domination over Ireland and made Irish Americans particularly keen to disassociate themselves from African Americans. When Rhode Island's suffragists, many of whom either were Irish immigrants or had adopted the cause of enfranchising Irish immigrants, worked with Locofoco Democrats, whiteness was the primary element that united them.[19]

Locofoco harangues against wealth and privilege sometimes made them allies with abolitionists, and commonalities in their views of oppression left a narrow opening for potential cooperation among Black and white suffrage activists. The *Colored American* had supported Locofocos in some states during the 1838 elections, citing Wall Street as a common enemy for bringing on the economic panic and hoping that northern Democrats would secretly support abolitionist causes should abolitionist votes keep them in power. Further, when the Suffrage Association began publishing its own newspaper, the *New Age and Constitutional Advocate*, the *Colored American* noticed that there was no distinction of race in its call for the extension of the franchise. The *Colored American* certainly overreached when it determined that the new paper would be "warring against all invidious distinctions set up to graduate political right" but saw in the ambiguity real opportunity for Black suffrage, which had seen setback after setback around the North. The rest of the antislavery press was less optimistic; Garrison devoted no ink to the Suffrage Association in the *Liberator* in 1840. The *National Anti-Slavery Standard*, the AASS's newly founded official paper and allied closely with Garrison, hoped the Suffrage Association and its newspaper would accept abolition and Black rights as part of its activism but cautioned its readers to take a wait-and-see approach.[20]

Around the same time that the Suffrage Association was formed, one to two hundred unnamed African Americans in the city met under the banner of the Providence Union Anti-Slavery Society and heartily endorsed Garrison as its national champion. The archives are almost completely silent on this society, which in 1840 met for the second time. Publicly, it seems to have remained on the sidelines regarding the question of suffrage, perhaps following Garrison's lead in keeping his branch of abolitionism out of politics. Barber James E. Crawford, who would represent Providence in the AASS national meeting later that year, was one of its leaders, authoring the resolution pledging "hearty co-operation" with Garrison. Black Rhode Islanders also continued to fundraise for the AASS, earning the thanks of Garrison and Charles Lenox Remond. Black Rhode Islanders' interests were also represented by former community leader John W. Lewis in Boston, who along with leading Black Boston intellectual William Cooper Nell, advocated continued agitation in desegregating railroad cars into and out of the city. Their efforts may have led to a moderate concession from railroad managers. At a Providence First of August celebration commemorating the end of slavery in the British empire, another Black Boston leader named Thomas Cole praised the fact that seats in first-class cars were now being appropriated for travelers of color but lamented that he was "colonized" into the designated seats rather than allowed to ride where he wanted. Small changes like these buoyed hopes that chipping away at the color line would lead to the day when "these paltry distinctions will be done away."[21]

Some of Providence's Black leaders saw opportunity in the new suffrage agitation. George McCarty submitted a petition to the General Assembly's January 1840 session whose text has been lost, but according to the assembly's recording secretary it made quite a stir. The McCarty petition, perhaps written with Alfred Niger, George C. Wyllis, and other abolitionist allies, was asking for "an alteration of laws in relation to persons of color"—most likely the abolition of distinctions of color in statutory law, which existed mainly in the licensing of businesses that sold liquor and in the voting requirement. The petition reinstated the previous year's request by abolitionist women for the formal abolition of slavery in the state and the guarantee of a jury trial for those accused of being escaped slaves, and now also asked the assembly to perform a historical survey of slavery in Rhode Island. This latter request may have been an attempt to coax the state into recognizing that its discriminatory laws had their statutory basis in slavery and were unnecessary where slavery was outlawed. The committee tasked with receiving the petition continued its recent trend of signaling a distaste for slavery generally, regretting that the South was moving away from its view of slavery as a "necessary evil" and adopting more of the "positive good" theory, and renouncing the congressional gag. However, it reverted to what historian Joanne Pope Melish deems "a kind of erasure by whites of the historical experience of local enslavement" toward the end of rationalizing white supremacy. "It is believed," wrote the committee, "that while slavery existed in Rhode Island, the slaves were always treated with humanity, and they were generally rather a burden than a source of profit for their owners." Emancipation, they seemed to have thought, was a favor to Black Rhode Islanders and African Americans should be grateful for limited freedom rather than agitating for more. This historical dissonance helped perpetuate the racism that might have disappeared along with slavery but instead persists through today.[22]

The committee denounced what they deemed interference with slavery in the South, something they felt was unconstitutional and therefore intolerable, and so it rejected the idea of personal liberty for accused slaves. In a response that covered both the formal abolition of slavery in the state and the erasure of the statutory color line, the committee sought to downplay the existence of racial designations as insignificant. Simultaneously, it understood the maintenance of the color line as politically expedient, stating that "in the state of society and of public feeling among us," whether the color line was repealed was of little consequence. These laws were very few, and few people would be helped by the race distinction's repeal, they determined; no action on the color line would be forthcoming. They may have been correct that it would not immediately benefit many people when it came to voting, given Rhode Island's high property requirement for freemanship. However, Black Providence leaders understood citizenship was multifaceted, and knocking down one barrier meant that more could fall. Further, extension of the franchise to Black men and keeping the requirement for whites unchanged may have fanned the flames already flickering among white suffragists. After the election season of 1840, the conservative establishment would have a much more difficult time defending its racial exclusivity on one hand and its property requirement on the other.[23]

Chipping Away, 1840–1841

Without participation from either the white artisan class or African Americans, the Whig candidates for political office dominated 1840. The "Log Cabin and Hard Cider" excitement that carried William Henry Harrison into the presidency infected Rhode Island freemen, who voted in favor of the Whig ticket by more than 60 percent. In the gubernatorial election, Whig Samuel Ward King, a "firm and conciliatory" politician, ran slightly behind Harrison, but with 58 percent of the freeman vote he was able to trounce Locofoco Democrat Thomas Carpenter. Whigs controlled the state legislature, entrenching the interests of merchant and manufacturing magnates, whose industrializing enterprises threatened the economic security of artisans and factory operatives alike. This was a bitter defeat for the latter, who participated in the rousing version of electioneering pioneered by the 1840 campaign in every way—the parades, the speeches, mass rallies, and so on—except voting. Locofoco Democrat and staunch advocate for the disfranchised Thomas Dorr saw the Whig victory as an existential calamity.[24]

The Suffrage Association immediately got to work, starting the *New Age* just two weeks after the 1840 election results were announced. A newspaper entirely devoted to the cause of extending the right to vote in Rhode Island, the *New Age* advocated abolishing the property requirement and invited "all friends of equal rights" to join the fight.[25] Edited by John A. Brown, president of the Suffrage Association, the paper reflected Brown's decidedly waffling stance on Black voting. Brown would later favor Black suffrage, but from the beginning he allowed the paper to run editorials that denounced Black voting as antithetical to republican philosophy and declared Black voting an inexpedient political position, at least for the time being. Suffragists constantly compared white Rhode Islanders to southern slaves, ignoring, belittling, or using the plight faced by Rhode Islanders of color to augment their case for universal *white* manhood suffrage. Using similar language that abolitionists employed in their missions against slavery and in favor of Black rights suggested a window for an alliance, but the *New Age* nevertheless routinely accused abolitionists of advocating for Black supremacy. Despite its call to "all friends," a hopeful editorial by the *Colored American*, and a few columns written by abolitionists, the Suffrage Association was quite clearly dominated by men who had no interest in extending the right to vote across the color line.[26]

In the midst of the rapidly spreading suffrage agitation, George McCarty submitted yet another petition to the General Assembly in January 1841, this time on behalf of a group of fifteen leaders. Unfortunately, its text has also been lost, but it harkened back to his, Wyllis's, and Niger's petition of 1831. We can surmise that the premise was asking the assembly, as the leaders had ten years earlier, to either exempt people of color from taxation or permit them to vote on the same plane as whites, hoping that republican principle would lead to the latter. In a brief conversation, Locofoco Democrat Samuel Y. Atwell moved that people of color be relieved from taxation, "cotton" conservative capitalist Whig John Whipple agreed but had questions about where to draw the line between races, and antislavery Whig James F. Simmons determined that "the best we can do . . . for them" was exempt people of color from taxation because they could not be made equal to whites. In a stunningly bipartisan fashion, the General Assembly rejected the idea of Black voting, passing "An Act in Relation to Blacks and People of Color." "*Be it enacted by the General Assembly, as follows*," the act read, that "the real and personal estate of Blacks and People of Color not freemen of this state or any town thereof, shall not be liable to town or state taxes in any manner whatever." It was a move that pleased no one.[27]

Aside from being an obvious setback for Black Rhode Islanders, it enflamed white suffragists who lambasted the state for applying the "taxation without representation" principle to African Americans but not disfranchised whites. White suffragists could have united behind this idea alongside Black Rhode Islanders, perhaps using this precedent to force the state into choosing between their large combined tax base and the right to vote; instead, white suffragists accused the state of caving to abolitionists and continued charging abolitionists with desiring African Americans rule over whites. More talk of "white slavery" and complaints that Black people—even those enslaved—were better taken care of than whites filled the pages of the *New Age*. The Suffrage Association was further incensed when, in response to the suffrage agitation, the General Assembly called for a constitutional convention to convene in

November 1841 to discuss voting qualification and reapportionment of legislative seats—but decided that only freemen could vote on delegates to attend. This prompted the association to issue its own call for a "People's Convention," or a mass meeting to determine next steps, to meet before the "Landholders' Convention." By early spring, the state government had alienated both white suffragists and Black activists, and white suffragists responded by alienating Black activists and the state government. There were now three bodies politic embroiled in a messy constitutional controversy: the decidedly conservative General Assembly (with suffragist Democrats and reformist Whigs sprinkled in) defending a conservative outlook on state politics; Black activists and their abolitionist allies, who had been organizing for over twenty years for more equitable citizenship and an erasure of the color line, especially when it came to the right to vote; and the Suffrage Association, rapidly growing in number and seeking to, by dint of its size, force the state to bend to their will.[28]

The *Colored American* spoke for many Black Rhode Islanders who were dismayed at the General Assembly's actions but also at the Black petitioner(s) whose tactic constituted "bad policy." Charles B. Ray, now the newspaper's editor, saw the utility of trying to leverage taxation without representation as a way to force the state to act in favor of Black suffrage, but the miscalculation in predicting the result was devastating.[29] Black activists were now further from gaining suffrage than ever, having handed the state an excuse to disfranchise them. Ray saw Black Rhode Islanders' best hope in the People's Convention, which despite the racism it often employed, had yet to make a definitive determination as to who would qualify for the franchise. He implored,

> We hope that our people in that State, having waked up to this matter, and commenced operations in one form, will keep an eye towards that convention, and make a general and a vigorous move throughout the State, and that their friends will take hold with them, and both see to it, that their rights are defended and maintained in that convention. Remember that now is the time, the Constitution once framed and established, it will take a half a century to move an alteration and an amendment to it. May the people of that State not so overlook the spirit of the age, as to disgrace the State in their contemplated Constitution, by restricting the rights of even the humblest individual.

To the Suffrage Association, he offered a warning that would echo throughout their campaign: "Can it be found possible, however, that a convention representing the workingmen of Rhode Island, will be found framing a constitution to measure and graduate rights, according to the color of the skin. We shall see. It ought not to be so, we hope it will not be."[30]

On April 17, the Suffrage Association held a massive parade and ox roast to kick off its campaign in earnest, drawing three thousand Rhode Islanders, many of whom marched with the tools of their trades, and winning the respect of some freemen and politicians. Although the movement was not formally aligned in the party system, Locofoco Democrats Samuel Atwell from Gloucester and Duttee J. Pearce—who, as the attorney general of Rhode Island, had prosecuted the Hard-Scrabble rioters—addressed the crowd and pledged their support. The association determined to hold their own constitutional convention, one that they would force the state legislature to recognize by showing a majority of Rhode Island men supported it. However strong this stand was, the association was still unable to fully determine to whom to extend the right of suffrage—an editorial published shortly after the rally hedged on the idea of "free" suffrage and said that the association was open to an "extension" of it. The author warned that unless the voting qualification was determined first, before any delegates to a convention would be voted on, the movement could fail on that very issue. The next month, the association held another rally in Newport and resolved that "every American citizen" should vote for delegates once a People's Constitutional Convention was announced. While there was no mention of race, the status of African Americans as non-taxpayers, non-militiamen, and on the wrong side of a persistent legal color line still left so much ambiguity in the Suffrage Association's use of the term "citizen" that Black Rhode Island leaders would not publicly support it.[31]

Sensing that their best hopes still lay with the state legislature, a group of Black leaders that did not include McCarty, Niger, or Wyllis sent a petition to the General Assembly, now under siege by the suffrage movement. The Whigs clearly had a stranglehold on legitimate state power—in the May–June session of the assembly, Whigs dominated the house and were unanimously elected to the senate, so the petition would be a calculated gesture couched in Whig sensibility.[32] It was submitted just four days after the mass rally in Providence. In a remarkable document, thirty-eight signees repudiated the McCarty petition, claiming that it did not represent the will of Black Providence residents, was the work of "a few private individuals," and was written and submitted "without the notice or authority of any public assemblage." The petitioners deprecated the act that removed them from the tax rolls, and while they desired "higher privileges and more enlarged right," they feared more immediately the harm such a move could do to their "educational and personal emolument." They asked that the act be repealed when the assembly met in its June session, believing that taxes assessed on their "real and personal estate in this state" to be "just and due to the government." Calling themselves "colored citizens," it is quite clear the petitioners were attempting to recoup ground lost in the citizenship fight by the McCarty petition, and to put themselves in a stronger position in the eyes of the General Assembly when the suffrage excitement reached a fever pitch, as the *New Age* was promising it would.[33]

If not the old triumvirate of McCarty, Niger, and Wyllis, who was this group of "colored citizens of the state, possessed of Real Estate and personal property?" Led by James Hazard, the wealthy clothing dealer, and Ichabod Northup, a laborer who had amassed sizeable real estate holdings, this leadership group much more resembled the committee of people of color in the Providence Anti-Slavery Society, who had published letters in the *Emancipator* during that organization's brief reign over abolition before the establishment of the RIASS. Hazard and Northup represented a business elite, somewhat outside—or at least alongside—the leaders of the African Union Meeting House, which by 1840 had spawned several denominational churches around the city. However, there were some connections between this group and the old leaders. Northup and James Harris, another signee, had been associated with McCarty, Niger, and Wyllis before—according to William J. Brown, they had been at the 1831 meeting that first petitioned the legislature asking for the vote or to be removed from tax rolls. There was one sexton among the group, Caesar Gardner, who was also involved in the mutual benefit society founded by William J. Brown and other young men in the 1820s. Perhaps he was related to an elder Caesar Gardner, who became a member of the African Union Society in Newport in 1797, marking an even deeper connection with past leadership. Further, educator and temperance advocate Ransom Parker appears on the list, representing some continuity with the old guard of leadership that tied education funding to taxation and the vote.[34]

Most of the committee reflected a commercial elite of Black Providence whose hard work and independence made their case for citizenship, not necessarily the respectability the barbers and ministers sought to weaponize. To be sure, in addition to Gardner, some had church leadership connections—Thomas Howland was a trustee, and waiter Abraham Bignell and clerk George Head were leaders of the newly organized Christ Church (Episcopalian), which splintered off of the African Union Meeting House. Twelve of the thirty-eight signees were listed as "Laborer" in the Providence city directory, but as all identified as property owners, they must have been the most financially successful. Some may have been children of those listed as heads of independent households in the 1822 census of people of color, as, for instance, George Head may have been the child of either Abraham or Thomas Head, both listed in 1822 as living with their children. Prince Congdon, one of the laborers, may have been the same Prince Congdon listed as a head of household that year. The next most common occupation among the petitioners was drayman, who in the nineteenth century quite literally moved the economic wheels of the city. Transporting goods from wharf to market, their visible presence in ever-more bustling streets, and their contacts with merchant and business elites, offered a potentially exploitable tie to the Whig power structure—as well as animosity from white artisans who saw them as competition for jobs in the economic downturn. There were also two men who must have applied for and received licenses to run their own businesses: Howland, who would later become the first Black elected official in the state, was listed as a grocer, and William Lee owned William Lee & Co., a victualling cellar on South Main Street.[35]

In a first for Black political petitions in the city, there were two women signees—Catherine Williams and Lucy Crawford. Williams might have been married to someone linked to the other petitioners, as there was one Black John Williams who appeared in the 1820 federal census and on the 1822 Providence census. Both appeared in federal censuses independently, Catherine Williams in 1830 and Lucy Crawford in 1840, as heads of households. Perhaps they entered the political arena through a similar path many Black women took, becoming activists after being raised in abolitionist families or rising to prominence alongside their abolitionist husbands. The exigencies of economic circumstance, as we have seen, also brought women like Elleanor Eldridge into the Providence commercial scene. Many women ran boardinghouses, some quite successfully, like Rosanna Jones. Jones boarded white and Black men, women, and children, and was able to steadily expand her real estate holdings in Providence and Cranston, despite having her home destroyed in the 1831 Snow Town pogrom. In a state where Black political activism took on a more carefully crafted tone to appeal to a General Assembly steeped in conservative republican ideology, the inclusion of businesswomen might have risked some scandalization. Widowhood, or at least the perception of carrying on a man's legacy, might have mitigated some of that risk for Williams and Crawford, affording women a voice in the fight for citizenship.[36]

The General Assembly took up the petition on June 24, 1841, when it was debated in the Committee on Finance. Unfortunately, it was Richard K. Randolph who moved the petition through the committee. The arch-conservative Newport Whig, a native Virginian and associate of Benjamin Hazard, strongly opposed it using Lockean degradations of people of color, determining that they were in a state of "pupilage" and that the state needed to exercise more "guardianship over their interests" than their "pretended friends," the abolitionists. They ought not to tax the "pittance" of wealth Black people had gained because they had not the means of expanding it. Chauvinistically, he moaned that taxing people of color would be a penalty on the "poor and humble." Finally, he deemed it granted that the assembly would not want Black people voting or holding office—he should want to tax them otherwise. Suffrage Association ally Samuel Atwell agreed, claiming—correctly—that adding them back to the tax rolls would be returning the "sword" with which they would contend for other rights. Whig Samuel Ames, a Federalist in the old, more philanthropic Providence tradition, rose to support the petition, giving Black citizenship at least a small voice in the legislature. He supported it not necessarily on its merits but on principle: first, the fifteen signees of the McCarty petition could hardly be representative of the city's whole Black population. Second, African Americans had been taxed all the way up until the previous January without regard to color; the distinction seemed to have been added so suddenly and was too antithetical to the primacy of the state's property-driven republicanism. The country conservative and white suffragist factions put their disagreements aside to block the petition, recreating the alliance of whiteness across class lines that had sustained white suffrage and defeated Black suffrage across the country over the previous decades.[37]

Over the summer of 1841, as the General Assembly prepared for freemen to vote on delegates to its November constitutional convention, the Suffrage Association was planning an election for delegates to its own People's Convention. This included, as many had agreed since the idea was first brokered, finally determining exactly who the franchise should be extended to. Most agreed that it should be "every American citizen" over the age of twenty-one, but the one question that nagged them throughout was whether African Americans were part of the citizenry. The pages of the *New Age* were saturated with debates as to who could even determine qualifications. The philosophy they settled on, which has been well-documented by historians, was that republican governments must be based on majority rule. When the majority of adult male Rhode Islanders owned land, they created a government that enfranchised themselves based on that common attribute. Now that the majority did not hold the amount of land required by the king's charter and confirmed after achieving U.S. statehood, the government must necessarily be altered to the will of the majority. This meant that government needed to be based on expediency rather than principle, for the majority's will might change from time to time while principles were inflexible. Despite the logical loophole of majority rule itself being a principle, this agreement was the first step in getting to the question of citizenship. Following this, the association determined that the majority of the people had the right to make and unmake citizens. On August 6, the call went out that elections would be held on August 28 for delegates to meet at the People's Convention in October. It invited "every American citizen, 21 years of age and upwards, residing in this state one year, and a resident of the Town six months preceding the election."

With no mention of race, it seemed that the election would be open to people of color. However, despite the rhetorical equivocation on race, the Suffrage Association took concrete steps to alienate Black leaders. Just prior to the call for their own elections to a constitutional convention, the Suffrage Association petitioned the General Assembly one last time, asking that the assembly's convention open itself up to delegates being voted on by "every free white male citizen over twenty-one years of age" who paid taxes. The assembly denied the request. Most of the editorials and correspondence published in the *New Age* was hostile toward Rhode Island's abolitionists, who association members accused of wanting to free Black people before, or even at the expense of, their white statesmen. Additionally, as Black Rhode Islanders understood, if the theory was that the majority could make themselves citizens, they could just as easily "unmake" Black citizens by adding a "white" provision when the October convention drafted formal voting qualifications—if they determined it expedient. Around this time, William J. Brown remembered Black leaders convening a meeting in the city at which it was determined that they would offer support to the association if they were allowed to vote in the August 28 election. They brought their offer to one of the regular association meetings, and after some debate the participants rejected the idea of including Black leaders. "Report to your people," they were told, "that we leave you just where we found you." The continued presence of abolitionists as association members, however, and the *New Age*'s publishing of several editorials in favor of Black voting—along with constant rejection from the General Assembly—kept the door open for talks. But the longer the Suffrage Association maintained a policy of inconsistency, the more wary Black Rhode Islanders remained of the white suffrage movement.

The General Assembly, which the Suffrage Association had rightly denounced for governing entirely on the principle of land ownership, also continued to alienate Black and white suffragists. Refusing to budge on loosening voting qualifications, the new Speaker of the General Assembly's House of Representatives, conservative Whig Charles Jackson, publicly stated that voting qualifications were either "arbitrary" or "indispensable." He regarded as "indispensable" that each voter should "be a resident for a reasonable time, 21 years of age, and a white male person." The fact that the "white" provision was only enacted nineteen years earlier might have seemed arbitrary, but he implied that the assembly was merely confirming what most white Rhode Islanders, freemen especially, deemed natural. However, the absence of a racial proscription through the first 157 years of the charter, and the main governing principle during that time being property, meant that the state legislature's logic when it came to race was also on shaky ground, perhaps more so than that of the Suffrage Association. Both the General Assembly and the white suffragists had largely brushed Black people aside, but with each desperate to defeat the other by exposing their opponents' ideological faults, opportunity was opening up for Black Providence leaders.[38]

In August 1841, the Suffrage Association made a sharp turn and published strong editorials endorsing Black voting. One correspondent wrote,

> I have yet to learn why a man should be robbed merely in consequence of the color of skin, of the right inherent in all men, to give his vote on the question to constitute the government under which he is to live, and which is to affect him in all his relations as a free man and a citizen and subject, as fully as though his complexion were a few shades lighter. A "*white*" skin is no more an indispensable qualification than a tract of land. The exception to the color is an arbitrary one, right or wrong; and I am fully persuaded, sir, that, on second thought, you will agree that it should be placed among the "*arbitrary qualifications.*"[39]

Another editorial, under the pseudonym "FOR THE RIGHTS OF ALL," sought to vindicate the state's abolitionists for even putting the cause of equitable citizenship for all non-freemen on the public's agenda. Should the Suffrage Association "plant their feet upon the prostrate bodies of the 1500 colored people of Rhode Island," the author wrote, they may "gain a temporary advantage in the strife after their own rights." In other words, keeping Black men disfranchised might be politically expedient in the climate of the time. However, the writer predicted—presciently—that the abandonment of the republican principle of the primacy of independence, and the addition of an arbitrary qualification like the color line, would lead to the eventual overthrow of the "whole enterprize." Still another editorial suggested the only disqualification for men over the age of twenty-one should be the commission of a crime, but this author's recognizing of the franchise as a "social right" to be bestowed by a constitutional legislature showed the hesitancy of the association to formally commit to Black voting. So too did reprints of articles from around the North, sometimes in the same column as pieces supporting pro-Black voting, denouncing abolition and "white slavery," and a bobalition-esque allegory of a Black "dandy" being ridiculed by the elite white people he was riding horses with—symbolically ridiculing the old Federalist-Black alliance.[40]

On the day of the People's Convention election, August 28, Alfred Niger, having some fences to mend after his disastrous petition that January, decided to force the Suffrage Association to finally make a definitive statement on Black voting. He showed up at the designated voting location in Providence's Sixth Ward and was accepted by the ward's electoral chairman initially, as were supposedly "light-skinned" people of color elsewhere in the city. However, Niger was soon rebuffed on the ground that "a colored man had no right to vote." Niger did not back down, and several abolitionists who were there to witness (or support) the spectacle declared that if Niger could not submit his ballot, then they would also withhold theirs. Niger and "his friends" told the chairman that because the call for elections on August 6 did not say anything about race, it implied that men of color could vote. He was again rejected, prompting the resignation of one of the clerks present at the poll. After more than twenty years of organization and careful probing, Providence's Black leadership had waited for the perfect moment to spring into action. In doing so, Niger was one of the first Rhode Islanders to significantly damage the color line.[41]

The Suffrage Association's first definitive statement on Black voting opened a torrent of criticism and left its message crafters scrambling. The pro-Whig *Providence Journal* led the way. In September, Whig assemblyman Samuel Ames, under the pseudonym "Town Born," began writing a series of influential editorials in the *Journal* denouncing the white suffragists and clarifying the holes in their logic. His most salient points were centered around the Suffrage

Association's inability to reconcile extending the franchise to white and not Black men. "It is said," he wrote, "if 'all men are born free and equal,' if 'the right to vote be a natural and inalienable right,' if the principles of the revolution and of democratic liberty apply in favor of American citizens generally upon this subject, why does the mere accident of color make a difference?" Speaking to his "colored friends," he asked rhetorically if, when a constitution drawn up by the Suffrage Association must be ratified by the whole state, and when they took into account the prejudice against people of color in the country and southern towns, did people of color really believe that the association would stand by them and include them in the voting qualification? A staunch supporter of the assembly's authority, Ames was quite clearly attempting to convince influential abolitionists like William Goodell and Francis Whipple Green, who had been sympathetic to the suffragists, to withdraw their support and deprive the association of powerful allies. Never saying anything about his own stance on Black voting, he instead used the idea as a bludgeon to destroy the association's legitimacy. He ridiculed them for toying with the idea of Black voting, claiming they viewed extending the franchise as inexpedient while holding it out to Black people and abolitionists should they need their votes "in a pinch." "Know your friends," he warned African Americans, and "be united and wait." It was hardly advice they needed, but Ames seemed to hint that Niger might have won over some powerful allies in the General Assembly.[42]

The *Journal* in September began resembling an abolitionist paper, though they were most likely trying to exploit the embarrassing ambiguity in the Suffrage Association that Niger had exposed. The paper published an article by "A Colored Man" decrying his treatment aboard a steamer in which he and two female companions had to stay on deck overnight. The editor appended to the article a statement that said the general public would not be offended by granting Black people equal treatment, and that any disturbance was usually caused by a white person. In a nod to what many of Providence's Black leaders had been advocating for decades, the editor asked that passengers of "respectability" be granted protection from the elements in the future. It also published a letter from "A Friend to Equal Rights," calling himself a "strenuous advocate of extension of suffrage to our colored fellow-citizens" and agreeing with Town Born's sentiments—all except his call for people of color to "wait." For too long, African Americans had been "strangers" in the state and must be "*freemen* in a land of *freedom*." The People's Constitution the Suffrage Association was going to draft, he said, would be "perilled . . . by timid compromises—by a pusillanimous desertion of principles—by a resort to the counsels of a wretched expediency."[43] For Providence's Black leaders, Town Born seemed to offer the first major opening for an alliance with the state's leading political party, the Whigs.

The denial of Niger's vote put the Suffrage Association squarely on the defensive throughout September, trying to answer the charges brought by the *Journal*. The group's messengers continued to equivocate, with one saying that the Niger issue was a "misunderstanding" and another decrying the *New Age* for not holding more public debate on a "white" provision. Thomas Dorr, having been both an abolitionist and an ally to white suffragists, published his first piece in the *New Age*, hoping that "every American Citizen" would be advocated for in the convention, but like his peers, not committing to defining the term any more clearly. Still others defended the idea of whiteness as a precursor to citizenship, with one claiming that because people of color were not specifically invited to vote on August 28, the implication was that "all American citizens" meant "white citizens." People of color did not serve in the militia or pay taxes, making their claims to citizenship irrelevant. Besides, it was better to cure one evil—that two-thirds of white men could not vote—than none. Another article, written under the pseudonym "Country Born," sought to answer Town Born and other critics by claiming that Black voting would open up the vote to women and children—"universality" in universal suffrage had to end somewhere! John A. Brown, editor of the *New Age*, frantically sought to keep the association united. He expressed sincere regret that his "one general rule," namely, that "*all men are created free and equal, and that suffrage is the birthright of every man, and that nothing but the majority can take from him this right, and that only for the good of the greatest number,*" had left room for so many interpretations that infighting over such a base principle could consume the whole project. The racial proscription specifically, he warned, could be "the rock" on which the movement split, sinking it.[44]

Alfred Niger's quest to make Black voting central to the brewing conflict was not finished. When the Suffrage Association met on September 24 to discuss how to proceed with the People's Convention scheduled for October 4, they were again confronted with their own inconsistency. Early in the meeting, they resolved not to discuss any topic "calculated to disturb the harmony so long and nobly preserved," clearly implying the issue of Black suffrage. One of the association's members, a man firmly against including Black voting in the constitution, circumvented this maneuver, moving that Niger be nominated as the convention's treasurer. It was a ruse, the delegate admitted, designed to force the association to adopt a policy on Black citizenship. The meeting erupted into chaos with several members inveighing against the "firebrand" that had just been thrown in, and others expressing support for Black voting. The latter included Caleb Mosher of Providence's Sixth Ward, the same ward where Niger had tried to vote, who said he had "an interest" in the Black population. Another said that the call for "all American citizens" to vote on August 28 implied that people of color should be included—both then and in the constitution they were to draft. John A. Brown quickly ruled the proceeding out of order, repeatedly pointing out the earlier resolution on discussing divisive issues and admitting that that had covered voting qualifications. In short order, a white "minority report" candidate was appointed treasurer, and Brown adjourned the meeting.[45]

The abolitionist press began to take notice of these developments, signaling that while the RIASS had remained largely on the sidelines of the suffrage agitation, William Lloyd Garrison's powerful influence would be deployed in defense of Black voting. Lydia Maria Child, abolitionist and proponent of women's rights, excoriated the Suffrage Association in the *National Anti-Slavery Standard* for even considering maintaining a "white" provision in the People's Constitution. A week before the convention was to meet, she wrote,

> We understand there is reason to fear that the word "white" will be inserted, with the view of excluding colored people from the privileges of citizenship. If this is done, it will be an eternal disgrace to Rhode-Island.—It is a foul blot on constitutions formed half a century ago; what, then, must it be now? We trust the friends of freedom will be vigilant and active in this matter. It is of vital importance to the honor of that State, and to the cause of general humanity. If that ugly, monopolizing word is inserted now, it will, ere long; most assuredly have to be erased, through much unpleasant conflict.—Let the evil be arrested at the beginning.
>
> At a meeting of the friends of suffrage, held in Providence, [members] unanimously resolved that "any form of Government depriving one class of citizens of privileges which are granted to another, is not only aristocratic, but oppressive and tyrannical; and should not be tolerated in a land professedly Republican."
>
> Men who sustained those sentiments, and published them to the world, ought to be ashamed to give a vote for the insertion of the word "white" in their constitution; it would indeed be a disgraceful contradiction. And who, in Rhode-Island, will deny that the above resolution is just and true?[46]

Ames, as Town Born, also predicted calamity over the color line. On the same day Child's article was published, Ames declared that by rejecting Alfred Niger at the polls and then for a position in the convention, Niger would become a "mustard seed," referring to a biblical parable that suggested something so seemingly insignificant would grow to overshadow all else. He again urged vigilance among Black and white abolitionists and activists, telling them to *"be united and wait."*[47]

* * *

As the summer of 1841 turned to fall, Providence's Black leadership had found its opportunity to strike. The General Assembly could brush off calls for the enfranchisement of Black Rhode Islanders during ordinary times, but the swift rise of suffrage agitation among poor and artisan whites brought up all kinds of questions about the limits of citizenship. Black leaders seized on this in their attempt to hold the Suffrage Association accountable to its democratic principles—and though Niger was rebuffed, he exposed the soft spots in the association's logic. Still, however, neither the suffragists nor the state government had accepted Black leaders' arguments. As the tension between the two white factions escalated and then boiled over, calls for Black suffrage became too sharply reasoned, too loud, and ultimately too important to be ignored. The constitutional conventions were about to meet, and Black leaders would make sure their movement's ideas about republican citizenship—which largely agreed with the state's definition but without Blackness as a disqualifier—would top the agenda in each.

CHAPTER 7

"The Mustard Seed," Part 2
CITIZENSHIP

Ichabod Northup had deep roots in Rhode Island. His father, Ichabod Northup Sr., was born into slavery in the plantation country of North Kingstown and earned his freedom by enlisting in the First Rhode Island Regiment during the American Revolution. He was captured during battle, and the British hung rope around his neck, threatening to hang him on the spot if he did not divulge his knowledge of troop movements. He did not flinch. Instead, he was imprisoned for two and a half years, the enemy releasing him after peace was established. Despite his willingness to sacrifice his life in defense of the new republic, he would not live to see the day when the state of Rhode Island would consider him eligible for citizenship. His son, who made Ichabod Sr.'s service a part of the Black community's case for equitable citizenship, leapt to the forefront of its leadership at a time when the state government faced its greatest peril since the Revolution.

Ichabod Jr., at various times, followed the sea, was listed as a laborer, and was employed as a gardener, porter, and clerk—and would eventually with his wife, Catherine, amass considerable wealth by investing in real estate and rental properties. By 1825, he had moved to Providence and begun a sixteen-year stint working as a porter for a wealthy merchant and militia commander named William P. Blodgett. Blodgett, who grew to value Northup's faithfulness, honesty, and character, commanded one of the militia units that quelled the Snow Town riot, and would again be called to defend the property and people of Providence when white suffragists escalated their movement toward armed insurrection. It was perhaps these kinds of connections—economic and transactional but also long-lasting and personal—that tied Providence's Black community leaders to the elite white power structure more strongly than to white suffragists.[1]

In the absence of hard evidence of formal agreements between Providence's Black leaders and the leaders of the republic they ended up defending, suggestive relationships like this help us understand the willingness of Black leaders to protect the very political structure that had disfranchised them two decades earlier. Historians have seemed to agree that the outcome of Black enfranchisement as the result of the state government having "incurred an obligation to the Black community which was repaid with the franchise."[2] One scholar has written that the Black community's "assertiveness" helped them win back the vote.[3] They are not wrong, but these claims only tell a part of the story. As we have seen so far, Black leaders' advantageous position was the result of a deep, carefully constructed campaign and utilized a long history of craftily cultivated alliances—some personal, like Northup's—with the state's white power brokers. In the end, Northup and his cohort of leaders carried forward the legacy of his father and his father's generation of Black Rhode Islanders. This chapter discusses how Black leaders were able to employ generations of well-honed tactics to hold Rhode Island's government to account, convincing them that the "white" provision in voting was inexpedient, unprincipled, and un-republican.

Black Leaders' Arguments before the Constitutional Conventions

The People's Constitutional Convention got underway as scheduled on Monday, October 4. On the second day, some of the delegates met in caucus to see if they could hammer out an agreement on their one tormenting dispute—where the line between voter and nonvoter would be. John A. Brown, the mouthpiece for the Suffrage Association, introduced to the group a resolution that affirmed their constitution would guarantee the right of Black men to vote. Providence's Benjamin Arnold, a grocer and former RIASS executive committee member, supported it, but Smithfield's Nathaniel Mowry opposed it, offering the horrifying prospect of Black officeholding—even a Black person in the chair of a constitutional convention! Brown then wavered, agreeing that while he supported Black voting, he was doubtful his fellow Rhode Islanders at large would. Another delegate suggested having the question sent directly to the voters, but Brown, waffling between trying to maintain control and not taking a stand that would divide the caucus, deemed Black voting a worthy sacrifice for white harmony. Using derogatory language fit more for South Carolina than Rhode Island, he agreed to drop his motion and the convention proceeded. Arnold then, on Thursday, October 7, spoke to the convention in support of Black voting, or at least if the delegates could not decide among themselves, to put the question to the people as suggested in caucus. Samuel Atwell, Democratic assemblyman and delegate to the convention, opposed on the grounds that further debate on the issue would only serve to grant a larger voice to abolitionists. Brown again stepped in, exclaiming that he had worked for months to keep everyone's mouth shut on the issue, and quashed all debate on the matter.[4]

Providence's Black leaders closely followed the debate. On Friday morning, delegate Thomas Dorr received a petition from Providence's Black leaders that he moved be read and debated. One member objected, supposing that the petition was written by a white person "unfriendly to the Suffrage cause"—perhaps, Samuel Ames (Town Born). Dorr replied that it was written by Alexander Crummell, the young minister of the newly organized Christ Church and veteran of abolitionist activism, someone Dorr deemed a "respectable colored man." Crummell, however, did not sign it; he may have had a hand in writing it, or been a sort of middleman, using his prominence as a minister in a Black church and an abolitionist connection with Dorr to ensure the petition would be handled fairly. The petition was signed by stalwart leaders Ichabod Northup, James Hazard, Ransom Parker, and also George J. Smith, a coachman and original committee member for the building of the African Union Meeting House, and Samuel Rodman, a man listed as a laborer in the 1841 city directory and later an "Indian Doctor" who owned substantial property according to the 1850 and 1860 U.S. Censuses. Satisfied by Dorr's endorsement of Crummell and seeing that the time had come to finally confront the issue, the motion to hear the petition was agreed to.[5]

What was read to the People's Convention was an extraordinary document: eloquent in its defense of people of color and firm in their warning about how the people of Rhode Island—and history—would judge them should "white" be added to the suffrage qualification. This latter element separated it from the previous, more deferential petitions that McCarty, Niger, and Wyllis had been sending to the General Assembly, though this could be expected as the People's Convention was not sanctioned by the state. The Northup-Hazard-Parker leadership group represented the business and intellectual elite (Parker was the first Black teacher supported by the state), perhaps most outwardly independent and in the best position to make the republican case for citizenship. They entered their "earnest remonstrance" against a proposed "white" provision, deeming it a "sore, grievous, and unwarrantable infliction . . . anti-republican, and in tendency destructive." Most people of color were native-born citizens, they said, both affirming their national identity as Americans, not "strangers" as some had said, and also alluding to the charge of the Suffrage Association's wanting the vote to extend to noncitizen Irish for political gain. They then alluded to all the organizing efforts of the past twenty years—"repulsed and disfranchised," they had nonetheless proven themselves "respectable and competent," and enabled themselves to access the "means and advantage of religion, intelligence, and property," all republican virtues that they had been charged with lacking. They continued, "Is a justification of our disfranchisement sought in our want of christian character? We point to our churches as our reputation. In our want of intelligence? We refer not merely to the schools supported by the State, for our advantage; but to the private schools, well filled and sustained and taught by competent teachers of our own people. Is our industry questioned? This day, were there no complexional hindrance, we could present a more than proportionate number of our people, who might immediately, according to the freeholders' qualification, become voters."

Because of all this, they surmised, it must be "insuperable objection of our color." They found no respectable political body having "the temerity to insult the common sense of mankind by promulgating such a sentiment." Nowhere in the Declaration of Independence or the Federalist Papers, the documents that best articulated the nation's founding philosophy, could rationalizations for a color line among free people be found. They then turned to the "harm and injury" they knew disfranchisement causes:

> If the nature of man opens the way for, and requires civil government and its various functions, as a means of good and blessing to him, and as an aid in the full development of his powers, how can it be otherwise than that the powers capacitated to civil duty, being diverted from their natural channel, should turn upon himself in hurtful inactivity, or active evil? And surely the State is to blame, and not the people, when invidious disfranchisement causes moral and civil degradation; and when the sympathies and sentiments capacitated to political duty are perverted and smothered. And herein lies the destructive tendency of this

measure.... The possession of the elective franchise is ever a stimulant to enterprise, a means of influence, and a source of respect. And will you help deprive us of this benefit? The want of it is the cause of carelessness, intellectual inertness, and indolence.

This passage might seem to belie all the gains that Black Providence residents claimed to have made since being disfranchised but it also served to, should the "white" provision be enacted, undercut any future claims about the supposed inherent inferiority of African Americans made by whites. Should they be accused of "carelessness, intellectual inertness, and indolence," the "white" provision would be to blame.

Their final warning struck an ominous tone and echoed the writings and speeches of many Black intellectuals. The petitioners tried to show the Suffrage Association the harm the arbitrariness of a color line could bring back to them. "We ask you, gentlemen," they challenged,

> What safeguard have you for your liberties, and the liberties of your children, if you are willing to pollute the pure and eternal principles of human liberty by a base admixture of the adventitious circumstance of human complexion? What security have you against some unexpected distinction which may at some future time arise, and, taking precedent in our proscription, sweep away your dearest rights, and most highly cherished prerogatives, as unconcernedly as you would ours? And it is the warrant of history when we say, that thus striking off from us the dearest boon—the precious birthright of freemen—that yet, in the course of God's providence, the poisoned chalice may be returned to the lips of those who departed from their principles, and retributive justice place them under severe restrictions and endurable chains.

They ended their petition with a flair of confident provocation: "If, in making known our views, we may appear unusually earnest, we trust to the candor and enlightenment of your respected body in presenting earnestness of feeling as an extenuation of strength of sentiment and expression."[6]

Benjamin Arnold was convinced. He moved that the word "white" be stricken from the constitution. The former RIASS executive committee member spent fifteen minutes reading resolutions and declarations of the state Suffrage Association and local chapters like Woonsocket's (a populous, supportive mill town) to show that "white" had not come before "American citizens"; it was therefore anathema to the principle of extension. He was glad that this committee of people of color had come forward and praised their timing. If the only argument in favor of adding a "white" clause in the voting qualification was expediency, discerning suffragists who favored sound principles would react negatively. He echoed the petitioners' warnings, asking if the conventioneers would wish to have their rights stripped because later the legislature imposed another arbitrary condition on voting? He cited the Town Born articles published in the *Providence Journal*, asking how they could possibly overcome the inconsistency their enemies pointed out. Finally, he disavowed his abolitionist past but said he was in favor of human rights, freedom, and justice—and, more practically, alienating abolitionists and people of color in what could be a close election could doom the whole project. If this was a "rock" on which the movement would split, why not remove the rock altogether?

The convention finally debated the question, with delegates from Providence and Smithfield and even Newport County supporting it. They claimed that their constituents were men of principle, men who knew plenty of people of color more worthy of the vote than whites, that Roger Williams himself would disapprove of the "white" provision, and that the word "white" would belie the "all men are created free and equal" statement of article 1 of the proposed constitution. One man from Portsmouth said the constitution would be "stained *Black* by the word *white*." Finally, a few claimed that those opposed to Black voting were assuming defeat without evidence. To this last charge, John A. Brown answered that a committee had contacted all towns the previous night and found that all but one were opposed to "let in the blacks." The opposition took the offensive, asking whether enfranchising "a few hundred" men of color was worth endangering the rights of fifteen thousand white men. The very constitution of society, one said, separated whites and Blacks; forcing them together into one body politic would be disregarding the laws of nature. The room erupted in thunderous applause for the opposition. Thomas Dorr then rose and closed the debate, and the former abolitionist harkened back to his RIASS days by passionately defending Black voting and citizenship. He used many of the arguments that Black leaders had been making for decades—that Rhode Islanders of color had fought and died in the American Revolution, that race prejudice had been brought up as a scare tactic to carry or defeat bills in the General Assembly, and that a color line was arbitrary and inconsistent with the founding principles of the country. Rhode Island voters were not "illiberal" like the General Assembly, and they might not forgive the People's Convention for bowing to expediency. He would vote alone if he had to against a "white" provision. However, at the end, cracks began to show in his strong defense. He said he would support any constitution passed at the convention, and that he regretted so much time had been taken to debate an undemocratic action at a supposedly democratic proceeding. Reading that the room was against him, he acknowledged they would now have to turn to defending a constitution passed on expediency at the expense of principle. He urged that Arnold's motion to strike "white" be voted on quickly so as to not open the convention up to more ridicule. The convention voted forty-six to eighteen to keep the "odious distinction." As bitter consolation for people of color, the subject of exempting them from the tax rolls was brought up but tabled; they had undercut themselves enough for one day. Still trying to keep abolitionists on their side, they did include a provision for trial by jury for accused runaway slaves.[7]

The Suffrage Association was then forced to, for the third time in two months, defend itself against accusations of ideological malpractice when it came to Black voting. In the Sunday, October 11, *Providence Journal*, a satirical "Address of the Suffrage Convention to the People of Providence" ran under Town Born's byline. In it, the author lamented that Black people had to sit in the galleries of meetinghouses and theaters, and so did they have to sit and watch the Suffrage Association gamble away their rights from afar. "*Wait for us*," Ames mockingly said to Providence's Black residents, "and if you can find time in the mean-while, *wait upon* us." Another editorial mocked the ineptness of the Suffrage Association because of their adding "white" to such a supposedly democratic document. Welcome Sayles, a delegate who opposed equal voting rights for people of color, erroneously claimed that Black people were disfranchised throughout the North. The *Colored American* called out the embarrassing error and confronted him with the truth about every state north of Rhode Island, including one "a ten minutes' ride" from Providence. Sayles then claimed he meant that Black people *did not* vote, which was also untrue, given public claims that they often tipped elections in Massachusetts. Benjamin Arnold desperately tried to defend the proceeding, saying he had to abide by the convention's vote, and that he would rather let the people decide the question. Dorr also told a meeting in Providence that while he was still in favor of striking "white," the constitution published by the convention was "one step" in the work of reform and contained enough good that it should be supported. On October 15, the People's Constitution was published with "white" as a qualification for voting in article 2, section 1. The convention then disbanded for one month, planning to reconvene after the state-sanctioned convention.[8]

Black Rhode Islanders' suffrage agitation had now fully rallied the abolitionist movement to its cause. After the convention, the *National Anti-Slavery Standard* lambasted the notion of "expediency" as the "old scape-goat of Satan," and observed that friends of freedom around the world would note the "disgraceful incongruity" of a movement claiming the mantle of democracy. Lydia Maria Child commented that race distinctions were "discordant" elements of free constitutions, producing "a perpetual and wearing friction in the wheels of the state," and were the very basis for just about all national and intrastate "bickerings." William Lloyd Garrison urged all abolitionists to oppose the People's Constitution, citing its "meanness, hypocrisy, [and] oppression!" The *Colored American* urged the RIASS to action, decrying their heretofore apolitical stance. Abby Kelley, a tireless abolitionist speaker and organizer who had followed the proceedings closely through her RIASS contacts, was dismayed that many of the state's abolitionists supported the Suffrage Association and the People's Constitution. She was especially disappointed that concessions to perceived "expediency" and those willing to sacrifice Black suffrage had nullified chances of a potentially powerful alliance among Black Rhode Islanders, abolitionists, and white suffragists. Now, she wrote, people of color and their allies were forced to look to the upcoming convention for a remedy. It was hardly a rosy prospect, but priorities were rapidly shifting, and the state government would soon have a chance to respond.[9]

The "Landholders" met for the General Assembly's authorized constitutional convention just a few weeks later, starting their work on November 1. Thomas Dorr and Samuel Atwell, on opposite sides of the Black suffrage debate, were the only two members elected to attend both conventions. On November 4, knowing that the convention was about to determine voting qualifications, Ichabod Northup and James Hazard submitted another petition, this time with a few different prominent co-signers.[10] Charles G. Brown was one of them; he was listed in 1841 as a confectioner, and in a few years would own a bathhouse and a home in which he boarded a white Brown University professor and student. Thomas Howland, the grocer, church trustee, and future elected official, also signed, as did James Gumes, a man who began his public service along with William J. Brown in the mutual benefit society they founded, and was now a laborer steadily increasing his wealth.[11]

Northup and Hazard had by this time fully taken over leadership of

Providence's Black community, at least when it came to voting rights. For this petition, they adopted a tone much closer to that of McCarty, Niger, and Wyllis in years past. Gone was the forceful, ominous language of their petition to the People's Convention; in its place was the strategically obsequious tenor of officialdom. "We beg with deference," they began, "to present our claims and to ask an equal participation in the rights and privileges of citizenship." The strongest case they made was tied to both their knowledge of the nativist sentiment in the conservative Whig body and the history of the elite-Black alliance in the old Federalist order. In characteristic eloquence, they affirmed, "We are native born Citizens descended from an Ancestry stretching back to a period almost coeval with the first settlers of the country." They continued,

> On American soil, beneath American skies, surrounded by American Institutions, we first beheld the light of the impartial sun.
> Born in no foreign clime, not accustomed to a political creed repugnant to democratic principles and republican usage; we are members of the state of Rhode Island under the Government of the United States, familiarized from Youth with the natures, features, and operations of our Government, whose excellencies and peculiarities are accordant with the flow of our feelings and the current of our thoughts.
> A foreign birth, and adverse usages, that might possibly beget uncongenial political sympathies, and sentiments; exists not in our case. We have been brought up under a Republican creed; we are acquainted with Republican law.

They then turned to the major aspects of republican citizenship, first and most importantly, their independently chosen paths toward wealth and prominence, and their role in protecting their fellow citizens whenever called upon:

> And we have done service for the Country. By the dint of our labour—by hard, and earnest activity, have we for years, lent our best strength in the cultivation of the soil, in the development of its resources, and in contributing to its wealth and importance.
> If at any time danger has threatened; the aid and defence we have contributed, has been more than proportionate. There is hardly a Battlefield in the Country but what is enriched with the blood and bones of Colored Men.
> Throughout the Revolution they contributed their aid. They were seen at Bunker Hill, they were present at York Town.
> The most splendid Naval achievements were owing to no small extent to the valor of Colored Americans.

> The fame of your own Perry was gained at the expense of the bleeding veins and mangled bodies of our neglected and disfranchised People.[12]

They also sought again to undo the damage wrought by the January petition that further removed them from citizenship, claiming, "As Citizens we have at all times taken our part in common burdens and expenses; we have always been ready and prompt tax-payers." Then came an analogue to their grievous warning to the People's Convention about what such arbitrary distinctions would do to those on both the right and wrong side of them. Keenly aware of their audience, however, they began a marked tone change:

> We beg that it may be remembered that integral portions of the body politic, we are affected by all the fluctuations of public adversity—and sufferers as we are, when others suffer—we become doubly so, when by law, we are made as a class, passive instruments of Government—subjected to the operation of law—just or unjust—enacted and put into operation without our acquiescence.
>
> We entreat a guarantee of those free born rights and immunities, the possession of which is the means of influence and respect, builds up the heart of a depressed people and begets a general consciousness of manly and generous feeling. We petition the abrogation of that odious feature of the statute, which, in making the right of citizenship identical with color, brings a stain upon the State, unmans the heart of an already injured people, and corrupts the purity of Republican Faith.
>
> That benefit, we ask with deference—what benefit can it be, that laws should be so framed, as to set a portion of the community—a whole and distinct class—beyond the pale of common human nature?

They closed by alluding to the People's Convention's and Suffrage Association's accession to perceived expediency, offering—deferentially—that the landholders had the chance to allow principle to rule the day:

> We submit to your honorable body, whether it is not the dictate of humanity—of correct political expediency—especially if it is not in accordance with the doctrines of the Government under which we all live;—to elevate the humblest class of its members to the duties of manhood and the prerogatives of citizenship, rather than debar them from the most efficient instrument of elevation on account of a matter beyond their control.
>
> We beg your honorable body, a candid consideration of our memorial. We trust the Constitution of the State may not be tarnished by so

Anti-Republican a feature, as a color qualification for the franchise right. We hope that the pure light of political justice may not be obscured amid the oblivious shades of unnatural distinctions and unreasonable prejudices.[13]

Dorr moved that the word "white" be stricken from the voting requirement if the statutory law, in addition to the property and residency requirements, was to be inserted into the new constitution. Richard K. Randolph, the native Virginian and Newport aristocrat, scoffed that "natural rights" were an overbroad theory, and that since they did not extend to women and children, what made people of color or non-freeholders so worthy? He answered the argument that Black people had served and died in the American Revolution by saying, yes, they won their freedom but that was not the same as winning political rights. Non-freeholders also served, as did Native people—why were the latter not being advocated for? Regardless of theoretical arguments, Randolph finished, there just wasn't enough support among the landholders to enfranchise others, as they were too conservative and protective of their own rights. Dorr's motion was voted down, as were most other reform measures, save the reapportionment of state legislature seats, the second most sought-after measure from suffragists who had decried Newport County's and the southern countryside's outsized influence in seat allocation. The convention disbanded with more work to be done but with a clear rejection of Black suffrage.[14]

Now central to the imbroglio the state found itself in, inconsistency in ideology on Black citizenship threatened to tear apart the Suffrage Association and ignite an abolitionist backlash against the state government. The RIASS, long on the sidelines, suddenly found itself at the epicenter when it met on November 11–13, 1841—between the end of the Landholders' Convention and before the People's Convention reconvened. Franklin Hall in Providence was packed with the state's Black leaders like Vice President Alfred Niger and rank and file alike, along with some of the foremost national abolitionist leaders. They included Garrison, Nathaniel P. Rogers of New Hampshire's abolitionist organ the *Herald of Freedom*, Abby Kelley, Stephen Foster, Wendell Phillips, and young Frederick Douglass, who had just recently entered the abolitionist lecture circuit and would go on to become the most prominent national Black leader of the nineteenth century. The first action taken, after an opening prayer and reading of the previous year's minutes, was the reading of a letter from Robert Purvis, a Black leader from Pennsylvania and veteran of the recent unsuccessful fight for Black voting rights in that state. In his letter, Purvis urged the RIASS to fight the "cowardly, mean, and despicable movers" of the "unrighteous proposition" of the "white" clause in the People's Constitution, a clause that performed the "dirtiest work, which the great charnel-house of slavery *can* afford, for those base spirits who seem to 'live, move, and have their being,' upon southern patronage and generosity"—perhaps an allusion to the Suffrage Association's Democratic Party leanings. Five Black speakers then stirred the audience with rousing speeches dedicated to Black equality, most notably Douglass, who reminded white members that "the colored man had a head to think, a heart to feel, and a soul to aspire to, like other men." When John A. Brown of the *New Age* tried to address the meeting on the merits of the People's Constitution, promising that when whites achieved universal suffrage, Black voting would become a priority. He was immediately shouted down by Garrison and a "colored brethren" who said that some members of the Suffrage Association were not worthy enough to "carry . . . old shoes." After a debate between a four-person delegation from the association with Garrison, Kelley, and Foster, the RIASS concluded that no person could call themselves an abolitionist and vote for a constitution with the word "white" in it. The notion of compromise on race backfired, helping the RIASS raise more than a thousand dollars on the spot, much of it from Black men and women, to fund a lecturing campaign against the People's Constitution. While Brown grumbled about the language used by Purvis (the "colored man from Philadelphia"), the RIASS passed resolution after resolution haranguing both the Suffrage Association and state legislature for disfranchising Black men and also vowing to support the state's Black communities against discrimination in all forms. The "axe was laid at the root" of slavery—the race ideology that perpetuated the institution and stained the northern states with unrepublican distinction of color.[15]

The RIASS meeting had a demonstrable effect on the proceedings of the People's Convention when it reconvened a few days later. A committee debated whether to have its resolutions read into the convention's record and decided in its favor. They were never read, however, as an RIASS delegation declined to show up, thinking that their memorial would remain tabled. Samuel Burgess of Little Compton spoke in favor of striking "white," pointing to the contradiction the word would cause with the association's democratic principles. Aaron White, a self-described abolitionist and property lawyer, lauded the service of Black troops in prior wars and said that harmony—or at least the prevention of mobs—would ensue from their having an interest in government. The *New*

Age published a table indicating, according to the 1840 census, that the state had 668 men of color over twenty-one, a small number but one that showed the association had continuously downplayed their strength in a state that often saw close elections. The association still, however, was determined to compromise: instead of revising the voting qualification, they added a provision at the end of the constitution providing for a binding referendum on the word "white" in the voting qualification after the first session of the General Assembly, which itself would meet after a majority of Rhode Islanders adopted the constitution as the legitimate governing document of the state. This, they hoped, would satisfy abolitionists, and they called for a mass meeting of antislavery suffragists on December 6, 1841, at which they would attempt to persuade the attendees to endorse it. They would then hold a referendum on December 27–29 to determine statewide support for the constitution.[16]

Their efforts were entirely unsuccessful however. The strength of the abolitionist movement was used to stir up opposition to any constitution, legitimate or otherwise, that contained a "white" provision in voting. The RIASS addressed a letter to the citizens of Rhode Island to that effect, and the AASS sent Abby Kelley, Stephen Foster, Parker Pillsbury, James Monroe, and Frederick Douglass on a tour of the state, speaking wherever they could find an audience, urging all to vote against the constitution because of its "white" provision. Beginning with the abolitionist-suffragist meeting on December 6, Foster determined that the "white" provision was so odious that Black Rhode Islanders had a better chance of winning the vote from the landholders—at least their commitment to principle and legitimacy as a recognized body offered a clearer path. Douglass then addressed the meeting with a speech that was well received, though the editor of the *New Age* determined, in a telling statement, that Douglass was just working "hard to say what his instructors had told him." After Kelley addressed the crowd, the meeting devolved into confusion, ending with no discernible movement either in favor of or against the constitution.[17]

Kelley's and Foster's presence in particular stirred controversy. Foster often openly provoked the crowds and spoke until he was thrown out of meetings, with Douglass writing that he was frequently "needlessly offensive," though "no white man ever made the Black man's cause so completely his own." Between South Kingstown and Westerly, Foster and Douglass rode together in a "Jim Crow car," with Douglass contracting a cold due to the car's exposure to the frigid winter air. Kelley recognized that while Foster's tactics at speaking engagements might have been distasteful, the vehemence with which he was denied podia or escorted from meetings drew attention to their cause and made it more powerful. Kelley herself aroused violent opposition, as she often faced eggs and brickbats on her way into and out of meetings. In Newport, mobs of five hundred to a thousand strong broke up several of the meetings she spoke at. In one of them, after Pillsbury called for unity among the laboring classes, former attorney general and prosecutor of the Hard-Scrabble rioters Dutee J. Pearce filibustered, using race prejudice and the idea that abolitionists and Black people were employed by the aristocracy to defeat the suffrage movement. In Providence, Kelley was confronted by a drunken antiabolitionist mob, but her meeting went on after Whig mayor Thomas Burgess and the city's police finally intervened. She had to make her way home, however, through a gauntlet of "howls and snow-balls." Reports in the antislavery press detailed mobs shutting down meetings in Woonsocket and elsewhere around the state and published resolutions of nearby branches of the AASS in Massachusetts announcing their support for Rhode Island abolitionists. One editorial in the *Emancipator* called on Dorr and Arnold to withdraw their support for the People's Constitution.[18]

Looking back half a century later, Douglass remembered his own activism as much more measured, similar to the Black leadership in Providence, with his focus, at least on the surface, on the narrow goal of eliminating "white" from the voting qualification while his companions felt that they were taking the axe to the very root of slavery. While his presence evoked heavy resistance—Kelley remembered being deeply impacted by the shouts of racial epithets when with him—when he spoke, he sought to disarm his audience rather than rile it. In doing so, he "stole the hearts of" many more than other speakers did. While he "cared nothing" for the landholders' government, he may have understood like Providence's Black leaders that the best hope for reform ran through the conservative legislature, and so he tuned his message accordingly. There were signs of this calibration elsewhere—the *Emancipator* noted that the Whig press in the state was covering Kelley's travails quite favorably. *Liberator* correspondent William Alpin wrote from one of these tense meetings that while abolitionists deplored both Democrats and Whigs, the mob connections with the Democratic Party seemed to be tilting Black and abolitionist sentiment toward the Whigs. Pawtucket abolitionist Susan Sisson wrote to Abby Kelley that her compatriots trusted the state government's commitment to principle over the whims of the white men of the state at large.[19]

Nearly fourteen thousand Rhode Island men cast ballots in favor of adopting the People's Constitution in the waning days of 1841, including a clear majority of the state's eight thousand freemen. Only fifty-two voted against it; hardly anyone who was not a suffrage supporter bothered to vote. Further, the number of affirmative votes was still less than half of the state's total white male population over the age of twenty-one.[20] Such a large number of people willing to vote for the constitution, however, prodded the state legislature into reconvening its own constitutional convention in February 1842. It took some of the air out of the sails of the Suffrage Association by adopting a clause that enfranchised all white males over the age of twenty-one, though it lengthened the residency requirement from one to three years, in a jab at the pro-Irish association. Stubbornly, however, it rejected Black voting again, shooting down an amendment that proposed to put "men of color" on the same qualification as naturalized foreigners. Another amendment was put forward giving the General Assembly the authority to admit people of color to vote and exempting their property taxes until such time. The convention, however, settled for a clause that gave the assembly the power to confer a freehold on anyone born in the country who was not included in the original qualification. It provided for elections to be held March 21–23 on adoption of the new constitution, with all who would be made a voter eligible to vote on its adoption. The RIASS executive committee issued a statement that directed their members and all abolitionists to vote against the document because of its retention of the "white" provision, and reiterated their opposition to any future constitution that should contain such a distinction. Nonetheless, one member of the RIASS said he would vote in its favor, citing the fact that Black people had a better chance of gaining the vote through the assembly (per the amendment noted above) than through a statewide referendum. Still, many abolitionists must have stuck with the executive committee's recommendation; they doubtless contributed to its defeat. The final tally was 8,689 against to 8,013 in favor. The constitution was defeated, much to the Suffrage Association's delight, but more people had voted in this election, a sign of the landholder government's firm grip on its legitimacy.[21]

Defense of the Republic and Enfranchisement

Events in March and April led to mass confusion and heightened tensions. The state consolidated its power while the suffragists for their part increasingly saw their constitution as vindicated by the principle of majority rule and the U.S. Constitution's guarantee of a republican form of government in each state, per article 4, section 4. Locofoco Democrats from New York had convinced the Suffrage Association that, should the state insist on maintaining the unrepublican Charter of 1664 as its basis for existence, they had the constitutional authority to replace it if a majority of citizens wished. As such, in the wake of their victory over the assembly's proposed constitution, they scheduled their own elections for General Assembly and governor for April 18, with Thomas Dorr at the head of the "Suffrage Party." The landholders, however, now dominated by a coalition of urban Whigs and rural aristocratic Democrats under the "Law and Order Party," had scored a victory in early March when a group of Providence citizens asked the state Supreme Court whether it would be legal to vote in the people's election. The court issued a constitutionally dubious yet forceful opinion that determined that voting in an election not authorized by the General Assembly would be considered "treason against this state, if not the United States." A group of "Nine Lawyers," including Dorr, Samuel Atwell, and Duttee Pearce, responded to this by issuing their own opinion stating that the American Revolution had passed sovereign power from the king and Parliament to the citizens of each state. As such, the charter was null and the people were without a constitutional republic—the suffragists were only fulfilling article 4, section 4's guarantee. The Law and Order Party then raised the stakes by passing through the General Assembly what the suffragists called the "Algerine Law" (because it was fit only for the draconian dey of Algiers), which prescribed harsh penalties for anyone found by the Supreme Court to have acted under the authority of the People's Constitution.[22]

Shortly before the April 18 election, the Law and Order and Suffrage Parties dispatched competing delegations to meet with President John Tyler, trying to gauge the Democrat-turned-Whig who had ascended to the office after Whig William Henry Harrison's death in 1841. Governor Samuel Ward King had written several letters to Tyler asking for troops should the situation devolve into an armed rebellion but had so far received no reply. Law and Order delegates John Whipple, John Brown Francis, and Elisha Potter represented the Whig–aristocratic Democrat coalition (Potter being a South Kingstown Democrat); John A. Brown was sent by the Suffrage Party. Tyler proved somewhat evasive. Not wanting to alienate Democrats, who he hoped would support him when he ran for president on his own, he deemed the issue one for the Whig-dominated state legislature to solve and declined to send the requested troops. However, also recognizing that the Suffrage Party had a large abolitionist following, he promised the Law and Order Party that, should the suffragists attempt what constituted a rebellion, he would send the army to crush it. The illegal April 18 election then went ahead, with the Law and Order Party unwilling to risk criticism for applying the "Algerine Law" too soon. Its sentiment seemed to have an effect, with just 6,604 turning out to defy the state. Dorr was elected governor and a slate of candidates were elected to the People's General Assembly, scheduled to meet on May 4.[23]

The People's General Assembly met for two days, with Dorr delivering an inaugural address but little else being accomplished. On May 4, Governor King announced that a state of insurrection existed and the fear of arrest kept them quiet. Rival delegations again met with Tyler in Washington, and he seemed to be won over to the Law and Order side by conservative Whig Richard K. Randolph's painting of the Suffrage Party as overrun with abolitionists—an easy task given Dorr's history with the RIASS and the support he had received from Garrison in the late 1830s. Dorr himself met with Tyler, who declared his movement treasonable. Washington Democrats could not offer much support, for Dorr's flirtation with abolition turned off the party's dominant, John Calhoun–led southern wing, and the conservative Whig establishment led by Daniel Webster was staunchly against such Locofocoism. On his way back to Providence, Dorr did find support among the New York Locofocos, and emboldened by a warm welcome back in his home city, decided that now was the time to act. As night turned to early morning on May 17–18, Dorr and a contingent of armed Suffrage Party members attempted to seize the state arsenal. But the arsenal having been reinforced earlier on the 17th, the insurrection was immediately overwhelmed by superior firepower. Dorr escaped the state, and his loyalists retreated to Chepachet in the northwest part of the state, a major suffragist base, where for over a month they contemplated their next steps.[24]

The recklessness with which the Suffrage Party undertook to implement the People's Constitution nullified any chance for Black leaders' support. As late as April, the *National Anti-Slavery Standard* could say when it came to either the suffragists or the Law and Order Party, as it concerned equal rights for people of color, "it is of no consequence which rules the roost." Dorr's turn to violence, however, opened a new opportunity for Black leaders to win support from the highest echelons of state power. After the attack on the arsenal, militia companies, most of which had been loyal to the state, were called in to patrol the streets of Providence.[25] Keenly aware of military service as an avenue toward citizenship, Black leaders in the city formed two companies themselves, with two hundred men joining. Shortly thereafter, the companies met to elect leaders. Thomas Howland and James Hazard, having guided the petition campaign through two constitutional conventions, came forward first. Howland, who William J. Brown remembered as having little education but a lot of money, was rejected after he thought his money could win him the coveted spot. Hazard too was rejected after thinking that the command belonged to him. The next man up was Abraham Peterson, a barber who had heretofore not registered any recognition as part of the city's leadership class. "He could not," according to Brown, "boast of money or influence, but had a good education, and thought that he should have the place on that account."[26]

What Peterson then did, seeing that neither money nor education alone could convince Providence's Black rank and file, was something that recalled the old Black leadership class. He urged Black Providence not to be "too fast" in selecting their leadership, for "colored people had often been deceived. When they were needed, great promises would be made, and when they were through with them, they would be forgotten." Such had been the case after the American Revolution. Peterson noted too Andrew Jackson's speech lauding Black troops after they had contributed mightily to his company's victory over the British in the War of 1812. Jackson, of course, had then abandoned them with his reckless warring against Natives and African Americans in the Creek and Seminole Wars, and again when his presidency riveted the chains of slavery more strongly by officially opening the expropriated land to King Cotton. Those in the assembled companies might have also remembered that emancipation had brought about much promise, which was quickly eroded by "warnings out" and a gradual re-hardening of the color line. They might have remembered that their parents and grandparents had largely rejected emigration and colonization, for the land of their birth had boasted founding documents that championed liberty and equality. They might have remembered their parents' generation building the African Union Meeting House as a tangible move toward citizenship, despite the legal disfranchisement that strained their relationships with the white elite around the same time. They might have been children during, or they might have been part themselves of, the resilience of their communities in the face of mob violence. Finally, they might have taken part in the meetings that pushed forward a petitioning campaign that sought the right to vote and the right to have their tax dollars used for the education of their children. Overall, they might have sensed that what they were undertaking was as momentous as any in the history of race relations in the state.

What they thought and felt was not recorded, but Peterson's oration caused "a sensation" among the assembled troops, and they decided that continuing as a segregated group was not in their best interest. Perhaps they sought, once again, to hold their former allies—the elite white power structure—to account by offering their services to defend the republic. They disbanded, determining to offer their bodies and weapons to the white militia companies already organized.[27] They were accepted into a hastily assembled Volunteer Police Corps, a body made up of dissident suffragists, militiamen, and fire companies, and which, according to one militiaman, were segregated not by race but by height. All seven Black men in this particular unit were treated with the "utmost respect." When one of the companies believed that Dorr might have been hiding out in Woonsocket and plans were drawn up for a daring mission against a desperate enemy, all five Black men serving in that company volunteered to go. For the next eleven weeks, they patrolled the city alongside white soldiers, stood guard at the city limits, served as firemen, and took part in periodic raids on suspected Dorr supporters. In one such raid, nine Black militiamen and three white men hauled Nathaniel Knight off to prison. When Knight objected that a Black man was the one handling him physically, the commander of the group allowed him to be guarded by a white man but threatened that at any moment he might allow the Black militiaman to handle him again. This incident, and undoubtedly others that remained undocumented, signaled that a palpable shift in race relations was occurring.[28]

On June 26, Governor King formally declared martial law in the state as the militia prepared to invade the Dorr camp in Chepachet. On the same day, the General Assembly called for yet another constitutional convention, this one to meet in September. Delegates would be elected at town meetings across the state on August 26, and this time "all male native citizens of the United States" over the age of twenty-one were allowed to vote. It seems that the protection of the city by African American volunteers played a large part in forcing the hand of the conservative General Assembly. For the past year, Black leaders and abolitionists had been holding the Suffrage Association to account on their ideological inconsistencies, dramatically undercutting support for the movement. They had also played an understated role in defeating the rebellion militarily, with at least one Dorr supporter derisively telling William J. Brown years later that they would have "whipped" the state militia had it not been for the prospect of four hundred Black troops scaring them into submission. The overstated numbers clearly show the impact Black service had on the psyche of Dorrites. For the General Assembly, their service at the end of twenty years of petitioning, critiquing, and searching for an opening to get Black voting rights a proper hearing was finally paying off in a demonstrable way. Of course, this was only an early step—the will of influential archconservative Whigs like Richard K. Randolph would have to be defeated once a convention got underway. The right to vote on delegates was one thing, but to prevent "white" from being added to a constitution written by the very same people who had added it in November 1841 and again in February 1842 was another battle altogether.[29]

Service in defense of the city was a public relations bonanza for Black Providence residents. By the end of July, one abolitionist could confidently report to the *Liberator* that because of their "brave deeds" during the crisis, they were now bowed to, welcomingly smiled at, and greeted cordially on every street corner by their white neighbors. It was almost as if everyone in Providence had suddenly become an abolitionist! At the Fourth of July parade in the city, a Black marching band attracted much attention, playing instruments seized from Dorr's forces at Chepachet. Outside the state, Providence's Black community was also being recognized. A writer from New York noted that Black troops had served in the American Revolution, were just as good as whites, and those from '76 would be proud of their sons in Providence. He hoped his hometown (Whig-affiliated) paper would never again deprecate people of color. In Congress, when debate over a bill to regulate U.S. Navy enlistment did not include a color provision, Senator Perry Smith, a Connecticut Democrat, supported the addition of "white" to the act, using the opportunity to score political points by mocking Rhode Island's Whig government for having to resort to using Black troops to defend itself. Rhode Island Whig James F. Simmons, who had recommended several abolitionist reforms three years earlier in the state legislature, was now a U.S. senator. Although he defended the state's Whig government by saying that Black troops were not used as a last resort, he nonetheless gratefully acknowledged that Black Providence men had volunteered to defend the property of Rhode Island and voted against the insertion of "white."[30]

While the Black community rallied around the Law and Order Party government, white abolitionists, whose popularity in mill villages meshed well with the Suffrage Party, were hotly divided. Some deemed the eschewal of a "white" provision in the call for a Law and Order constitutional convention a political stunt while still offering praise to the Black activists. William Goodell, a white abolitionist with Providence connections and an advocate for a political solution to slavery and race, one based on class unity across racial lines that would come only outside of the Whig-Democrat dynamic, followed the crisis closely. Late in the summer, he published a hearty defense of the suffragist cause, saying that it was equally wrong to deny the rights of citizenship to poor whites and Black people. The People's Constitution's provision for a later election to determine whether to strike "white" from its voting clause, he correctly claimed, went much further than the landholder constitution. Instead of acknowledging that the Law and Order Party had corrected this wrong by accepting Black troops into desegregated units, showing that their lack of a color provision in voting had more bite than the suffragists' call of August 1841, Goodell claimed that the Law and Order Party members were only allowing "their colored domestics" to vote in order to win the support of the "*pseudo*-abolitionists."[31]

While Goodell and others may have been right in characterizing the June 26 call a political calculation, abolitionist Suffrage Party supporters appeared somewhat blind to the real agency this created for Black suffragists. Merchant-abolitionist Asa Fairbanks responded to this viewpoint by saying the suffragists constantly underestimated the role race was playing in the crisis. The Law and Order Party had corrected themselves and finally listened to Black Providence leaders, and since African Americans were given the opportunity to defend the government as they had in the Revolution, no constitution containing the word "white" could possibly be adopted. Besides, was it not the suffragists who mobbed Abby Kelley, Frederick Douglass, and others who had spoken in favor of Black rights? Fairbanks recounted that at one Providence meeting in which the aforementioned spoke, Dorr was in attendance, remaining quiet and walking away when the mob began shouting down the speakers and pelting them with snowballs: "Five words from him might have made all quiet—*but no!*" Abolitionists had no reason to defend the suffragists if suffragists refused to defend Black rights. Garrison also took on Goodell, praising him for his integrity before deriding his suggestion that the word "white" was a mere blemish on an otherwise fine document. Goodell eventually backtracked, admitting that his light treatment of the suffragists on race was mostly designed to show that oppression of one was oppression of all. Others, like Frances Whipple Green, a staunch abolitionist who had written and promoted the *Memoirs of*

Elleanor Eldridge, continued to defend the suffragists in the years after the conflict ended. She vindicated them on the fact of their lack of a color provision in their constitutional convention call in August 1841, failing to mention the reality that people of color were barred from the polls on election day. She also took Goodell's defense of oppression of both white and Black people to a different, more problematic level. Referring to the marching of Dorr-allied prisoners from Chepachet to prison, she posited, if *"colored* men had been marched through the streets of Providence, *under the same circumstances* all New England would have been in a blaze. I have yet to learn, that Black men are better than white men, or that their rights are any more sacred." She even claimed that Black men were "dupes" for voting with the Law and Order Party under their constitution, before backtracking by saying that Black service was the "noblest" development "during the whole controversy."[32]

Vote Black men most likely did when called on to elect delegates to the convention, scheduled to meet in Newport in September. While no record has yet been found of that election, one *Providence Journal* correspondent noted that the suffragists had been using "deception, lying, flattery, and intimidation" to keep people of color from the polls. The Suffrage Party dubbed the convention the "Algerine Convention" because of the supposedly tyrannical suppression of suffragists by the state, though the racial connotation is certainly noteworthy. Despite this, the author could confidently say that "there is not among them a man, who is not a friend of the government." By the time the Law and Order convention got underway on September 12, it was clear that public opinion was still decidedly in favor of the elimination of the color provision in voting. The pro-Whig *Journal* had published a defense of Black Providence residents in response to a derisive article in the *Washington Globe*, the national mouthpiece for the Democratic Party. Providence merchant Thomas Stead and Brown University president Francis Wayland wrote to Senator Simmons, who returned to Rhode Island to take part in the convention. Stead confidently informed Simmons that the constitution must provide for Black suffrage or it would be voted down. Wayland wrote that Black men had "prov[en] themselves worthy of the right of suffrage" by protecting the government, and that "expediency" was now on their side.[33]

Still, Black voting faced stiff opposition. The first copy of the voting qualification that was reported contained the word "white." After this came out, the *Providence Journal* stepped up its lobbying campaign. One editorial published during the convention reiterated that public support was unmistakably in favor of Black voting. The author understood that race prejudice existed in the country, where conservative, aristocratic Democrats reigned, but the feeling in the city—home to more people and more votes—was entirely different. Another writer under the pseudonym "Thousands" said so many deemed the distinction between Black and white especially odious because Black people had voted on delegates to the convention; any constitution that now barred them would be the height of betrayal. Besides, the state had much more to fear from *"white"* ruffians" in the mill villages than people of color from Providence. The author was confident that Providence's weight would go against the constitution if it contained "white," dooming it statewide. Another, under the moniker "Equality," similarly made the argument that excluding the same voters who sent delegates to the convention would "decapitate their own constituents." One abolitionist writing to the *Emancipator* said he believed that Black people had "created a sympathy in their behalf never before aroused" in the freemen of the state, and that Goodell was a "blockhead or scoundrel" for supporting the mobocrats in the Suffrage Party. Joshua Leavitt, the paper's editor, defended Goodell's critique of the landholders as inconsistent allies to Black Rhode Islanders, appending a caution to the enthusiasm of the correspondent: "Promise is good, but performance is better."[34]

Joseph Childs of Portsmouth leveled the first blow at the "white" provision, moving simply that the word be stricken. It received a positive hearing, being supported by at least two other delegates, before Richard K. Randolph offered the resolution that people of color only be admitted with the old freehold qualification, reflective of the New York law of 1821 requiring $250 worth of property that applied only to Black men. That motion was laid on the table so Randolph could try to apply it to naturalized foreigners. Later in the convention, Childs again slipped in a "suggestion" that the word "white" be omitted, to which Charles Jackson, a Whig delegate from Providence—and one who had just the year earlier scolded the Suffrage Association that whiteness was an "indispensable" qualification—replied that he would favor Black voting if they were re-added to the tax rolls and paid a poll tax (as he was suggesting all should do). Charles F. Tillinghast of Providence then moved three petitions to the floor, the first of which was the one Black leaders Ichabod Northup, James Hazard, and colleagues had sent to the November Landholders' Convention requesting "equal participation in the rights and privileges of citizenship." To it was appended two more signed by many of the leading white citizens of Providence: one simply asking that "white" not appear in the voting qualification and another that declared the word as antithetical to the founding principles of the country. The convention hurriedly moved on to other business, but some delegates would not remain silent.³⁵

Later, after William Ennis of Newport again moved that "white" be stricken, Jackson suggested a compromise that would please both the Randolph faction, which had allied with conservative, aristocratic country Democrats like Elisha Potter and former governor (and president of the convention) James Fenner, and those who pushed for striking "white": they would in some way admit people of color to vote but they would also put the question to the people in a separate referendum. Randolph then moved that a poll tax be levied on all white male citizens, and only those who paid should vote. Nearly unanimously panned, the convention adopted the Jackson compromise, supporting by a vote of fifty-three to twelve a resolution that "the question of whether native colored male citizens shall have the right to vote, if possessed of the qualifications required of native *white* male citizens, be submitted to the qualified voters." The next step was to determine whether the constitution itself would contain "white," after which they would ask the voters whether or not to strike it, or if the constitution should not contain "white," asking the voters whether or not to add it. Senator Simmons, back from Washington to represent his hometown of Johnston at the convention, who controlled much of the state's Whig agenda, had clearly been swayed by his powerful backers. Believing that the constitution would not be adopted with "white" in it—a proposition that threatened more unrest—he teamed with Jackson and Childs to advocate putting the version without "white" to the voters while simultaneously asking whether the word should be inserted. This passed forty-five to fifteen. Because all who the constitution *would* enfranchise were allowed to vote on its adoption, this provision also confirmed that Black voters would have their say on their own enfranchisement.³⁶

The constitution that was proposed to voters contained the following provision for who would qualify as a voter (article 2, section 2):

> Every [ ] male native citizen of the United States, of the age of twenty-one years, who has had his residence and home in this state two years and in the town or city in which he may offer to vote, six months next preceding the time of voting... shall have a right to vote in the election of all civil officers, and on all questions in all legally organized town or ward meetings, until the end of the first year after the adoption of this constitution, or until the end of the year eighteen hundred and forty-three.

All would be eligible to vote who could pay either a real estate or poll tax of one dollar. Despite the glaring gap between "Every" and "male," whose meaning was abundantly clear, the only place the word "white" appears in the document is in the enactment clause, confirmed when the convention reassembled in November:

> In the first line of the second section of article second, relating to the qualification of electors, when the constitution is enrolled, there shall be a blank space left between the words *every* and *male*; and at the meetings hereinbefore appointed for voting upon the constitution, the following question shall also be separately submitted to be voted upon by those who may be authorised to vote for or against said constitution, viz: "In case the constitution framed by the convention assembled at Newport in September, 1842, be adopted, shall the blank in the first line of section second of article second of said constitution, be filled by the word '*white*;' and a sufficient number of affirmative and negative ballots for this purpose shall be printed and distributed by the secretary."

Town clerks would keep separate the ballots on the constitution itself and the question on the "white" provision. If there were more affirmative ballots, "white" would fill the blank space, and if there were more negative ballots, the gap would simply be eliminated in the document's official printing. A vote on each—whether the constitution should be adopted and whether the "white" provision should be included—would be held statewide from November 21–23, 1842.[37]

Adoption of the constitution became a foregone conclusion when the Suffrage Party and Dorr himself from exile urged their supporters to boycott the vote. Given the near-unanimous praise of Black Providence for defending the city and helping secure peace, the "white" provision was similarly doomed.[38] One commenter in the *Providence Journal* brought some much-needed, if partisan, context to the situation. "No: No: No!" refreshed the memories of Rhode Island voters by bringing up Primus Bailey of Little Compton, who voted in an 1817 election and who Democratic-Republicans blamed for their one-vote loss. Bailey was still alive, the writer noted, and only a "NO" vote on the question of adding "white" would restore to him and other people of color the promise of "liberty and equality" they had been denied. Tinged with a yearning for old Federalism, the commenter's partisanship nevertheless underscored the significant truth about the Black and elite-white alliance that lay at the root of Black Providence leaders' hopes and frustrations. Federalists had pushed through the end of slavery. They also kept Black leaders at arm's length, apparently refusing to admit most to freemanship—as Anthony Kinnicutt's exasperated pleas, together with little evidence of Black voting prior to 1822, showed. Democratic-Republicans had pushed through formal disfranchisement, and their descendants in the Suffrage Association were largely to blame for exclusion of Black leaders in their ranks, which led to Alfred Niger's forcible removal from the voting booth in August 1841. Black leaders always had to make difficult, calculated choices. Although this was one of them, the path to citizenship, the one they had been on since the rejection of emigration, clearly ran through forcing the hands of their old allies.[39]

The November 1842 vote on both the constitution and the word "white" showed that Providence's Black leaders had calculated the right time to act. The constitution passed 7,024 to 51, with Dorr supporters boycotting. The "white" provision was defeated by a closer, yet decisive vote of 4,031 against to 1,798 in favor of adding "white" to the blank space. Preliminary results showed that about half the difference was made in Providence, where voters rejected "white" by a ratio of thirteen to one and by a margin of over a thousand. The Quaker and abolitionist hotspots of Smithfield and Coventry, the towns surrounding Providence, and Newport all voted against the "white" provision, while the votes in favor of it mainly came from the rural and former plantation areas of the state. The committee tasked with reporting on the votes enumerated that eighty-two people of color had voted to adopt the constitution and presumably against the "white" provision. With over seven hundred men of color of voting age, we can also presume that this is a drastic undercount.[40] Notably, the RIASS meeting that took place shortly before the vote reported no discussion on the new constitution. Niger was elected vice president and Ransom Parker earned a spot on the executive committee, while Fredrick Douglass and Charles Lenox Remond addressed the assembly. At this meeting, a more urgent matter had gripped abolitionist activists: all of the resolutions recorded were related to supporting George Latimer, a man who had escaped slavery and been apprehended in Massachusetts, setting off a firestorm of abolitionist activism. The abolitionist presses had moved on as well, though both the *Emancipator* and *National Anti-Slavery Standard* praised the triumph of democracy and the adoption of equal suffrage in the state—a rare setback to the rising tide of white supremacy in national politics.[41]

In the first General Assembly session following the victory of the new constitution, in January 1843, the act "exempting blacks and people of color from taxation" was formally repealed. Providence's Black community, having already organized into a body politic despite disfranchisement, began formal political activity immediately. On March 29, a "very large" meeting of Providence's people of color "friendly to law and order," chaired by Thomas Howland, formally registered their approval of the new constitution and the Law and Order Party. James Hazard offered a resolution favoring the "Rhode Island prox," a slate of Law and Order candidates for state office, including former governor and Democrat-turned–Law and Order leader James Fenner for the governorship, in the upcoming election. Their reasons for doing so were, first, because the party "gives us our rights, or, in other words, it gives us all the rights we do enjoy." Second, they valued these rights so highly because they had "receive[d] them through the forms of law; and through that same form we may receive all other rights."[42]

This last provision perfectly reflected the terms on which the battle for the right to vote had been fought over the past twenty years. The African Union Meeting House was built during the threat, then enactment, of disfranchisement, with the Black community in Providence continuing a long-heralded tradition of mutual benefit organizing and forging ties with elite white allies. A leadership class committed to planting firm roots in the republic had formed during this process and continued in various guises through the lean years that saw two nasty pogroms, numerous drawbacks, and moderate gains. The strategy was always clear: prove that the color line was an arbitrary disqualification for citizenship by holding the state government accountable to the revolutionary principles it had endorsed, specifically linking taxation with representation, and publicizing an adherence to intellectual rationality, independence, property accumulation, and Christian morality—all major tenets in the republican tradition of citizenship. African Americans especially had recognized that the right to vote was central to everything they wished to accomplish, and since that was legally stripped from them, all of their activism—the campaign to access equal education, temperance organization, and abolitionism—was geared toward that goal. In the end, they engineered the only movement in the nation that removed a color qualification for the right to vote before the Civil War.

Epilogue
"FRIENDS TO SOCIAL ORDER, TRUE TO OUR FELLOW MAN"

The movement by Providence's Black leaders to win back the right to vote was undoubtedly successful and one of the rare instances in antebellum America that involved Black leaders' forcing the elite white establishment to bend toward its will. It is an instructive event because it can help us understand what a successful movement looks like in a political culture dominated by a mythological adherence to its founding documents' ideals regarding liberty and equality. The founding of the republic as a form of government was one in which the vote was almost entirely the province of white, property-owning men, and which defined people of color at varying times as slaves, outsiders, "strangers," and even a separate species from whites. Yet, the professed commitment to freedom and the republican notion of self-government were always ideological openings that Black intellectual leaders found exploitable. In Providence, Rhode Island, the capital of the smallest state in the union, Black leaders were able to engineer a campaign that promoted their own professed commitment to the founding ideals, and one that achieved the elusive goal of altering the mindset of the white power structure. The exclusion of these leaders—particularly George McCarty, George C. Wyllis, Alfred Niger, Ichabod Northup, James Hazard, Ransom Parker, and Thomas Howland—from the pantheon of antebellum Black leadership is a gap in the historical record that this work seeks to close.

It would not be fair to scholarship, however, to omit the sacrifices the leaders consciously made in order to ensure their movement's success. The strict adherence to republican respectability left little room for advocacy in favor of those who, because of discriminatory practice, were forced into the underground economy. This included unlicensed selling of goods, odd-jobbing, domestic work, or those who were otherwise forced to live lives and earn money in what historian of Providence Joanne Pope Melish calls "strangerhood," or in what Cincinnati historian Nikki Taylor calls the "shadow community."[1] While inside Black communities, people in these circumstances were often supported by mutual benefit societies, republican ideals held them outside the bounds of respectability and citizenship. Therefore, while Black leaders correctly pointed to the persistence of the color line as the reason many Black people lived in dire conditions, these leaders eschewed some of the radical critiques of Black leaders outside the state. The deferential language in which Providence leaders' petitions were couched almost certainly was inserted over some objection at the African Union Meeting House. The fact that opposition went unrecorded in order to promote unity silenced what could give historians a more well-rounded view of the relationships between leaders and the rank and file.

The notion of "respectability" has a fraught history in the long Black freedom struggle, and has been identified as an uplift strategy by many academics in the African American Studies tradition.[2] Internally, respectability campaigns could help individuals lead healthier lives and reflected the growing complexities of African American communities decades after the nominal end of slavery. Such efforts provided Black community leaders with a vocabulary and ideological ammunition for protesting the rising tide of white supremacy and racial pseudoscience. When tied to republican ideals, however, they could be exclusionary for women, the propertyless, and those who espoused radically egalitarian views in a society that valued its hierarchy. In a sense, while the abolitionist movement became more widespread and its visions for a more democratic distribution of rights and wealth were becoming more forcefully articulated, Providence's Black leaders were seeking elevation within the state's accepted hierarchy—the only major tweak they sought was the removal of the word "white." While the breaking of the color barrier in the voting statute was an enormous feat, it most likely would have failed without Black leaders' constant reminders of the community's striving for wealth, education, and religious virtue, and the history of their fighting to protect the conservative government.[3]

The success of the movement to win back the right to vote on terms of republican respectability tied Providence's Black leaders more formally to the state's white elite establishment. This was not an easy alliance. While the Law and Order Party implemented the new voting law and repealed the statute barring Black people from taxation, they left on the books other laws forbidding Black people from obtaining licenses to sell liquor, oysters, and other victuals. They also refused to remove special protections for slaveowners who brought their captives to the state. They ridiculed some Black voters for not being able to sign their own names, and harassed and threatened others who signaled an unwillingness to vote the party line. The Law and Order Party could scarcely lose Black support; the Suffrage Party continued to dominate much of the white population in Providence County. The Suffrage Party, at least once, tried to court Black voters—however, when one agent tried to address the "colored citizens of Providence," only nine showed up. In the first major election in which Black voters participated, that for governor in April 1843, Black voters accounted for much of the margin of victory for Law and Order Party chieftain former Democrat James Fenner, over a Locofoco, Suffrage-aligned Democrat.[4]

By the fall of 1844, after delivering Fenner another term as governor, the first presidential election in which Black voters could participate under the new constitution led Providence's Black leaders to declare publicly their allegiance to the Whig Party. Although Fenner was a Democrat, the Law and Order Party was dominated by Whigs who, nationally, tolerated antislavery sentiment within its ranks and opposed the fanatic nature of Democratic racism. Providence's Black leaders brushed aside the explicitly abolitionist Liberty Party in favor of Whig candidate Henry Clay, helping deliver the state for the slaveholder who sought the political middle over the Democratic slaveholder James Polk, who promised to deliver for the Slave Power.[5] Black citizens' opting for party loyalty over an explicitly abolitionist choice earned an "abusive and vehement" denunciation from Frederick Douglass at an RIASS meeting shortly after the election. *Liberator* correspondent Henry Clapp deemed that Black Clay supporters were "led on evidently by designing Whigs," pointing to the seeming vote against their own interests that baffled Douglass and the RIASS. Douglass would later make the difficult choice to engage in establishment politics when he became a national leader, but at this moment he and the state's Garrison-dominated antislavery society could not fathom the accommodationist stance taken by Providence's Black leaders.[6]

What Clapp mistook for gullibility and Douglass mistook for abandonment was actually yet another calculated decision by Providence's Black leaders to ally themselves with the dominant political party of Providence's elite. The evening after Douglass's "insulting remarks," a "committee of the Whig colored population" met and drafted resolutions defending their votes for Clay, sending them to the *Providence Journal* for publication. The committee representing the meeting included veteran leader Thomas Howland; Abraham Peterson, the barber whose speech inspired Black militiamen to join the Law and Order Party forces during the late rebellion; and newcomer to leadership ranks Richard Nichols. Explaining their motivations, they wrote,

> We do publicly say that we discountenance the means adopted by the abolitionists of the convention being holden in this city, to erase the evil of Southern Slavery from our land—to speak in slanderous terms of our most influential men, men who have labored arduously to advance the true interests of this nation, and for the promotion of the happiness of its citizens, will have a direct tendency to rivet still stronger the chain of tyranny and oppression. We would not wish the world to think we, as freemen, participate in such outbreaks, but that, as men, we are true Whigs, friends to social order, true to our fellow man, to our God, and to our country.

They followed with eight resolutions mostly admonishing those who resorted to "indignation" when evaluating these men's course of action. "We, as freemen," they declared, "know our rights, and knowing dare maintain them," signaling that they were sensitive to the tenuousness of their alliance with the Whig establishment, lest a move into radical camps cause either the Whigs to disfranchise them again or lead to a Democratic takeover that could do the same. Statements like "friends to social order" and "'wisdom without justice' [is] craftiness" fit neatly with the Whig doctrine of defending "middle-class morality," according to one historian, lending credence to their claim as "true Whigs." Finally, they pleaded, "trust we are governed by as holy and upright principles as any of the advocates of the liberty party, and that we will ask the sympathy of them when needed." They were abolitionists, of course, but they thought their best chances to end slavery and improve their own place in the body politic was through the Whig Party.[7]

This rupture probably caused Black leadership to withdraw support for the RIASS. As other state and local societies largely depended on the financial backing of Black communities, it is perhaps no coincidence that the RIASS basically ceased to function outside of its annual meeting after Black leaders broke with Garrison and Douglass. By 1847, the American Anti-Slavery

Society no longer deemed it as one of its auxiliaries.⁸ The slave's cause, however, was supported in other ways. Although the society was never viably resuscitated, calls for activism ramped up around watershed events like the passage of the Fugitive Slave Act of 1850 and John Brown's raid on Harper's Ferry in 1859. Women like Aramancy Paine and Elizabeth Chace continued to raise money and sponsor speakers such as Douglass, ex-slave and author William Wells Brown, and others, while Black and white leaders participated in the local and regional AASS.⁹

Black Providence leaders remained involved in Whig Party politics through at least the end of the 1840s. The *Providence Journal* reported on a meeting of Providence's Black leadership, chaired by Niger and Wyllis, that resolved to support the Law and Order Party because of the improvement they saw in their community that accompanied the right to vote.¹⁰ It would be one of the last elections of the Law and Order alignment. The presidential election of 1848 promised a difficult test for Black leaders, as this contest featured the Free Soil Party, which was much more forceful than the Liberty Party in siphoning abolitionist votes from the Whigs and Democrats. The Whigs again nominated a slaveholder, Mexican War hero Zachary Taylor, and this time the nominee ran in a three-way race against Northern Democrat Lewis Cass and former president, enemy to New York Black voters, and Democrat-turned-Free Soiler Martin Van Buren. The Free Soil Party was made up of a coalition of antislavery Democrats and Conscience Whigs mainly from New York, the upper Midwest, and Boston—and their main tie was opposition to slavery's spread westward. Van Buren had as his running mate Charles Francis Adams, a Whig and son of the party's antislavery hero John Quincy Adams. Some Black leaders like Frederick Douglass and formerly enslaved Black political activist Henry Bibb joined the cause seeking to blunt the Slave Power ascendancy. Douglass and Bibb went to Providence to try and persuade Black voters to defect from the Whigs and join the Free Soilers, while the Whig *Providence Journal*, in a bid to keep the Black community in the fold, alternated between flattery and chauvinistically reminding Black voters of the Whigs' support for Black voting rights in 1842. Henry Bowen, the chair of Providence's Whig central committee, hired William J. Brown to convince Black voters to turn out for Taylor. The party sponsored an election day festival in which crackers, cheese, shaved beef, and coffee was to be served. Black men were encouraged to attend, and then the whole gathering would go to the polls en masse to vote for Taylor. Black leaders, torn between loyalty to their local allies and pressure from national Black leaders, did what they had done time and again when put in a difficult position by outside circumstance: they turned inward, finding strength in their common purpose. They called a meeting to determine their next steps.[11]

According to Brown, about 250 people crowded a packed meeting hall on South Main Street for a gathering chaired by Thomas Howland. No one seemed to favor Cass, the official Democratic nominee, who though a northerner, was identified as a tool of the Slave Power. Stalwart leader George C. Wyllis spoke first, and after remarking on the "very curious position" the community found itself in, declared he would support Taylor as a lesser evil than Van Buren. Many members of the community remembered that Van Buren had led the Democratic Party for the better part of the past two decades before defecting in a power struggle with the southern faction. Further, with little chance of national success for the Free Soil Party, a vote for Van Buren could only help Cass. Brown then rose to speak and recommended Taylor as well, though "it was a bitter pill for us to vote for a man who was a slaveholder." He understood that must be "the feeling of every colored voter" but added that "we are identified with the Whig party." Although paid to take this position, his reasoning was nonetheless cogent: Taylor was merely a "servant for the party." This proved to be prescient. After helping deliver the state for Taylor, the Virginia aristocrat by blood and owner of a plantation in Louisiana nonetheless fell under the sway of leading Senate Whig William Seward, a leader in the "Conscience" faction, and the party adopted much of the Free Soil platform before Taylor's death ushered in a more moderate administration under Millard Fillmore. Perhaps this was coincidence, but more likely Providence's Black leaders understood the inner workings of the Whig Party better than most.[12]

The Fight Continued

The 1850s were a decade of constant political upheaval, both in Rhode Island and the country at large. A number of setbacks plagued Black leaders early in the decade, beginning with the Fugitive Slave Law of 1850, which erased the Whig-passed proscription against Rhode Island state officers assisting in the capture of fugitive slaves.[13] One of the first major tests on voting was met and passed when Democrats controlled the assembly and governorship between 1851 and 1854 and took no steps to disfranchise the pivotal Black electorate. The Kansas-Nebraska Act of 1854 all but destroyed the Whig Party nationally, ushering in a political whiplash in which the American, or Know-Nothing, Party suddenly—and briefly—wedded antislavery voters in general, nativists, and old Whigs, wrenching power from Democrats across the North. In Rhode Island, William Hoppin won election to the governorship as a Whig in 1854 and then crushed his Democratic opponent the next year as a Know-Nothing, winning an astounding 81.5 percent of the vote. Soon after, however, the state's Know-Nothings bolted to the newly minted Republican Party, organized largely around the Free Soil platform of 1848, providing Black leaders with a political party they had many fewer qualms about uniting with. It was into this situation they forged a resurgence of the activist spirit that had won them the right to vote in 1842.[14]

The year 1857 brought a surprising triumph and setback for one of the stalwart leaders—Thomas Howland, the stevedore who had accumulated enough wealth and cache to become a church and community leader. That year, he was nominated for election warden of Providence's Third Ward, in a way by accident. In an area apparently dominated by the new Republican Party, most of the party voted according to the old custom of *viva voce*, unaware of a law that had been passed recently requiring the election of wardens by ballot. Democrats, seeing this, printed ballots with a Democrat-turned-Republican they despised as "clerk" and Howland as "warden," the former being subservient to the latter. This ticket actually ended up winning, and in the process Howland became the first Black elected official in the state. Despite the nature of the election, Howland served as warden on election day with dignity.[15]

Howland's election came just a few months after the U.S. Supreme Court handed down its *Dred Scott* decision, which used the same logic that Benjamin Hazard had in 1829, determining that because the ancestors of African Americans were enslaved, they were not considered citizens by the founding framers of the government. Therefore, despite the existence of "free states" and the fact that some states invested some African Americans with rights of citizenship, they were not to be considered citizens of the country. Roger Taney, the chief justice and author of the majority opinion, also cited the racial nature of republican philosophy as articulated by Locke and Rousseau; citizenship was a condition for the "civilized portion of the white race," as agents able to reduce things of nature to property. The reduction of people of African descent to property marked them as a race ineligible for civilization, and the freedom bestowed on the lucky few only afforded them the privilege of living among—and according to the rules of—whites. The Declaration of Independence's profession of the belief of men's equal creation had given African Americans a basis for equitable citizenship, and the attempt at closing that gave African Americans and antislavery whites everywhere a new rallying cry. Howland, having been elected to an office that oversaw one of the most central rights of republican citizenship, then tried to exercise another right of citizenship—obtaining a U.S. passport. He had "decided to try his fortunes in Liberia," and when he applied for a passport, he was rejected by the State Department on the grounds that "passports are not issued to persons of African extraction." Despite the rejection of his emigration endeavor, the near-simultaneous affirmation and denial of citizenship was emblematic of what Black Rhode Islanders had been up against for decades.[16]

The rest of Providence's Black leadership that year turned their attention to another contour of citizenship—equitable education. The very basis for the early suffrage petitions had been the right to access the public education system their tax dollars supported, and the two schools for Black children that the public coffers supported were becoming an ever-growing, glaring blot on the notion of equitable citizenship. As the city was sprawling away from the waterfront, Black children from other wards were forced to travel longer distances while white children could attend the schools closest to them. There remained little distinction among primary, grammar, and secondary levels in Black schools like there were in white schools, and Black students were barred from high school altogether. Teachers at the Black schools were paid less than those at the white schools. While in the beginning Black parents had supported the Black-only schools, as they shielded children from the racism of their white peers, and the schools consistently were praised for their educational outcomes, by the 1850s the tide among the city's Black leaders began to shift in favor of integration.

Clearly emboldened by the new unity of the Free Soil platform with an establishment political party, a combination of old and new Black leadership took the helm one last time before the Civil War. Newcomer George T. Downing, a wealthy man who owned a catering company in Providence and a restaurant and hotel in Newport, and a veteran of desegregation on the railroads, was dismayed at the appalling conditions of the schools his children were forced to attend because of their race. As early as 1855, he had reached out to prominent Republican senator Charles Sumner from Massachusetts, who had won a court case that outlawed school segregation in that state. In December 1857, at "a large and enthusiastic meeting of colored persons opposed to proscribed schools," Downing and Ichabod Northup, one of the authors of the petitions for enfranchisement in 1841–1842, among others, pushed through several unanimous resolutions in support of integration. They affirmed their status as "free men and women, of our own rights and interests in connexion with our children's education, like all others in the community," and though they did not expressly say it, they were also some of the wealthiest men of color in the city. In other words, they were independent republican citizens who were arbitrarily denied the right to educate their children on equal terms with whites. They compiled a series of letters of support from Black and white education leaders around the Northeast, and specifically pointed to former Brown University president Francis Wayland's support for universal, equitable public education in the late 1820s and early 1830s. They then bundled the meeting notes and letters of support with a formal petition, and sent the whole document, titled *Will the General Assembly Put Down Caste Schools*, to the General Assembly's January 1858 session. The petition claimed that the present law forbade people of color, as citizens of Rhode Island, from exercising the duties of citizenship because of the distinction of color in public education. Downing and Northup even testified before the Providence School Committee and the General Assembly, but this first attempt came to naught; no action was taken on the petition.[17]

The *Providence Journal*, now the main Republican newspaper in the state, strongly resisted school integration—another betrayal in a long series of betrayals by the Black community's necessary but unreliable allies. The paper had otherwise provided significant positive press since the summer of 1842, warmly covering First of August festivities celebrating British emancipation and showing some support for an abolitionist meeting at Mechanic's Hall that decried the abuses of African Americans on railroads. However, when it came to this issue, the newspaper played on whites' fears of Black boys going to school with white girls and claimed that the presence of Black children would drive rich whites to pull their children from the schools and wield their influence to stop the flow of tax dollars into the school system. Downing, Northup, and Ransom Parker, a leader in the education fight from the 1830s, authored a broadside titled "We Would Ask, Why Deny Us Our School Rights?" and a longer piece titled *To the Friends of Equal Rights in Rhode Island*, in which they refuted the arguments lobbed at them by the *Journal* in preparation for another campaign to be undertaken in 1859–1860. Parker's daughter Clementia testified in front of a General Assembly committee in June 1859 about the arbitrariness of the color line in education, using language similar to the leaders of her father's generation. By this time, the country's inability to square its adherence to slavery and race with its professions of liberty and equality had brought it to the precipice of civil war, and soon even the most conservative of Republican allies, like the Whigs before them, would be forced to knock down this barrier only after Black men were called on to defend the republic. In 1866, a full year after nearly 200,000 Black union troops helped quell the Slave Power's rebellion and end slavery—1,800 of them in the celebrated Fourteenth Rhode Island Heavy Artillery (Colored)—Black Rhode Islanders won school integration.[18]

One final appeal from Providence's Black leadership in the antebellum era stands out. In the midst of the school integration fight, Ichabod Northup wrote and published *An Appeal from a Colored Man Whose Father Fought in the Revolution*, a broadside that included many of the same arguments leadership had made in their other, larger appeals on behalf of their children: their taxes went into the public education coffers at the same rate as whites' so they should have access to the same schools, the color line had been rescinded in all other matters of law, and the state's Republican establishment appeared to be implementing the *Dred Scott* decision it so roundly denounced. It is perhaps most useful for historians because it profoundly, yet in such an understated way, links the activism of the 1850s with that going back to earlier leadership. Northup lamented the fact that white "Foreigners" were allowed into white public schools—playing to the nativist tint in the Republican Party—while he, "whose father fought with *Washington*, [was] driven from their doors." More than eighty years after the First Rhode Island Regiment began recruiting men of color to defend the republic, and almost two decades after the son of one of those men led a movement that both defended that body politic and confirmed that Black Providence had an equal voice in it, Northup was still fighting. Black Providence leaders between the Revolution and the Civil War had always had to plan their activism carefully, craftily holding their allies to account and choosing the right moments to make their stands. In the heady days before the Civil War, when all Americans questioned the survival of a republic that professed ideas about liberty and equality and yet still held millions in captive bondage and deemed hundreds of thousands unequal citizens, Northup understood the utility of pointing again to the revolutionary principles—principles passed down through the generations of his city's Black leaders.[19]

Black leaders of the late eighteenth century, whether they fought for the republic like Northup's father or were seeking out ways to emigrate, were working out ideas for self-liberation that would set the stage for their children. Some of this generation, and almost all of the next, decided to stay in the place of their birth, founding the African Union Meeting House and laying tangible roots both *in* the body politic and *as* a body politic. They absorbed the sting of disfranchisement and protected their homes from mobs, and out of the ashes of the turbulent 1820s and 1830s they organized and launched a campaign for citizenship. So situated, they were prepared for the right moment to capitalize on an opportunity to do what they had always done—defend the republic and show that the existence of the color line could not be reconciled with the country's founding principles, though republican citizenship had been philosophically developed in racialized terms. As has occurred throughout American history, however, the movement's successes were limited by the tensions created by the simultaneous desire to bend the conservative establishment toward it while seeking to join that very establishment. Providence's Black leaders altered the republic yet they were absorbed by it, and so they inherited its limitations too.

The long Black freedom struggle has been defined by the incomplete successes of abolition, emancipation, and the civil rights movement. The addition to the scholarship of the actions and words of Providence's Black leaders, their earnest remonstrances against the color line and in favor of their "precious birthright," the right to vote, is both long overdue and valuable to our understanding of the devastatingly central role race has played in the evolving conception of citizenship in the American republic.

Notes

Introduction

1 Henry Trumbull, *The Life of Robert the Hermit* (Providence, RI: H. Trumbull, 1829). For context on the hermit trope in early American literature and politics, see Eric Slauter, "The American Hermit and the British Castaway: Voluntary Retreat and Deliberative Democracy in Early American Culture," *Early American Literature* 46, no. 1 (2011): 121–56.
2 *Providence Journal*, August 19, 1867 (in a "supplement" entitled "A Glance at the Town of Providence in 1812, Revised and Annotated").
3 Trumbull, *The Life of Robert the Hermit*.
4 Harris, *In the Shadow of Slavery*, 61. While in many cases a Federalist–African American alliance was an accusation made by Jeffersonians, Republicans, and then Democrats to vent frustration in close election losses or to vilify their opponents, there is certainly some truth to this—and this alliance was recast starkly in the Whig–African American partnership in Rhode Island following the re-enfranchisement of Black voters in 1843.
5 See especially Sean Wilentz, *The Rise of American Democracy: Jefferson to Lincoln* (New York: Norton, 2005).
6 Burke, *Interference of the Executive in the Affairs of Rhode Island*, 113.
7 Horton and Horton, *In Hope of Liberty*, xi.
8 Of course, women and people of color did own property and serve in militias—that is, until the Militia Acts of 1792 barred them from duty. Women's property was often seen as "moveable," meaning either inherited from generation to generation or to be absorbed into a male-headed household when she married. See Laurel Thatcher Ulrich, *The Age of Homespun: Objects and Stories in the Creation of an American Myth* (New York: Random House, 2001), 128–42.
9 Women in New Jersey could vote until 1807.

10 Robin Blackburn, *The Making of New World Slavery: From the Baroque to the Modern, 1492–1800* (New York: Verso, 1997), 263–65.
11 Masur, *Until Justice Be Done*; Gosse, *The First Reconstruction*, 3–28. Gosse elides much of the early community activism of Black leaders in his chapter on Rhode Island, but it nonetheless adds value to the conversation. Bonner, *Remaking the Republic*, 4–5 (quotation). For other work on citizenship and Black rights in the early republic period, see Polgar, *Standard-Bearers of Equality*.
12 Litwack, *North of Slavery*, 180.
13 Douglas Bradburn, *The Citizenship Revolution: Politics and the Creation of the American Union, 1774–1804* (Charlottesville: University of Virginia Press, 2009), 1–18, 235–71.
14 Winch, *Philadelphia's Black Elite*, 2.
15 See Parker Pillsbury's rather crude description of Reverend John W. Lewis, a member of Providence's leadership class in the late 1830s, in Pillsbury, *Acts of the Anti-Slavery Apostles* (Boston: Cupples, Upham, 1884), 88.
16 See Melish, *Disowning Slavery*, 171–79, for a thorough examination of "bobalition" broadsides.
17 For more on how political and social messaging began explicitly defining whiteness and Blackness in the early national period, see Roediger, *Wages of Whiteness*, and Ignatiev, *How the Irish Became White*.
18 Jackson, *A Short History of the African Union Meeting and School-House*, 5.
19 Providence was incorporated as a city in 1831.

Chapter 1

1 Robinson, *Proceedings of the Free African Union Society*, 20.
2 Hopkins, Harding, and Park, *Works of Samuel Hopkins, D.D.*, 135.
3 Robinson, *Proceedings of the Free African Union Society*, 20.
4 While artisanry among enslaved African Americans in urban areas was common, after emancipation free Black men were often squeezed out by white artisans who saw them as competitors for business.
5 Robinson, *Proceedings of the Free African Union Society*, 42–43.
6 Horton and Horton, *In Hope of Liberty*, 60.
7 Greene, *The Negro in Colonial New England*, 190; Clark-Pujara, *Dark Work*, 70.
8 Pierson, *Black Yankees*, 118. For more on Pinkster and its role in New York City, see Harris, *In the Shadow of Slavery*, 40–41, 69–70, and Horton and Horton, *In Hope of Liberty*, 31–32.
9 Elleanor Eldridge of Warwick and Providence, according to her biographer, had a brother who was elected governor; she would accompany "His Excellency" to events and stood "in the very highest niche of the aristocracy" among Black Rhode Islanders. See Green, *Memoirs of Elleanor Eldridge*, 35–36.
10 See Greene, *The Negro in Colonial New England*, 249–55; Melish, *Disowning Slavery*, 45–47; and Horton and Horton, *In Hope of Liberty*, 22–27.
11 Horton and Horton, *In Hope of Liberty*, 23.
12 Pierson, *Black Yankees*, 117. There was a huge influx of enslaved people brought to Rhode Island directly from Africa or the Caribbean between 1750 and the

Revolutionary War, as opposed to those who were born in the colony, the latter of whom had been an increasing proportion of enslaved people before 1750. See Melish, *Disowning Slavery*, 46, and Clark-Pujara, *Dark Work*, 45.

13 The drumming may also have been a cultural syncretism of Narragansett Indians, who lived close to the plantations of King's County, Rhode Island, and often worked side by side with, were enslaved with, and married Africans and African Americans. See Pierson, *Black Yankees*, 117–28, 157.
14 Greene, *The Negro in Colonial New England*, 86–88.
15 Melish, "The Racial Vernacular"; Sweet, *Bodies Politic*, 9–10.
16 Cottrol, *The Afro-Yankees*, 18–19, 23–24; Brown, *Life of William J. Brown*, 12–15.
17 Staples, *Documentary History of the Destruction of the Gaspee*, 37–38.
18 The reward was up to £1,000 by August 1772. York, "The Uses of Law and the Gaspee Affair," 13; Staples, *Documentary History of the Destruction of the Gaspee*, 74–75.
19 Staples, *Documentary History of the Destruction of the Gaspee*, 63, 32.
20 Melish, *Disowning Slavery*, 78.
21 Staples, *Documentary History of the Destruction of the Gaspee*, 30.
22 Horton and Horton, *In Hope of Liberty*, 60–62.
23 Quarles, *The Negro in the American Revolution*, 10–11.
24 Sweet, *Bodies Politic*, 197–98.
25 Nell, *Colored Patriots of the American Revolution*, 11–13.
26 Horton and Horton, *In Hope of Liberty*, 60.
27 Quarles, *The Negro in the American Revolution*, 73.
28 The General Assembly met in a rotation in all five counties (Newport in Newport County, Providence in Providence County, Bristol in Bristol County, East Greenwich in Kent County, and South Kingstown in King's/Washington County). The Old State House in Newport, however, was the building that housed the colony's records, etc., making Newport the de facto capital.
29 Greene, "Observations of the Black Regiment," 147–55.
30 Geake and Spear, *From Slaves to Soldiers*, 51.
31 Greene, "Observations of the Black Regiment," 161–62; Robinson, *The Hazard Family of Rhode Island*, 57–60; Sweet, *Bodies Politic*, 184.
32 Greene, "Observations of the Black Regiment," 159; Geake and Spears, *From Slaves to Soldiers*, 58–60; Sweet, *Bodies Politic*, 209.
33 Popek, *They "... Fought Bravely, but Were Unfortunate*," 899–903; Geake and Spears, *From Slaves to Soldiers*, 84–85.
34 Bartlett, *From Slave to Citizen*, 17–24; Horton and Horton, *In Hope of Liberty*, 68; Nell, *Colored Patriots of the American Revolution*, 130.
35 McBurney, *Abductions in the American Revolution*, 48–53; *Providence Patriot, and Columbian Phoenix*, October 31, 1821; *Rhode Island American*, November 2, 1821; *Colored American*, February 27, 1841.
36 Popek, *They "... Fought Bravely, but Were Unfortunate*," 727–28; Sweet, *Bodies Politic*, 221–23.
37 Popek, *They "... Fought Bravely, but Were Unfortunate*," 811–12.
38 Clark-Pujara, *Dark Work*, 19.
39 Berlin, *Many Thousands Gone*, 55–57.

40 Clark-Pujara, *Dark Work*, 44.
41 See Cottrol, *The Afro-Yankees*, 11–35; Clark-Pujara, *Dark Work*, 10–60; and Melish, *Disowning Slavery*, 11–49, for the clearest descriptions of how enslaved people lived in colonial Providence and Newport.
42 For the most complete works on this idea, see Jordan, *White over Black*, and Eze, *Race and the Enlightenment*.
43 *The Public Laws of the State of Rhode-Island and Providence Plantations . . . in January, 1822*, 371, 444.
44 Sinha, *The Slave's Cause*, 10–14; Melish, *Disowning Slavery*, 52–53.
45 See Thompson, *Moses Brown*, for more on Brown's life and conversion.
46 Sinha, *The Slave's Cause*, 37–39.
47 Wroth, *The First Press in Providence*, 368–69; *An Act for Prohibiting the Importation of Negros into This*; Thompson, *Moses Brown*, 98–99.
48 Greene, "Observations of the Black Regiment," 165; Clark-Pujara, *Dark Work*, 76.
49 In the absence of a colony-wide court system, the General Assembly often ruled on such matters as a body. Sweet, *Bodies Politic*, 247–48.
50 *1779 Act Banning the Export of a Slave without Consent*.
51 Coughtry et al., *The Notorious Triangle*, 236.
52 Conley, *Democracy in Decline*, 72.
53 *Providence Gazette*, December 20, 1783.
54 *Providence Gazette*, January 9, 1784.
55 *An Act Authorizing the Manumission of Negroes, Mulattoes and Others*.
56 *An Act Authorizing the Manumission of Negroes, Mulattoes and Others*.
57 *Act Repealing Part of Act Respecting the Manumission of Slaves*.
58 Hopkins, Harding, and Park, *Works of Samuel Hopkins*, 130; Pierson, *Black Yankees*, 58; Sweet, *Bodies Politic*, 78; Robinson, *Proceedings of the Free African Union Society*, 21–22.
59 Pierson, *Black Yankees*, 42; Bamberg, "Bristol Yamma and John Quamine in Rhode Island," 14–25.
60 Caleb Gardner was also a ship captain who traded around the world. No sources seem to make the connection, but it is within the realm of possibility that Caleb was the ship captain who kidnapped Marycoo.
61 Mason, *Reminiscences of Newport*, 154–56; Pierson, *Black Yankees*, 42; Greene, *The Negro in Colonial New England*, 278.
62 Hopkins, Harding, and Park, *The Works of Samuel Hopkins*, 133; Brooks, "The Providence African Society's Sierra Leone Emigration Scheme," 185–86.
63 Robinson, *Proceedings of the Free African Union Society*, x–xi.
64 See Sinha, *The Slave's Cause*, 131, and Clark-Pujara, *Dark Work*, 112—they are two among many who have made this claim.
65 Prinz, *On the Chocolate Trail*, 54–55.
66 See Berlin, *Many Thousands Gone*, 240–41, and Horton and Horton, *In Hope of Liberty*, 78–79, for discussions of naming patterns among enslaved people during the revolutionary era. Berlin argued that both retaining African names or those adopted under enslavement could serve practical purposes depending on the situation a slave or ex-slave found themself in. Names adopted during enslavement,

whether forced or not, often retained patterns known to exist in the African communities from which enslaved people came.
67 Robinson, *Proceedings of the Free African Union Society*, 21–27.
68 Robinson, *Proceedings of the Free African Union Society*, 21–27. Apparently, Cato Gardner left the leadership ranks in the group shortly after it began, for he was no longer mentioned in any of the correspondence after the initial two letters.
69 Cottrol, *The Afro-Yankees*, 48.
70 See U.S. Census, 1790, 1800, 1810, and Rhode Island Census, 1782, ancestry.com. See also Providence Direct Tax, 1798 List A and B, for a list of homeowners; most "Black" or "mulatto" homeowners were identified as such.
71 Definitive proof of enslavement was only found for five of the men: Cudge/Cudgo and Bonner Brown were enslaved and then freed by Moses Brown, Felix Holbrook coauthored a petition of enslaved people to the Massachusetts governor in 1773, Cato Mumford had been enslaved to Nathaniel Mumford and freed in the Revolutionary War, and Bristol Yamma was enslaved up until he was sent to Princeton for his education in preparation for his missionary trip. It is very likely that others in the group were enslaved, but no definitive proof has been found as of yet.
72 Williams, *Slavery and Freedom in Delaware*, 117–19.
73 U.S. Census, 1790, 1800, 1810; Coughtry et al., *Creative Survival*, 52–53; Melish, "Black Labor at the Nightingale-Brown House"; Popek, *They ". . . Fought Bravely, but Were Unfortunate*," 1038–39.
74 For all his philanthropy, Moses Brown was either deceitful or careless when it came to documenting ownership of the land he gave to his former captives. Cudge's son and grandson saw most of it sold off when Moses could not produce its deed, and Bonner was listed as an "occupant" when his land was sold to a third party in 1807. This is discussed further in chapter 2.
75 Brown, *Life of William J. Brown*, 5–19; Brown, Receipt from Joseph Johnson to Moses Brown.
76 Providence Town Papers, series 1, vol. 19, p. 542.
77 Melish, "Black Labor at the Nightingale-Brown House."
78 Coughtry et al., *Creative Survival*, 52.
79 Hopkins, *The System of Doctrines Contained in Divine Revelation*, xi.
80 Hopkins, Harding, and Park, *Works of Samuel Hopkins*, 132.
81 Bracey and Sinha, *African American Mosaic*, 53–55; Robinson, *Proceedings of the Free African Union Society*, 27; Jay Coughtry, "Holbrook, Felix (ca. 1743–ca. 1794)," in Miller and Smith, *Dictionary of Afro-American Slavery*, 336–37.
82 Hall agreed that the two branches of the Free African Union Society and his masonic lodge should keep in touch and acknowledged that he had heard of their "proceedings," but did not elaborate on how he felt about them. Wheatley, having been offered a place in the original missionary plan led by Hopkins, Quamine, and Yamma in the early 1770s, declined respectfully but wished the Rhode Islanders well. See Robinson, *Proceedings of the Free African Union Society*, 25–26, and Shields, *The Collected Works of Phillis Wheatley*, 184.
83 *First Report of the Providence Record Commissioners*, 167.
84 Brooks, "The Providence African Society's Sierra Leone Emigration Scheme," 191–202.

85 For more information on Thornton and his ideas for colonizing free Africans and African Americans, see Hunt, *William Thornton and Negro Colonization*.
86 Robinson, *Proceedings of the Free African Union Society*, 27–35; Brooks, "The Providence African Society's Sierra Leone Emigration Scheme," 187–92; Hopkins, Harding, and Park, *Works of Samuel Hopkins*, 148–49.
87 Robinson, *Proceedings of the Free African Union Society*, 25–30; Sinha, *The Slave's Cause*, 133.
88 Allen and Jones were both born enslaved in Delaware. Winch, *Philadelphia's Black Elite*, 5–7; Sinha, *The Slave's Cause*, 135–38.
89 *Constitution of the Providence Society for Abolishing the Slave Trade*.
90 A resolve of the General Assembly had supported the anti–slave trade resolutions of the Continental Congress in 1774, which Moses Brown viewed as legal precedent for its abolition within the state. The U.S. Constitution was ratified in 1787 allowing the slave trade for at least twenty-one years. When Rhode Island accepted statehood in 1790, the slave trade was made legal. Brown had to resort to moral suasion, petitioning, and sponsoring of freedom suits thereafter. See Thompson, *Moses Brown*, 200.
91 Thompson, *Moses Brown*, 180–202; Brooks, "The Providence African Society's Sierra Leone Emigration Scheme," 188.
92 Robinson, *Proceedings of the Free African Union Society*, 43–47.
93 Conley, *Democracy in Decline*, 45–50.
94 Brooks, "The Providence African Society's Sierra Leone Emigration Scheme," 192–202.
95 Sinha, *The Slave's Cause*, 160–71. For Black communities' and leaders' responses to colonization schemes, see Power-Greene, *Against the Wind and Tide*.
96 "Anthony Kinnicutt Petition for the Right to Vote," Providence Town Papers, series 1, vol. 4, p. 1520.
97 "Anthony Kinnicutt Petition for the Right to Vote"; Coughtry et al., *Creative Survival*, 30–32.
98 Conley, *Democracy in Decline*, 45–50.
99 Coughtry et al., *Creative Survival*, 32.

Chapter 2

1 John Quincy Adams to William Jones, July 5, 1811, in Ford, *The Writings of John Quincy Adams*, 129–31.
2 Bartlett and the Rhode Island Department of State, *Census of the Inhabitants of the Colony of Rhode Island*; U.S. Census, 1790, 1800, 1810; Curry, *The Free Black in Urban America*, 245–57.
3 Cottrol, *The Afro-Yankees*, 48–49.
4 Sullivan, "Reconstructing the Olney's Lane Riot," 50.
5 Coleman, *The Transformation of Rhode Island*, 218–28.
6 Unsigned, undated biography of William Jones, William Jones Papers; *Manufacturers' and Farmers' Journal*, January 3, 1820; "A Glance at Providence in 1812," *Providence Journal*, August 19, 1867.

7 "A Glance at Providence in 1812."
8 John Quincy Adams, diary entry, August 5, 1812, in Charles Francis Adams, ed., *Memoirs of John Quincy Adams, Comprising Portions of His Diary from 1795 to 1848* (Philadelphia: J. Lippincott, 1874), 2:395.
9 John Quincy Adams to William Jones, July 5, 1811, in Ford, *The Writings of John Quincy Adams*, 130.
10 *An Act to Establish an Uniform Rule of Naturalization; Scott v. Sandford.*
11 *Militia Act of 1792.*
12 *The Public Laws of the State of Rhode-Island and Providence Plantations . . . in January, 1822*, 371, 444; Sweet, *Bodies Politic*, 180.
13 Acts like the one passed in the January 1704 General Assembly session prohibiting "Negroes and Indians from being abroad at unseasonable times of the Night, and for *Punishing* those that shall Entertain them contrary hereto" were no longer in the public laws digest by 1822. See *Acts and Laws, of His Majesty's Colony of Rhode-Island*, 34–36.
14 Herndon, *Unwelcome Americans*, 4–22, 223.
15 Brown, *Life of William J. Brown*, 28–31.
16 Coughtry et al., *Creative Survival*, 40.
17 "A Glance at Providence in 1812"; *Manufacturers' and Farmers' Journal*, January 3, 1820; May, "Obtaining a Decent Livelihood,'" 115.
18 "A Glance at Providence in 1812"; Bristol, *Knights of the Razor*, 2.
19 For this and the previous two paragraphs, see "A Glance at Providence in 1812," and Herndon, *Unwelcome Americans*, 155–57, 170–73.
20 Brown, *Life of William J. Brown*, 46.
21 For a more in-depth analysis on pew-selling and the crossing over of social class into Providence worship life, see Schantz, *Piety in Providence*, especially his reproduction of a diagram of pew prices in the Richmond Street Baptist Church on page 130.
22 *Providence Gazette*, July 3, 1810.
23 Allen, "The Federal Ascendancy of 1812."
24 Malone, *Between Freedom and Bondage*, 118; *Providence Patriot, and Columbian Phoenix*, March 23, 1811.
25 *Providence Patriot, and Columbian Phoenix*, February 16, 23, 1811. The text of the act was published as an appendix to Frieze, *A Concise History of the Efforts to Obtain an Extension of Suffrage*, 145–46. Maxey, "Suffrage Extension in Rhode Island Down to 1842," 562–63.
26 *Journal of the House of Representatives of Rhode Island; Journal of the Senate*, June 1811 session.
27 "A List of Names of 'Colored' Heads of Families and the Owners of Their Residences, June 24, 1822," Providence Town Papers, series 3, vol. 112, no. 0039155, RIHS; Martin, "Forever and Hereafter a Body Politic," 30.
28 *Providence Patriot, and Columbian Phoenix*, January 9, 1813; Dwight, "Slave Representation, by Boreas."
29 *Rhode Island American*, March 15, 1811. See also Ignatiev, *How the Irish Became White*, 34–46, for a discussion on how Irish immigrants and Black Americans were often seen by elite whites as one in the same and seldom fought until pitted against each other by political and social authorities.

30 Harris, *In the Shadow of Slavery*, 89–92.
31 *Providence Patriot, and Columbian Phoenix*, January 9, 1813.
32 See Sinha, *The Slave's Cause*, 182–83, for an overview of partisan politics and antislavery in the early years of the nineteenth century.
33 *Rhode Island American*, November 2, 9, 1810; November 26, 1811.
34 *Providence Patriot, and Columbian Phoenix*, March 23, 1811; Rogers, *The Biographical Cyclopedia of Representative Men of Rhode Island*, 182.
35 *Providence Patriot, and Columbian Phoenix*, February 12, October 8, 1814; "Minutes of the Meetings of the Committee of Defence."
36 *Providence Patriot, and Columbian Phoenix*, April 12, 1817; Allen, "The Federal Ascendancy of 1812," 394.
37 *Providence Patriot, and Columbian Phoenix*, May 17, 1817. The *Providence Journal*, November 22, 1842, identified the voter as Primus Bailey.
38 *Rhode Island American*, November 3, 1818; *Providence Patriot, and Columbian Phoenix*, February 24, 27, November 3, 1819. See also Stark, "Universal Suffrage, the 'Stand-up Law,' and the Wallingford Election Controversy," for Connecticut's suffrage movement, which disfranchised African American voters by successfully having "white" inserted into the state's voting requirements in May 1818.
39 Richards, *The Slave Power*, 49–53.
40 *Rhode Island American*, January 11, 1820, written under Evarts's pseudonym, "William Penn"; *Rhode Island American*, December 15, 1820, in an article summarizing and agreeing with Federalist congressman John Sergeant from Pennsylvania's speech on the House floor on December 7.
41 *Rhode Island American*, May 30, 1820. See also Forbes, *The Missouri Compromise and Its Aftermath*, 98–99, for Randolph's use of "doughface," and the rest of the book for a detailed account of the debates surrounding the Missouri Compromise.
42 *Rhode Island American*, May 2, 1815; August 14, 1818.
43 *Rhode Island American*, July 9, 13, 1819; December 29, 1820.
44 *Providence Patriot, and Columbian Phoenix*, July 29, August 26, 1820.
45 The *Providence Patriot, and Columbian Phoenix* printed Burrill's speech—in a rare instance of the paper's printing a Federalist's speech—on February 9, 1820.
46 I say "again" because I, like many contemporaries and historians, view the Constitutional Convention's compromises with proslavery delegates, namely the "three-fifths compromise" and the agreement to allow the slave trade to continue for twenty years, as a betrayal to African Americans, who had fought in disproportionately greater numbers and for longer than their white fellow citizens in the Revolutionary War. There were certainly other acts, like the Northwest Ordinance's fugitive slave provision and nominal Black exclusion or bond-posting provisions for the states carved out of the "Old Northwest," but the Missouri question so forcefully pushed the country to discuss race, slavery, and citizenship that I feel comfortable with the claim that this was the first major conversation about these ideas since the Constitutional Convention. See Sinha, *The Slave's Cause*, 76–78, and Richards, *The Slave Power*, chapters 1–2.
47 *Providence Patriot, and Columbian Phoenix*, August 19, 1820.
48 *Providence Patriot, and Columbian Phoenix*, August 26, December 9, 30, 1820.
49 *Providence Patriot, and Columbian Phoenix*, July 14, 1821. This issue reprinted Lyman's

report in its entirety, along with the brief *Richmond Enquirer* editorial. *Providence Patriot, and Columbian Phoenix*, August 22, 1821.
50 *Providence Patriot, and Columbian Phoenix*, September 29, 1821. See also Melish, *Disowning Slavery*, 171–78, for a more detailed explanation of "bobalition" tropes and broadsides.
51 Malone, *Between Freedom and Bondage*, 40–53; Gosse, *The First Reconstruction*, 357–76.
52 *Rhode Island American*, October 9, 1821.
53 *Providence Patriot, and Columbian Phoenix*, September 1, October 6, December 8, 1821.
54 Conley, *Democracy in Decline*, 195; Malone, *Between Freedom and Bondage*, 119–20.
55 *The Public Laws of the State of Rhode-Island and Providence Plantations . . . in January, 1798*, 114; *The Public Laws of the State of Rhode-Island and Providence Plantations . . . in January, 1822*, 89–90.
56 See Roediger, *Wages of Whiteness*, 56–60, and Horton and Horton, *In Hope of Liberty*, 177–80, especially, for this thesis.
57 Melish, *Disowning Slavery*, 115–20; Malone, *Between Freedom and Bondage*, 122–29; Sweet, *Bodies Politic*, 362–63; Cottrol, *The Afro-Yankees*, 43.

Chapter 3

1 Curry, *The Free Black in Urban America*, 245.
2 See Bartlett, *From Slave to Citizen*, 37; Clark-Pujara, *Dark Work*, 126–30; and Chaput, *The People's Martyr*, 54–56.
3 Jackson, *A Short History of the African Union Meeting and School-House*, 2–4.
4 Sinha, *The Slave's Cause*, 117.
5 See chapter 1 for this event.
6 Brown, *Life of William J. Brown*, 24–26.
7 Sweet, *Bodies Politic*, 348–49.
8 Coughtry et al., *Creative Survival*, 55.
9 Horton and Horton, *In Hope of Liberty*, 125–26; Davis, *A History of Freemasonry among Negroes in America*, 82–84. In two major speeches, one in 1792 and one in 1797, Hall urged the formation of other lodges to serve as mutual benefit organizations. In 1792, he specifically thanked representatives from Providence in the audience and urged them to continue to communicate. He spoke on June 24, 1797, and the Providence lodge was formed one day later; this hardly seems a coincidence. See the full text of the speeches and commentary in Foner and Branham, *Lift Every Voice*, 38–52, and Grimshaw, *Official History of Freemasonry among the Colored People in North America*, 96.
10 Lemons, *Black in a White Church*; King and Wilcox, *Historical Catalogue of the First Baptist Church in Providence*, 45 (George Willis), 53 (Henry Greene), 56 (Warwick Sweetland).
11 For the text of the petition, see "Blacks, African Society of Prov., Abraham Gibbs, Josiah Wicks, et al—for Charter," Rhode Island General Assembly—Petitions Failed/Withdrawn, box 6, no. 3. For a discussion of racial consciousness, see Rael, *Black Identity and Black Protest in the Antebellum North*, and Cornish, "The Title of This Journal," *Colored American*, March 4, 1837, for a deeper discussion about racial identity and signifying titles like "African," "Colored," "Black," etc. For the

disfranchisement of African Americans in Rhode Island and New York, which happened during the same Republican ascendancy in both states and across the country, see Malone, *Between Freedom and Bondage*, chapters 2, 4.

12 Jackson, *A Short History of the African Union Meeting and School-House*, 4.
13 Cottrol, *The Afro-Yankees*, 48–60; Jackson, *A Short History of the African Union Meeting and School-House*, 23–24.
14 For a gendered analysis of Rhode Island's communities of color and the idea of "disorder," see Melish, *Disowning Slavery*, 61–63, and Green, *Memoirs of Elleanor Eldridge*.
15 Jackson, *A Short History of the African Union Meeting and School-House*, 24.
16 See Winch, *Philadelphia's Black Elite*, for an excellent study of Black ministers as leaders of communities. The beginning of Black churches under community leaders Richard Allen, Absalom Jones, and others is a useful comparison to Providence, albeit on a larger scale.
17 *Providence City Directory, 1824*.
18 See Horton and Horton, *In Hope of Liberty*, for the evolution of class in Black communities in the North in general; Winch, *Philadelphia's Black Elite*, for the same in Philadelphia specifically; and Harris, *In the Shadow of Slavery*, for the same in New York City.
19 Gilkeson, *Middle-Class Providence*. Some Black men were able to earn vast wealth and influence—for example, James Forten, who owned and managed a sailmaking factory in Philadelphia and became a community leader, or Paul Cuffe, who had African and Wampanoag ancestry and who owned a fleet of merchant ships, becoming a leading proponent of African colonization.
20 Jackson, *A Short History of the African Union Meeting and School-House*, 5. Pews specifically to be owned by African Americans were also sold to raise money. See also Schantz, *Piety in Providence*, 101–2.
21 For the most comprehensive looks at Nathaniel Paul's career, see Quarles, *Black Abolitionists*, and Blackett, *Building an Anti-Slavery Wall*.
22 Jackson, *A Short History of the African Union Meeting and School-House*, 9.
23 Johnson, "A Brief Historical Sketch of the Congdon Street Baptist Church."
24 Raboteau, *Slave Religion*, 201.
25 See Asher, *Incidents in the Life of the Rev. J. Asher*, and Schantz, *Piety in Providence*, 172–74. Lewis's educational and temperance activism is documented numerous times in *The Liberator* between the years 1835 and 1839.
26 Jackson, *A Short History of the African Union Meeting and School-House*, 4; *Providence City Directory*, 1828, 1836; U.S. Census, 1850
27 Brown, *Life of William J. Brown*, 60–61.
28 Brown, *Life of William J. Brown*, 150; Cottrol, *The Afro-Yankees*, 68.
29 *A List of Persons Assessed in the City Tax, Ordered by the City Council*, 94.
30 King and Wilcox, *Historical Catalogue of the First Baptist Church in Providence*, 56.
31 "A List of Names of 'Colored' Heads of Families and the Owners of Their Residences, June 24, 1822," Providence Town Papers, series 3, vol. 112, no. 0039155.
32 See Bolster, *Black Jacks*, for an in-depth discussion on Black mariners and their places in communities of color throughout the country.
33 *Ships and Shipmasters of Old Providence*, 32–34.

34 Brown, *Life of William J. Brown*, 47–48.
35 Popek, *They "... Fought Bravely, but Were Unfortunate,"* 277, 670–71, 1058.
36 "U.S., Revolutionary War Rolls"; *1798 Direct Tax List A and B for Providence*.
37 Fairclough, *Better Day Coming*, 148–50.
38 *Rhode Island American*, May 2, 1815.
39 Jackson, *A Short History of the African Union Meeting and School-House*, 23–24.
40 Rammelkamp, "The Providence Negro Community," 23.
41 *The Liberator*, May 14, 1836.
42 Coughtry et al., *Creative Survival*, 47.
43 U.S. Census, 1820, 1830; "A List of Names of 'Colored' Heads of Families and the Owners of Their Residences, June 24, 1822."
44 Brown, *Life of William J. Brown*, 221; National Park Service, National Register of Historic Places Continuation Sheet, College Hill Historic District, section 8, 36n113.
45 Hinks, *To Awaken My Afflicted Brethren*, 152.
46 Cottrol, *The Afro-Yankees*, 69; Brown, *Life of William J. Brown*, 48.
47 *Owners and Occupants of the Lots, Houses and Shops in the Town of Providence*; "Blacks, African Society of Prov."
48 *Providence Patriot, and Columbia Phoenix*, May 17, 1820.
49 Brown, *Life of William J. Brown*, 50.
50 "Blacks, African Society of Prov."
51 Schantz, *Piety in Providence*, 79. Schantz does a masterful job outlining the connections between class development and religion among white Rhode Islanders, but at a few points conflates white class development with the Black community, putting African Americans at large into the white working class.
52 Schantz, *Piety in Providence*, 3.
53 Cathcart, *The Baptist Encyclopaedia*, 589–90; Sinha, *The Slave's Cause*, 109; Jackson, *A Short History of the African Union Meeting and School-House*, 23–25. George Benson's daughter Helen would marry Garrison.
54 Melish, *Disowning Slavery*, 61.
55 Stockwell, *A History of Public Education in Rhode Island*, 19–24. The "Act to Establish Free Schools" is reprinted on page 19 and the provision for religious education by Providence's school department is reprinted on page 22. See also Sweet, *Bodies Politic*, 363, and Jones, *A Dreadful Deceit*, 101.
56 Coughtry et al., *Creative Survival*, 61.
57 Cottrol, *The Afro-Yankees*, 50.
58 Brown, *Life of William J. Brown*, 73–80.
59 "Blacks, African Society of Prov."
60 Brown, *Life of William J. Brown*, 48–49, 88–89; Jackson, *A Short History of the African Union Meeting and School-House*, 6–7; Curry, *The Free Black in Urban America*, 244–45.

Chapter 4

1 *Providence Journal*, January 29, 1830; Brown, *Life of William J. Brown*, 89–90; *Hard-Scrabble Calendar*, 23
2 *Providence Journal*, January 29, 1830.

3 Nathaniel G. Metcalf, the lone man who was seen razing Hall's home, was one of the "laborers" tried for tearing down the home of Henry T. Wheeler, another Black homeowner, the night of October 18. He appears only in the federal censuses of 1850 and 1860, and in each was boarding in the home of someone else.
4 For some of the clearest expositions of this, see Roediger, *Wages of Whiteness*; Wilentz, *Chants Democratic*; Montgomery, *Citizen Worker*; and Horton and Horton, *In Hope of Liberty*, chapters 5–7
5 Sweet, *Bodies Politic*, 358; Coleman, *The Transformation of Rhode Island*, 264–65.
6 Melish, *Disowning Slavery*, 124–34, 204–5; Brown, *Life of William J. Brown*, 32–35, 88–90.
7 *Providence Patriot, and Columbian Phoenix*, September 11, 1824.
8 Conley, *Democracy in Decline*, 184–213. The votes from the October 11, 1824, referendum are tallied by town on page 212.
9 *Providence Patriot, and Columbian Phoenix*, December 30, 1820; July 27, 1822. See chapter 3 for Providence's census of Black household heads.
10 *Rhode Island American*, March 21, 1823; February 6, 1824.
11 Sweet, *Bodies Politic*, 353–54.
12 *Hard-Scrabble Calendar*, 3.
13 Brown, *Life of William J. Brown*, 126–27; *Providence City Directory*, 1824, 12.
14 Ten men were charged, but only four reached the trial stage.
15 *Hard-Scrabble Calendar*, 12, 23.
16 *Hard-Scrabble Calendar*, 15–16; Sweet *Bodies Politic*, 383–87.
17 *Providence City Directory*, 1824, 1826, 1830, 1832.
18 This perhaps proves the point argued in Richards, *Gentlemen of Property and Standing*, in which the author claims that, despite contemporary accounts and previous historical scholarship regarding these mobs which asserted that they were undertaken by propertyless or poor whites, the riots were mostly either led or undertaken by those considered "middle class" or elite at the time.
19 *Hard-Scrabble Calendar*, 19–21. See also Ratcliffe, *The One Party Presidential Ticket*, chapter 8, for the racial dimension of the election, and Smith, *Dominion of Voice*, 56–57. Smith posits that much antebellum rioting in the North was seen by authorities as poor and artisan white men venting "their hostility to the norm of humble submission to social superiors," something that paralleled the rise of Andrew Jackson to prominence in the political discourse. Her analysis is apt when it comes to this riot, as it was both an attack on the Black community and outside the bounds of the law, and thus can be read as an assertion by poor whites lashing out at both of their perceived enemies—African Americans and elites—at the same time.
20 *Hard-Scrabble Calendar*, 21, 24–25, 30–32.
21 *Providence City Directory*, 1824, 65.
22 Rogers, *The Biographical Cyclopedia of Representative Men of Rhode Island*, 236–37; Bouseman, "The Meaning of the Right of Petition," 166; *The Liberator*, January 21, 1842.
23 *Providence Patriot, and Columbian Phoenix*, January 22, 1820.
24 Power-Greene, *Against the Wind and Tide*, 3–4.
25 *The Religious Intelligencer for the Year Ending May 1826*, 342–43; Wilkeson, *A Concise History of the American Colonies in Liberia*, 21–22.

26 *Providence Patriot, and Columbian Phoenix*, June 14, 1826 (reprint of the *Newport Mercury*). See also Power-Greene, *Against the Wind and Tide*, and Sinha, *The Slave's Cause*, chapter 6.
27 I have been unable to find origins for many of those in the ship's and colony's manifest, notably the Chavers and Clark families, so the possibility exists that there were people from Providence. The list of passengers (cited below) includes information that all were from Rhode Island but nothing more specific than that.
28 The rumor of Hall's emigration appears to have been started by William J. Brown in *Life of William J. Brown*, 90, and has been reproduced by other historians. See *Information Relative to the Operations of the United States Squadron*, for the full passenger list, where Hall does not appear.
29 Pope, "Our Segregated Brethren, Prince Hall Masons," 17; "The Constitution of Harmony Lodge No. 1 in Providence"; *Rhode Island American*, February 7, 1832; *Providence City Directory*, 1831, 1836, 1841, 1854; U.S. Census, 1860.
30 *Petition and Act of the Providence African Society for Mutual Relief*, with the attached constitution for the society, "Formed and subscribed to on the 2d of January, 1828."
31 Roediger, *Wages of Whiteness*, 55–58; Conley, *Democracy in Decline*, 218–21.
32 Price and Stewart, *To Heal the Scourge of Prejudice*, 8–9; Sinha, *The Slave's Cause*, 201.
33 *Providence Journal*, December 2, 1829.
34 Price and Brewer, *To Heal the Scourge of Prejudice*, 10–24; Rael, *Black Identity and Black Protest in the Antebellum North*, 242–47. See also Minutes of the National Conventions of People of Color.
35 Price and Brewer, *To Heal the Scourge of Prejudice*, 50; the address is published on pages 49–62. For more on his later activism, including a close analysis of his *Treatise*, see Rusert, *Fugitive Science*, chapter 2.
36 Price and Brewer, *To Heal the Scourge of Prejudice*, 54.
37 Rael, *Black Identity and Black Protest in the Antebellum North*, 130–33.
38 Price and Brewer, *To Heal the Scourge of Prejudice*, 54–62.
39 Price and Brewer, *To Heal the Scourge of Prejudice*, 54–62.
40 Price and Brewer, *To Heal the Scourge of Prejudice*, 59.
41 Rael, *Black Identity and Black Protest in the Antebellum North*, 283.
42 Sweet, *Bodies Politic*, 296–97.
43 Stockwell, *A History of Public Education in Rhode Island*, 163–69; Stachiw, *The Old Brick Schoolhouse*, 26.
44 Conley, *Democracy in Decline*, 221–23.
45 Luther, *An Address on the Right of Free Suffrage*. The petition mentioned here was appended to publication of the *Address*; Providence assemblymen agreed to propose different voting prerequisites in local elections, but those freemen later reneged; see Conley, *Democracy in Decline*, 224.
46 Rogers, *The Biographical Cyclopedia of Representative Men of Rhode Island*, 176–77.
47 Benjamin Hazard, *Report of the Committee on the Subject of an Extension of the Suffrage*, in Chaput, DeSimone, and Landry, "The Dorr Rebellion Project."
48 Hazard, *Report of the Committee*, 19–20; Pole, "Suffrage and Representation in Maryland," 218; Wang, "Make Every Slave Free," 119; Ratcliffe, "The Right to Vote and the Rise of Democracy," 231.

49 Hazard, *Report on the Committee*, 20–22.
50 Curtis, "Reconsidering Suffrage Reform in the 1829–1830 Virginia Constitutional Convention."
51 Coleman, *The Transformation of Rhode Island*, 112–15; Conley, *Democracy in Decline*, 230–34.
52 Here, they may either be specifically referring to liquor, which they were barred from being licensed to sell by statute, or a de facto prohibition on being licensed to sell other things because license-granting for "keeping taverns, ale-houses, victualling-houses, cook-shops, oyster-houses, or oyster-cellars" was the sole responsibility of each respective town council. See *The Public Laws of the State of Rhode-Island and Providence Plantations . . . in January, 1822*, 295, 297.
53 *Rhode Island American*, October 30, 1829.
54 *Rhode Island American*, June 7, 1830.
55 *Rhode Island American*, June 7, October 15, 26, 1830; *Providence Journal*, September 28, 1830.
56 Alfred Niger et al., "Petition for Relief against Taxes," Rhode Island General Assembly—Petitions Failed/Withdrawn, no. 435.
57 Sweet, *Bodies Politic*, 329.
58 See chapter 2.
59 Hinks, *To Awaken My Afflicted Brethren*, 116–20.
60 Niger et al., "Petition for Relief against Taxes."
61 *Providence Journal*, January 29, 1831.
62 *The Liberator*, January 29, 1831.
63 *History of the Providence Riots*, 18.
64 *Providence Patriot, and Columbian Phoenix*, April 13, 1830; April 20, 23, 1831.
65 Curry, *The Free Black in Urban America*, 244–46.
66 Howe, *The Political Culture of the American Whigs*, 134–35.
67 *Providence Journal*, February 12, July 28, August 10, September 25, 1830.
68 *Rhode Island American*, July 27, September 28, 1830; April 22, 1831; Lancaster, "Encouraging Faithful Domestic Servants," 79–80.
69 *Providence Patriot, and Columbian Phoenix*, January 19, 1831; Lancaster, "Encouraging Faithful Domestic Servants," 72, 75; Jones, *A Dreadful Deceit*, chapter 3; Green, *Memoirs of Elleanor Eldridge*.
70 *Providence Journal*, January 5, 1830.
71 *Rhode Island American*, August 28, 1829; Taylor, *Frontiers of Freedom*, 32–34, 63–64.
72 *Providence Journal*, October 1, 1830; D'Amato, *Warwick*, 76.
73 *Providence Patriot, and Columbian Phoenix*, February 17, 1830; Schantz, *Piety in Providence*, 40.
74 *Providence Patriot, and Columbian Phoenix*, April 30, 1831.
75 Roediger, *Wages of Whiteness*, 70; Wilentz, *Chants Democratic*, 175.
76 *Freedom's Journal*, March 16, 1827; Sinha, *The Slave's Cause*, 203–5.
77 Easton's advertisement appeared throughout the winter of 1829–1830 in the *Providence Journal*; Hinks, *To Awaken My Afflicted Brethren*, 152.
78 See Peter Wood, "Nat Turner: The Unknown Slave as Visionary Leader," in Litwack and Meier, *Black Leaders of the Nineteenth Century*, 21–40, for a broad description of Nat Turner's rebellion.

79 Sinha, *The Slave's Cause*, 210–14; Williams, *Capitalism and Slavery*, 181–84.
80 See Richards, *Gentlemen of Property and Standing*, for an exposition of the violence in the 1830s.
81 Brown, *Life of William J. Brown*, 93–96.
82 Sullivan, "Reconstructing the Olney's Lane Riot," 52–53; Brown, *Life of William J. Brown*, 90.
83 Johnson, Deposition; Sullivan, "Reconstructing the Olney's Lane Riot," 55–56; *Rhode Island American*, September 23, 1831.
84 Johnson, Deposition; *History of the Providence Riots*, 8–9.
85 *History of the Providence Riots*, 10–19.
86 *History of the Providence Riots*, 10–19; *Providence Patriot, and Columbian Phoenix*, September 28, 1831; "Providence Directory," in *The Rhode Island Register and United States Calendar for the Year of Our Lord Christ 1826* (Providence, RI: Carlile and Brown, 1826). One white man who died was a mariner, and the other wounded man was listed simply as "Mr. Davis," so it is impossible to know his occupation.
87 *City Charter*, section 3; Sweet, *Bodies Politic*, 395.
88 See Sinha, *The Slave's Cause*, introduction, and especially 160–61.

Chapter 5

1 Brown, *Life of William J. Brown*, 150; *Providence Journal*, January 21, 1858.
2 Sinha, *The Slave's Cause*, 213–20; Rockman, *Scraping By*, 231–32; *The Liberator*, January 8, 29, March 4, 1831.
3 Rappleye, *Sons of Providence*, 296, 314; Sinha, *The Slave's Cause*, 109; Van Broekhoven, *The Devotion of These Women*, 21–22; *The Liberator*, April 16, 1831.
4 *The Liberator*, November 5, 1831.
5 "Constitution of the American Society of Free Persons of Colour, for Improving Their Condition in the United States; for Purchasing Lands; and for the Establishment of a Settlement in Upper Canada" (Philadelphia: J. W. Allen, 1831), Colored Conventions Project Digital Records, https://omeka.coloredconventions.org. While African colonization was rejected firmly, the delegates did agree to propose funding for a community in Upper Canada; see "Minutes and Proceedings of the First Annual Convention of the People of Colour, Held by Adjournments in the City of Philadelphia, from the Sixth to the Eleventh of June, Inclusive, 1831" (Philadelphia: Committee on Arrangements, 1831), Colored Conventions Project Digital Records.
6 *The Liberator*, November 5, 1831.
7 See Welburn, *Hartford's Ann Plato and the Native Borders of Identity*, for Native, Black, and white intermarriage and family in the Missinnuok region (Connecticut, Rhode Island, and Long Island); Brilvitch, *A History of Connecticut's Golden Hill Paugussett Tribe*, for an example of Bridgeport's majority-Black neighborhood growing up in and around a Native community; and Barsh, "'Colored' Seamen in the New England Whaling Industry," for coastal New England communities of color that were heavily populated by people of African and Native ancestry.
8 Sinha, *The Slave's Cause*, 378.

9 *The Liberator*, November 5, 1831.
10 Popek, *They ". . . Fought Bravely, but Were Unfortunate*," 486; MacGunnigle, "Ichabod Northup," 124–27.
11 *The Liberator*, November 5, 1831.
12 *Rhode Island American*, October 22, 1831; February 3, May 23, June 1, 8, 1832.
13 *Rhode Island American*, May 23, June 11, 1832.
14 *The Liberator*, July 21, 1832.
15 Sinha, *The Slave's Cause*, 204; Van Broekhoven, *The Devotion of These Women*, 17–18, 272; *The Liberator*, July 14, 1832; Elizabeth Brewer, Providence, RI, to William Lloyd Garrison and Isaac Knapp, February 6, 1833, Digitized Anti-Slavery Collection.
16 *The Liberator*, September 22, 1832.
17 *The Liberator*, September 22, 1832; June 1, 1833; Jones, *All Bound Up Together*, 23–24.
18 *The Liberator*, September 22, 1832.
19 Schantz, *Piety in Providence*, 149; Gilkeson, *Middle-Class Providence*, 26–28.
20 *The Liberator*, October 13, 1832.
21 Chace, *Anti-Slavery Reminiscences*, 6–7; Sinha, *The Slave's Cause*, 181, 209, 222–23, 229; *The Liberator*, September 8, 22, October 27, 1832.
22 Brown, *Life of William J. Brown*, 122; *The Liberator*, October 27, 1832.
23 Brown, *Life of William J. Brown*, 128–29.
24 Brown, *Life of William J. Brown*, 157, 170–73; *The Liberator*, October 27, 1832.
25 *The Liberator*, November 17, 1832; March 9, 16, May 18, June 1, 1833.
26 *The Report and Proceedings of the First Annual Meeting of the Providence Anti-Slavery Society*, 1, 5–7, 12.
27 Hoffmann and Hoffman, *North by South*, 89–92; Van Broekhoven, *The Devotion of These Women*, 18–21.
28 *The Emancipator*, July 27, 1833. For discussions on "slave votes" or "slave seats," both historical and contemporary, see Balinski and Young, *Fair Representation*, 29–35, and Richards, *The Slave Power*, chapters 4–6.
29 *The Emancipator*, July 27, 1833.
30 *The Emancipator*, November 30, 1833; Sinha, *The Slave's Cause*, 172–73, 225; *The Report and Proceedings of the First Annual Meeting of the Providence Anti-Slavery Society*, 12; Bourne, "Rev. George Bourne, the Pioneer of American Antislavery," 84
31 *The Liberator*, December 28, 1833; Pryor, *Colored Travelers*, 2.
32 *The Emancipator*, March 11, 1834.
33 Richards, *Gentlemen of Property and Standing*, 25–30; Sinha, *The Slave's Cause*, 232–33.
34 The *Providence Patriot, and Columbian Phoenix* contained pro-suffrage articles in almost every issue between April 1833 and March 1834, while the *Providence Journal* did not dedicate much space to colonization.
35 *The Emancipator*, January 4 (reprint from *Zion's Herald*), June 14, 1838 (reprint from *Boston Times*).
36 *The Liberator*, March 22, 1834.
37 This was most likely James Scott, the white Quaker from North Providence who had married into the abolitionist Sisson family, as the letter was addressed from that town. There was also a Black James Scott, listed as a barber on North Main

Street in the city directory of 1836, but it is unlikely that this was written by him because of the former's attachment to organized abolitionism, and the lack of proof of the latter's involvement. See *Collections of the Rhode Island Historical Society*, 636, and Dyer, "The Old Schools of Providence."
38 *The Emancipator*, August 12, 1834.
39 *The Liberator*, June 28, December 6, 1834; January 10, April 25, May 23, June 27, December 19, 26, 1835; *The Emancipator*, December 1, 1836.
40 *The Liberator*, June 13, July 11, 1835; Sinha, *The Slave's Cause*, 202–3, 300–5; Foner, *Gateway to Freedom*, 208.
41 "Minutes of the Fifth Annual Convention for the Improvement of the Free People of Colour in the United States; Held by Adjournments, in the Wesley Church, Philadelphia; from the First to the Fifth of June, Inclusive; 1835" (Philadelphia: William P. Gibbons, 1835), Colored Conventions Project Digital Records. For more on Augustus Price, see Rogers and Sneed, "The Missing Chapter in the Life of Thomas Day."
42 *The Liberator*, December 26, 1835; April 2, May 7, July 30, September 3, 1836; Brown, *Life of William J. Brown*, 135; Sherer, "Negro Churches in Rhode Island before 1860," 20–21; Chaput and DeSimone, "The End of School Segregation in Rhode Island."
43 Stachiw, *The Old Brick Schoolhouse*, 26–29; *Colored American*, September 9, 1837.
44 Edward Martin Stone, "A Concise History of the Rise and Progress of the Public Schools in the City of Providence," in Stockwell, *A History of Public Education in Rhode Island*, 177–86; *Republican Herald*, May 16, 1838.
45 *The Liberator*, May 7, 1836; Brown, *Life of William J. Brown*, 139; *Acts and Resolves Passed by the General Assembly of the State of Rhode-Island and Providence Plantations*; Grover, *The Fugitive's Gibraltar*, 88, 112, 132, 134, 137, 144; Gura, *The Life of William Apess, Pequot*, chapter 5.
46 *The Liberator*, August 20, 1836.
47 *The Liberator*, October 29, 1836.
48 *The Liberator*, September 29, 1837; September 14, 1838.
49 *The Liberator*, July 28, 1837; Sinha, *The Slave's Cause*, 231; *Herald of Freedom*, June 3, 24, July 1, 15, 22, 1837.
50 *The Liberator*, November 9, 1838; September 6, 1839.
51 See Roediger, *Wages of Whiteness*, 66–68, for a discussion on the complications of "white slavery" or "wage slavery"; Van Broekhoven, *The Devotion of These Women*, 92–102. Stanton was part of the group that walked out of Lane Seminary in Cincinnati amid its administration's attempt to shut down debates over slavery. See Sinha, *The Slave's Cause*, 241–42.
52 Record Book, Kent County Female Anti-Slavery Society.
53 *Proceedings of the Rhode-Island Anti-Slavery Convention*.
54 "Anniversary of the Rhode-Island Anti-Slavery Society," *The Liberator*, November 19, 1836.
55 *The Liberator*, October 18, 1839.
56 *The Liberator, October 18, 1839*; *Providence City Directory*, 1836–1837; Mills, *Cutting across the Color Line*, 42–43; Horton and Horton, *In Hope of Liberty*, 116–17.
57 *Colored American*, November 25, 1837; Sinha, *The Slave's Cause*, 217–18, 238, 342, 346–47; Quarles, *Black Abolitionists*, 26, 132–34. See also Brownlee, "Out of Abundance of the Heart."

58 *The Emancipator*, November 16, 1837; *The Liberator*, November 17, 1837; *Colored American*, November 25, 1837.
59 Pryor, *Colored Travelers*, 59–60.
60 Foner, *Gateway to Freedom*, 63; *The Emancipator*, August 16, November 8, 1838; *The Liberator*, May 24, 1839.
61 Pryor, *Colored Travelers*, 76–78; *The Emancipator*, August 23, 1838; *The Liberator*, March 29, 1839.

Chapter 6

1 *The Liberator*, November 17, 1837; Sinha, *The Slave's Cause*, 222–23.
2 For the definitive scholarly biography on Dorr and the suffrage movement he came to lead, see Chaput, *The People's Martyr*, and for more dated accounts that downplay the influence of Providence's Black community but investigate the radicalism through the lens of the white class structure, see Gettleman, *The Dorr Rebellion*, and Dennison, *The Dorr War*.
3 Mowry, *The Dorr War*, 3.
4 Gettleman, *The Dorr Rebellion*, xx–xxii; Dennison, *The Dorr War*, 6–7.
5 Chaput, *The People's Martyr*.
6 Howe, *The Political Culture of the American Whigs*, 17–18; Litwack, *North of Slavery*, 86–88.
7 Gettleman and Conlon, "Responses to the Rhode Island Workingmen's Reform Agitation of 1833"; Conley, *Democracy in Decline*, 236–39; Roediger, *Wages of Whiteness*, 55, 87; *Providence Patriot, and Columbian Phoenix*, April 27, June 22, 1833; Luther, *An Address on the Right of Free Suffrage*.
8 Schantz, *Piety in Providence*, 110–11; *Providence Patriot, and Columbian Phoenix*, October 12, 1833.
9 Conley, *Democracy in Decline*, 252–68; Chaput, *The People's Martyr*, 32; *Providence Patriot, and Columbian Phoenix*, July 6, 20, September 7, 21, 28, November 9, 1833; February 15, March 8, 1834. Dorr's address is printed in Burke, *Interference of the Executive in the Affairs of Rhode Island*, 151–85.
10 *The Liberator*, July 2, 1836; Chaput, *The People's Martyr*, 34; Mowry, *The Dorr War*, 148; Rogers, *The Biographical Cyclopedia of Representative Men of Rhode Island*, 214–15.
11 Malone, *Between Freedom and Bondage*, 147, 165; Sinha, *The Slave's Cause*, 251–52; Earle, *Jacksonian Anti-Slavery and the Politics of Free Soil*, 8; Miiler, *Arguing about Slavery*, 375–77; Van Deburg, "Henry Clay, the Right of Petition, and Slavery in the Nation's Capital," 132–33.
12 *Colored American*, March 4, March 11, April 29, 1837; Litwack, *North of Slavery*, 114; Sinha, *The Slave's Cause*, 318; Moses, *Alexander Crummell*, 40–41.
13 *Colored American*, March 4, March 11, April 29, 1837; Litwack, *North of Slavery*, 114; Sinha, *The Slave's Cause*, 318; Moses, *Alexander Crummell*, 40–41.
14 Malone, *Between Freedom and Bondage*, 90–99; Fox, *Opinion of the Honorable John Fox*; Litwack, *North of Slavery*, 85–86; *Providence Journal*, July 13, 1837; Gosse, *The First Reconstruction*, 126–41.

15 Yates, *Rights of Colored Men to Suffrage, Citizenship and Trial by Jury*, 3–75, especially 36–37; *Colored American*, January 22, March 22, 1838; Jones, *Birthright Citizens*, 1–11; Quarles, *Black Abolitionists*, 51–52.
16 Purvis et al., *Appeal of Forty Thousand Citizens Threatened with Disfranchisement*; *Colored American*, March 29, 1838.
17 *The Emancipator*, January 3, February 7, 1839; Conley, *Democracy in Decline*, 291; Van Broekhoven, *The Devotion of These Women*, 154–58.
18 *The Emancipator*, February 7, August 29, 1839; *The Liberator*, August 19, 23, 1839; *Colored American*, July 13, 1839; Gettleman, *The Dorr Rebellion*, 34–37; Chaput, *The People's Martyr*, 43, 45–46; Conley, *Democracy in Decline*, 284.
19 Conley, *Democracy in Decline*, 293; Roediger, *Wages of Whiteness*, 77–80; Ignatiev, *How the Irish Became White*, 76–82.
20 *Colored American*, October 27, 1838; December 26, 1840; *National Anti-Slavery Standard*, December 24, 1840; Sinha, *The Slave's Cause*, 263.
21 *The Liberator*, March 27, April 3, May 22, June 5, August 21, 1840.
22 *Providence Journal*, January 15, February 8, 1840; Melish, *Disowning Slavery*, 3.
23 *Providence Journal*, February 8, 1840.
24 Conley, *Democracy in Decline*, 298; Rogers, *The Biographical Cyclopedia of Representative Men of Rhode Island*, 219; Chaput, *The People's Martyr*, 47–50; *The Emancipator*, November 12, 1840.
25 *New Age*, November 20, 1840.
26 Conley, *Democracy in Decline*, 299. For some of the few articles that showed abolition in a positive light, see *New Age*, January 22, 1841, for a reprint from the *Friend of Massachusetts* that compared the abolitionist cause favorably to the "political emancipation" of Rhode Island as a whole, and February 5, 1841, for an editorial written by an abolitionist, likely a Black man, who vowed support for suffrage for white and Black men.
27 *Providence Journal*, February 8, 1841; *New Age*, February 12, 19, 1841.
28 *New Age*, February 26, March 5, 19, 26, 1841; Conley, *Democracy in Decline*, 302.
29 Although this editorial is uncredited, Ray most likely authored it, as he had taken over editorship when Cornish left the paper in 1839. See Sinha, *The Slave's Cause*, 304–5, and Penn, *The Afro-American Press and Its Editors*, 32–47.
30 *Colored American*, March 27, 1841.
31 Gettleman, *The Dorr Rebellion*, 39–41; Chaput, *The People's Martyr*, 53; *New Age*, April 15, 23, 30, May 7, 1841.
32 Potter, *Considerations on the Questions of the Adoption of a Constitution*, 15–16.
33 Hazard et al., "Petition That Their Property May Be Taxed."
34 Hazard et al., "Petition That Their Property May Be Taxed"; *Providence City Directory*, 1836, 1841; Brown, *Life of William J. Brown*, 54, 86; Robinson, *Proceedings of the Free African Union Society*, 150.
35 Christ Church Records; "A List of Names of 'Colored' Heads of Families and the Owners of Their Residences," June 24, 1822, Providence Town Papers, series 3, vol. 112, no. 0039155. For the import of draymen, or cartmen, to nineteenth-century cities, see Hodges, *New York City Cartmen*, 3–5, and *Providence City Directory*, 1841.
36 U.S. Census, 1820, 1830, 1840. For Rosanna Jones's real estate accumulation, see *A List of Persons Assessed in the City Tax of $90,170.58*, 41; *List of Persons Assessed in the*

City Tax of $178,612.65, 53; and *Providence Patriot, and Columbian Phoenix*, September 28, 1831.

37 For this and the next two paragraphs, see *Providence Journal*, June 25, 1841, and Sirgo, "Samuel Ames."

38 *New Age*, May 14, 21, 28, June 14, 18, 25, July 2, 9, 16, 23, 30, August 6, 1841; Rogers, *Cyclopedia of Representative Men of Rhode Island*, 133–34; Brown, *Life of William J. Brown*, 171–72.

39 *New Age*, August 13, 1841.

40 *New Age*, August 20, 27, 1841.

41 *Providence Journal*, August 30, 1841.

42 *Providence Journal*, September 15, 17, 1841.

43 *Providence Journal*, September 17, 1841.

44 *Providence Journal*, September 18, 1841; *New Age*, September 3, 17, 24, 1841.

45 *Providence Journal*, September 27, 1841; *New Age*, October 1, 1841. Mosher's "interest" may have included a young woman of color, possibly a servant, living in the Mosher household in 1830 and 1840. He may have also seen Black people in the Sixth Ward as a potential allied voting bloc. See U.S. Census, 1830, 1840, 1850.

46 *National Anti-Slavery Standard*, September 30, 1841.

47 *Providence Journal*, September 30, 1841.

Chapter 7

1 MacGunnigle, "Ichabod Northup," 116–28; Chambers, "'Neither Justice nor Mercy,'" 433.

2 Lemons and McKenna, "Re-Enfranchisement of Rhode Island Negroes," 12. This is the main piece of scholarship that centers Black Rhode Islanders' winning back the right to vote, but it does not dive deeply into the activism of Black leaders. This accurately sums up the way re-enfranchisement is described in Gettleman, *The Dorr Rebellion*, and Dennison, *The Dorr War*. Chaput, *The People's Martyr*, more accurately describes the importance of race and Black activism in re-enfranchisement.

3 Horton, *The Tide Taken at the Flood*, 38. See also Chaput and DeSimone, "Strange Bedfellows," for an analysis that provides more details about Black leaders' rejection of the Suffrage Association than the rapprochement between Black leaders and white elites.

4 *Providence Journal*, October 8, 9, 1841. See also Gettleman, *The Dorr Rebellion*, 46–47.

5 *New Age*, October 22, 1841.

6 The full text of the petition is in Burke, *Interference of the Executive in the Affairs of Rhode Island*, 111–13.

7 *Providence Journal*, October 11, 1841; *New Age*, October 22, 1841; *The Liberator*, October 29, 1841. Each article that described the debate had some of the same elements, but each also slanted it toward its mission. The *New Age* gave much more ink to those opposed to Black suffrage and trumpeted Dorr's courageousness in bowing to the majority, the *Journal* played up those who supported Black suffrage and dwelled more on their pointing out the convention's inconsistencies, and the *Liberator* gave

more time to Arnold's and Dorr's speeches, both having been RIASS members. The retelling above was done with information gleaned from all three articles. The proposed People's Constitution was published in the *New Age,* October 15, 1841.
8. *Providence Journal,* October 11, 12, November 3, 1841; *New Age,* October 22, 29, 1841; *Colored American,* October 30, 1841.
9. *National Anti-Slavery Standard,* October 21, November 4, 1841; *The Liberator,* October 29, 1841; *Colored American,* October 30, 1841. See Sterling, *Ahead of Her Time,* for more on Kelley's life and activism.
10. *Memorial of Colored Citizens.*
11. *Providence City Directory,* 1841; U.S. Census, 1850, 1860; Brown, *Life of William J. Brown,* 54–55.
12. The "Perry" referred to was Oliver Hazard Perry, Rhode Islander and naval officer regarded as a hero in the War of 1812's Battle of Lake Erie, in which African Americans played a prominent role, suffering severe casualties in the victory over the British.
13. *Memorial of Colored Citizens.*
14. *Providence Journal,* November 13, 1841; Chaput, *The People's Martyr,* 63–64.
15. *The Liberator,* November 19, 1841; *New Age,* November 12, 19, 1841; *Providence Journal,* November 13, 14, 1841; *National Anti-Slavery Standard,* November 25, 1841. The Report of the RIASS meeting in November was published in *National Anti-Slavery Standard,* December 23, 1841. Burke, *Interference of the Executive in the Affairs of Rhode Island,* 114–15; Chaput, *The People's Martyr,* 66–68; Sinha, *The Slave's Cause,* 122, 208, 316.
16. *New Age,* November 19, December 3, 1841; Burke, *Interference of the Executive in the Affairs of Rhode Island,* 279; Chaput, *The People's Martyr,* 73.
17. *New Age,* December 10, 1841; Douglass, *Life and Times of Frederick Douglass,* 272–73.
18. *National Anti-Slavery Standard,* December 30, 1841; January 13, 1842; *The Liberator,* December 24, 1841; January 14, 21, 1842; *The Emancipator,* December 16, 1841; Sterling, *Ahead of Her Time,* 140–43; Chaput, *The People's Martyr,* 74–76.
19. Douglass, *Life and Times of Frederick Douglass,* 274; Sterling, *Ahead of Her Time,* 142; *The Emancipator,* December 31, 1841; *The Liberator,* January 14, 1842; Chaput, *The People's Martyr,* 70, 165.
20. Gettleman, *The Dorr Rebellion,* 54–55.
21. *Providence Journal,* February 4, 22, March 11, 19, 1842; *The Liberator,* March 18, 1842; Burke, *Interference of the Executive in the Affairs of Rhode Island,* 103–4; Gettleman, *The Dorr Rebellion,* 78–79.
22. Gettleman, *The Dorr Rebellion,* 63–95; Dennison, *The Dorr War,* 32–33.
23. Gettleman, *The Dorr Rebellion,* 95–97; Chaput, *The People's Martyr,* 88–92.
24. Chaput, *The People's Martyr,* 119–42; Gettleman, *The Dorr Rebellion,* 119–35.
25. *National Anti-Slavery Standard,* April 21, 1842; Gettleman, *The Dorr Rebellion,* 127–28.
26. Brown, *Life of William J. Brown,* 173.
27. Brown, *Life of William J. Brown,* 173–74; *Providence City Directory,* 1844.
28. Burke, *Interference of the Executive in the Affairs of Rhode Island,* 311, 318–19; *The Emancipator,* July 28, August 11, 1842; Gosse, *The First Reconstruction,* 263–67.

29 Gettleman, *The Dorr Rebellion*, 129; Chaput, *The People's Martyr*, 158–59; *Journal of the Convention Assembled to Frame a Constitution for the State of Rhode Island*, 3–4; Brown, *Life of William J. Brown*, 162–63.
30 *The Liberator*, July 22, August 19, 1842; Chaput, *The People's Martyr*, 159; *The Emancipator*, July 28, 1842.
31 *The Liberator*, July 22, 1841; Goodell, *The Rights and Wrongs of Rhode Island*, 4–6, 80; Sinha, *The Slave's Cause*, 261–62, 352.
32 *The Liberator*, August 19, September 30, October 14, 1842; Green, *Might and Right*, 287, 291–94; Chaput and DeSimone, "Strange Bedfellows."
33 *Providence Journal*, August 24, 26, 1842; Chaput, *The People's Martyr*, 165.
34 *Providence Journal*, September 20, 21, 1842; *The Emancipator*, September 22, 1842.
35 *Journal of the Convention Assembled to Frame a Constitution for the State of Rhode Island*, 29, 36, 45–49.
36 *Journal of the Convention Assembled to Frame a Constitution for the State of Rhode Island*, 67–68.
37 *The Constitution of the State of Rhode-Island and Providence Plantations*.
38 Gettleman, *The Dorr Rebellion*, 146–47; Burke, *Interference of the Executive in the Affairs of Rhode Island*, 762–63.
39 *Providence Journal*, November 22, 1842.
40 Burke, *Interference of the Executive in the Affairs of Rhode Island*, 652; *Providence Journal*, November 24, 1842.
41 *The Liberator*, December 2, 1842; *The Emancipator*, December 8, 1842; *National Anti-Slavery Standard*, December 22, 1842.
42 *Providence Journal*, March 30, 1843.

Epilogue

1 Melish, *Disowning Slavery*, 206. According to Melish, "Strangerhood implied a lack of substantive claim to a residence, any property within it, or a community of such dwellings." Taylor, *Frontiers of Freedom*, chapter 10. Taylor defines the "shadow community" as those forced to turn to unsteadily available or illicit occupations in Cincinnati after being excluded from the expanding industrial order.
2 See Higginbotham, *Righteous Discontent*, chapter 7, and Gates, "The Trope of the New Negro," for some of the original and detailed discussions on image and respectability in the field of African American Studies.
3 See Rael, *Black Identity and Black Protest in the Antebellum North*, chapter 4, and Sinha, *The Slave's Cause*, 131–32, 220–22, for discussions on antebellum notions of respectability and their utility for Black communities.
4 Brown, *Life of William J. Brown*, 157; *National Anti-Slavery Standard*, April 27, 1843; Cottrol, *The Afro-Yankees*, 77–79.
5 Cottrol, *The Afro-Yankees*, 79–84; Howe, *The Political Culture of the American Whigs*, 92–93.
6 *Providence Journal*, November 23, 1844; *The Liberator*, December 13, 1844.
7 *Providence Journal*, November 23, 1844; Howe, *The Political Culture of the American Whigs*, 16.

8 *The Emancipator*, December 29, 1847.
9 *The Liberator*, November 17, 1843; November 28, 1845; October 1, 1847; November 1, 1851; Van Broekhoven, *The Devotion of These Women*, 218–19, 223–24.
10 *Providence Journal*, March 31, 1846.
11 Brown, *Life of William J. Brown*, 157–60; Cottrol, *The Afro-Yankees*, 77–89. The order of events in Brown's retelling are often confusing, and Cottrol tells it in a bit different order than I do. Brown seems to mix up the Liberty Party and Free Soil Party as, while Bibb was involved in Liberty politics, he never made a visit to New England during the two elections when that party formed the main abolitionist opposition. Cottrol seems to interpret Brown as saying this election day ritual was a regular occurrence, but the way Brown tells it, it seems as though, while he certainly had some ongoing connections with Bowen and the Whig Party, this festival was specific to the 1848 election.
12 Brown, *Life of William J. Brown*, 160–63; Sinha, *The Slave's Cause*, 483; Howe, *The Political Culture of the American Whigs*, 204; Cottrol, *The Afro-Yankees*, 88–89. See also Potter, *The Impending Crisis*, chapters 2–3.
13 *Providence Journal*, January 29, 1848.
14 Cottrol, *The Afro-Yankees*, 92–93; Rogers, *The Biographical Cyclopedia of Representative Men of Rhode Island*, 315–16; Holt, *The Rise and Fall of the American Whig Party*, 919–20.
15 *National Era*, May 28, 1857; Cottrol, *The Afro-Yankees*, 93.
16 *New York Times*, October 23, 1857; *Scott v. Sandford*.
17 *Providence Journal*, August 2, 20, 1845; August 3, 1846; April 4, August 2, September 1, 1848; *Will the General Assembly Put Down Caste Schools?* (1857), and *To the Friends of Equal Rights in Rhode Island* (1865), Samuel J. May Anti-Slavery Collection; Chaput and DeSimone, "The End of School Segregation in Rhode Island."
18 Grossman, "George T. Downing and Desegregation of Rhode Island Public Schools"; Cottrol, *The Afro-Yankees*, 97–101; Sinha, *The Slave's Cause*, 326; Edward Martin Stone, "A Concise History of the Rise and Progress of the Public Schools in the City of Providence," in Stockwell, *A History of Public Education in Rhode Island*, 164–68; *Will the General Assembly Put Down Caste Schools?*; *To the Friends of Equal Rights in Rhode Island*; Baumgartner, *In Pursuit of Knowledge*, 165–66, 267n; Chaput and DeSimone, "The End of School Segregation in Rhode Island"; Grzyb, "The Fourteenth Regiment Rhode Island Heavy Artillery (Colored)."
19 Northup, *An Appeal from a Colored Man Whose Father Fought in the Revolution*.

Bibliography

Abbreviations

RIHS   Rhode Island Historical Society, Providence
RISA   Rhode Island State Archives, Providence
SCUA   Special Collections and University Archives, University of Massachusetts Amherst

Newspapers and Periodicals

Colored American (New York)
The Emancipator (New York)
Freedom's Journal (New York)
Herald of Freedom (Concord, NH)
The Liberator (Boston)
Manufacturers' and Farmers' Journal (Providence, RI)
National Anti-Slavery Standard (New York)
National Era (Washington, DC)
New Age and Constitutional Advocate (Providence, RI)
New York Times
Newport [RI] Mercury
Providence [RI] Gazette
Providence [RI] Journal
Providence [RI] Patriot, and Columbian Phoenix

Republican Herald (Providence, RI)
Rhode Island American (Providence, RI)

Government Documents

1779 Act Banning the Export of a Slave without Consent. C#0210, Acts and Resolves of the General Assembly. Volume 18, #164. RISA.

1798 Direct Tax List A and B for Providence. RIHS.

An Act Authorizing the Manumission of Negroes, Mulattoes and Others, and for the Gradual Abolition of Slavery. 1784. RISA.

An Act for Prohibiting the Importation of Negros into This Colony. 1775. RISA.

Act Repealing Part of Act Respecting the Manumission of Slaves. 1785. RISA.

An Act to Establish an Uniform Rule of Naturalization. 1st Congress, 1st session. Chapter 3. March 26, 1790.

Acts and Laws, of His Majesty's Colony of Rhode-Island, and Providence-Plantations, in New-England, in America. Newport, RI: "The Widow Franklin," 1745.

Acts and Resolves Passed by the General Assembly of the State of Rhode-Island and Providence Plantations. Providence, RI: State Printer, 1842. January Session.

Bartlett, John Russell, and the Rhode Island Department of State. *Census of the Inhabitants of the Colony of Rhode Island and Providence Plantations, Taken by Order of the General Assembly in the Year 1774.* Providence, RI: Anthony Knowles, 1858.

Burke, Edmund. *Interference of the Executive in the Affairs of Rhode Island.* 29th Congress, 1st session, 1844. House Report No. 546.

City Charter: Proposed for the Adoption of the Freemen of Providence, at a Town Meeting to Be Holden October 22, 1831. Providence, RI: Cranston and Hammond, 1831.

The Constitution of the State of Rhode-Island and Providence Plantations, as Adopted by the Convention, Assembled at Newport, September 1842. Providence, RI: Knowles and Vose, 1842.

First Report of the Providence Record Commissioners Relative to the Early Town Records. Providence, RI: Providence Press, 1892.

Hazard, James, et al. "Petition That Their Property May Be Taxed." June 1841. C#869. RISA.

Information Relative to the Operations of the United States Squadron on the West Coast of Africa, the Condition of the American Colonies There, and the Commerce of the United States Therewith. Washington, DC: Gales and Seaton, 1845. 28th Congress, 2nd session. S. Doc. 150, serial 458.

Johnson, Richard. Deposition. In *Rhode Island vs. John Gardner, William Jordan, and Richard Johnson.* MSS 562, series 6, box 14, folder 53, RIHS.

Journal of the Convention Assembled to Frame a Constitution for the State of Rhode Island at Newport, September 12, 1842. Providence, RI: Knowles, Anthony, 1859.

Journal of the House of Representatives of Rhode Island. RISA.

Journal of the Senate of Rhode Island. RISA.

A List of Persons Assessed in the City Tax of $90,170.58; Being the Amount Produced by an Assessment of 38 Cts. on Each $100 of Ratable Property. Providence, RI: H. H. Brown, 1845.

List of Persons Assessed in the City Tax of $178,612.65; Being the Amount Produced by an Assessment of 53 Cts. On Each $100 of Ratable Property. Providence, RI: H. H. Brown, 1852.

A List of Persons Assessed in the City Tax, Ordered by the City Council, March 1851. Providence, RI: H. H. Brown, 1851.

Memorial of Colored Citizens. November 4, 1841. RI Constitutional Convention Records, RISA.

Militia Act of 1792. 2nd Congress, 1st session. Chapter 28. May 2, 1792. https://www.constitution.org.

National Park Service. National Register of Historic Places Continuation Sheet, College Hill Historic District. 2018, Providence, RI.

Owners and Occupants of the Lots, Houses and Shops in the Town of Providence Rhode Island in 1798. RI GenWeb Project. http://www.rootsweb.ancestry.com.

Petition and Act of the Providence African Society for Mutual Relief, June 1833. Petitions Received, 1725–1890, RISA.

Providence City Directory. 1824, 1826, 1830, 1831, 1832, 1836, 1837, 1841, 1844, 1854. RIHS.

Providence Direct Tax, 1798 List A and B. RIHS.

Providence Town Papers. RIHS.

The Public Laws of the State of Rhode-Island and Providence Plantations: As Revised by a Committee, and Finally Enacted by the Honourable General Assembly, at Their Session in January, 1798. Providence, RI: Carter and Wilkinson, 1798.

The Public Laws of the State of Rhode-Island and Providence Plantations: As Revised by a Committee, and Finally Enacted by the Honourable General Assembly, at Their Session in January, 1822. Providence, RI: Miller and Hutchens, 1822.

Rhode Island General Assembly—Petitions Failed/Withdrawn. C#1179. RISA.

Scott v. Sandford. 60 U.S. 393. Supreme Court Collection. Legal Information Institute, Cornell University School of Law, Ithaca, NY. https://www.law.cornell.edu.

U.S. Census. 1790, 1800, 1810, 1820, 1830, 1840, 1850, 1860, 1870, 1880. Ancestrylibrary.com.

"U.S., Revolutionary War Rolls, 1775–1783" [online database]. Provo, UT: Ancestry.com, 2007.

Primary Sources: Monographs, Edited Collections, Archival Materials

Anti-Slavery Collection (digitized). Boston Public Library.

Asher, Jeremiah. *Incidents in the Life of the Rev. J. Asher, Pastor of the Shiloh (Coloured) Baptist Church, Philadelphia, U.S. and a Concluding Chapter of Facts Illustrating the Unrighteous Prejudice in the Minds of American Citizens toward Their Coloured Brethren.* London: Charles Gilpin, 1850.

Bracey, John H., Jr., and Manisha Sinha, eds. *African American Mosaic: A Documentary History from the Slave Trade to the Twenty-First Century.* Volume 1. Upper Saddle River, NJ: Pearson, 2004.

Brown, Moses. Receipt from Joseph Johnson to Moses Brown for Educating Cudge, Prime, and Pero, Three Men before Their Emancipation, ca. March 22, 1769. Moses Brown Papers (MS 930). SCUA.

Brown, William J. *The Life of William J. Brown of Providence, R.I.* 1883; reprint Freeport, NY: Books for Libraries Press, 1971.

Cathcart, William. *The Baptist Encyclopaedia: A Dictionary of the Doctrines, Ordinances, Usages.* Philadelphia: Louis H. Everts, 1881.

Chace, Elizabeth Buffum. *Anti-Slavery Reminiscences.* Central Falls, RI: E. L. Freeman and Son, 1891.

Chaput, Erik, Russell DeSimone, and Christiane Marie Landry, eds. "The Dorr Rebellion Project." Phillips Memorial Library, Providence College, Providence, RI. http://library.providence.edu.

Christ Church Records, 1841–1851. Mss 9001-C, box 7. RIHS.

Collections of the Rhode Island Historical Society. Volume 5. Providence, RI: Knowles and Vose, 1843.

"The Constitution of Harmony Lodge No. 1 in Providence, RI by African Grand Lodge of Boston." Records of African Lodge No. 459 Boston and Philadelphia (microfilm). Providence, RI: Quill and Sword, 1950.

Constitution of the Providence Society for Abolishing the Slave Trade (1789). Moses Brown Papers, MS 930. SCUA.

Douglass, Frederick. *Life and Times of Frederick Douglass, Written by Himself.* Boston: DeWolfe and Fiske, 1892.

Dwight, Sereno Edwards. "Slave Representation, by Boreas," 1812. Antislavery Pamphlet Collection (RB 003). SCUA.

Foner, Philip S., and Robert James Branham, eds. *Lift Every Voice: African American Oratory, 1787–1900*. Tuscaloosa: University of Alabama Press, 1998.

Ford, Worthington Chauncey, ed. *The Writings of John Quincy Adams*, vol. 4, *1811–1813*. New York: Macmillan, 1914.

Fox, John. *Opinion of the Honorable John Fox against the Exercise of Negro Suffrage in Pennsylvania*. Harrisburg, PA: Packer, Barrett, and Parke, 1838.

Frieze, Jacob. *A Concise History of the Efforts to Obtain an Extension of Suffrage in Rhode Island, from the Year 1811–1842*. 1842; reprint Providence, RI: Thomas Hammond, 1912.

Goodell, William. *The Rights and Wrongs of Rhode Island: Comprising Views of Liberty and Law, of Religion and Rights, as Exhibited in the Recent and Existing Difficulties in That State*. Whitesboro, NY: Oneida Institute, 1842.

Green, Frances Harriet Whipple. *Memoirs of Elleanor Eldridge*. Providence, RI: B. T. Albro, 1843.

———. *Might and Right; by a Rhode Islander*. Providence, RI: A. H. Stillwell, 1844.

Hard-Scrabble Calendar Report of the Trials of Oliver Cummins, Nathaniel G. Metcalf, Gilbert Humes, and Arthur Farrier; Who Were Indicted with Six Others for a Riot, and for Aiding in Pulling Down a Dwelling House, on the 18th of October at Hard-Scrabble. Providence, RI: N.p., 1824. American Antiquarian Society Digital Archives.

History of the Providence Riots, from Sept. 21 to Sept. 24, 1831. Providence, RI: H. H. Brown, 1831.

Hopkins, Samuel. *The System of Doctrines Contained in Divine Revelation, Explained and Defined*. Volume 1. Boston: Isaiah Thomas and Ebenezer T. Andrews, 1793.

Hopkins, Samuel, Sewall Harding, and Edwards A. Park, eds. *The Works of Samuel Hopkins, D.D.* Boston: Doctrinal Tract and Book Society, 1852.

Jackson, Henry, comp. *A Short History of the African Union Meeting and School-House, Erected in Providence (R.I.) in the Years 1819, '20, '21; with Rules for Its Future Governance*. Providence, RI: Brown and Danforth, 1851.

King, Henry Melville, and Charles Field Wilcox. *Historical Catalogue of the First Baptist Church in Providence, Rhode Island*. Providence, RI: F. H. Townsend, 1908.

Luther, Seth. *An Address on the Right of Free Suffrage*. Providence, RI: Samuel R. Weeden, 1833.

Mason, George Champlin. *Reminiscences of Newport*. Newport, RI: Charles E. Hammet, Jr., 1884.

"Minutes of the Meetings of the Committee of Defence," 1814. Mss 9001-C, box 11. RIHS.

Minutes of the National Conventions of People of Color. Colored Conventions Project. https://omeka.coloredconventions.org.

Nell, William Cooper. *Colored Patriots of the American Revolution*. Boston: Robert F. Wallcut, 1855.

Northup, Ichabod. *An Appeal from a Colored Man Whose Father Fought in the Revolution*. Providence, RI, 1859. In Lawrence Grossman, "George T. Downing and Desegregation of Rhode Island's Public Schools," *Rhode Island History* 36, no. 4 (November 1977): 98.

Potter, Elisha. *Considerations on the Questions of the Adoption of a Constitution, and Extension of Suffrage in Rhode Island*. Boston: Thomas H. Webb, 1842.

Proceedings of the Rhode-Island Anti-Slavery Convention, Held in Providence on the 2nd, 3rd, and 4th of February, 1836. Providence, RI: H. H. Brown, 1836.

Purvis, Robert, et al. *Appeal of Forty Thousand Citizens Threatened with Disfranchisement, to the People of Pennsylvania*. Philadelphia: Merrihew and Gunn, 1838.

Record Book, Kent County Female Anti-Slavery Society. MSS 9001-K, box 1. RIHS.

The Religious Intelligencer for the Year Ending May 1826, Containing the Principle Transactions of the Various Bible and Missionary Societies, with Particular Accounts of Revivals of Religion. Volume 10. New Haven, CT: Nathaniel Whiting, 1826.

The Report and Proceedings of the First Annual Meeting of the Providence Anti-Slavery Society with a Brief Exposition of the Principles and Purposes of the Abolitionists. Providence, RI: H. H. Brown, 1833.

Robinson, William H., ed. *The Proceedings of the Free African Union Society and the African Benevolent Society: Newport, Rhode Island, 1780–1824*. Providence: Urban League of Rhode Island, 1976.

Samuel J. May Anti-Slavery Collection. Division of Rare and Manuscript Collections, Cornell University Library, Ithaca, NY.

Shields, John H., ed. *The Collected Works of Phillis Wheatley*. New York: Oxford University Press, 1988.

Staples, William R., ed. *Documentary History of the Destruction of the Gaspee*. 1845; reprint East Providence: Rhode Island Publications Society, 1990.

Trumbull, Henry. *Life and Adventures of Robert the Hermit of Massachusetts, Who Has Lived 14 Years in a Cave, Secluded from Human Society*. Providence, RI: H. Trumbull, 1829.

Wilkeson, Samuel. *A Concise History of the American Colonies in Liberia*. Washington, DC: The Madisonian, 1839.

William Jones Papers. MSS 520. RIHS.

Yates, William H. *Rights of Colored Men to Suffrage, Citizenship and Trial by Jury: Being a Book of Facts, Arguments, and Authorities, Historical Notices and Sketches of Debates—with Notes*. Philadelphia: Merrihew and Gunn, 1838.

Secondary Sources

Allen, Samuel H. "The Federal Ascendancy of 1812." *Narragansett Historical Register* 7 (1899): 381–394.

Balinski, Michael L., and H. Peyton Young. *Fair Representation: Meeting the Ideal of One Man, One Vote*. 1982; reprint Washington, DC: Brookings Institution, 2001.

Bamberg, Cherry Fletcher. "Bristol Yamma and John Quamine in Rhode Island." *Rhode Island History* 73, no. 1 (Spring 2015): 5–25.

Barsh, Russell Lawrence. "'Colored' Seamen in the New England Whaling Industry: An Afro-Indian Consortium." In *Confounding the Color Line: The Indian-Black Experience in North America*, edited by James F. Brooks, 76–107. Lincoln: University of Nebraska Press, 2002.

Bartlett, Irving. *From Slave to Citizen: The Story of the Negro in Rhode Island*. Providence, RI: Urban League of Greater Providence, 1954.

Baumgartner, Kabria. *In Pursuit of Knowledge: Black Women and Educational Activism in Antebellum America*. New York: New York University Press, 2019.

Berlin, Ira. *Many Thousands Gone: The First Two Centuries of Slavery in North America*. Cambridge, MA: Belknap Press of Harvard University Press, 1998.

Blackett, R. J. M. *Building an Anti-Slavery Wall: Black Americans in the Atlantic Abolitionist Movement, 1830–1860*. Baton Rouge: Louisiana State University Press, 2002.

Bolster, W. Jeffrey. *Black Jacks: African American Seamen in the Age of Sail*. Cambridge, MA: Harvard University Press, 1997.

Bonner, Christopher. *Remaking the Republic: Black Politics and the Creation of American Citizenship*. Philadelphia: University of Pennsylvania Press, 2020.

Bourne, Theodore. "Rev. George Bourne, the Pioneer of American Antislavery." *Methodist Quarterly Review* (January 1882): 67–91.

Bouseman, Russell. "The Meaning of the Right of Petition: Northern Opinion and the Antislavery Gag Rule, 1836–1844." PhD diss., Oklahoma State University, 2016.

Brilvitch, Charles. *A History of Connecticut's Golden Hill Paugussett Tribe*. Charleston, SC: History Press, 2007.

Bristol, Douglas Walter, Jr. *Knights of the Razor: Black Barbers in Slavery and Freedom*. Baltimore, MD: Johns Hopkins University Press, 2009.

Brooks, George E. "The Providence African Society's Sierra Leone Emigration Scheme, 1794–95." *International Journal of African Historical Studies* 7, no. 2 (1974): 183–202.

Brownlee, Sibyl Ventress. "Out of Abundance of the Heart: Sarah Ann Parker Remond's Quest for Freedom." PhD diss., University of Massachusetts Amherst, 1997.

Chambers, Stephen. "'Neither Justice nor Mercy': Public and Private Executions in Rhode Island, 1832–1833." *New England Quarterly* 82, no 3 (September 2009): 430–451.

Chaput, Erik. *The People's Martyr: Thomas Wilson Dorr and His 1842 Rhode Island Rebellion*. Lawrence: University Press of Kansas, 2013.

Chaput, Erik, and Russell J. DeSimone. "The End of School Segregation in Rhode Island." *Small State, Big History*, August 2016, http://smallstatebighistory.com.

———. "Strange Bedfellows: The Politics of Race in Antebellum Rhode Island." *Common-place*, no. 10.1 (January 2010), https://commonplace.online.

Clark-Pujara, Christy. *Dark Work: The Business of Slavery in Rhode Island*. New York: New York University Press, 2016.

Coleman, Peter J. *The Transformation of Rhode Island, 1790–1860*. Providence, RI: Brown University Press, 1963.

Conley, Patrick T. *Democracy in Decline: Rhode Island's Constitutional Development, 1776–1841*. Providence: Rhode Island Historical Society, 1977.

Cottrol, Robert. *The Afro-Yankees: Providence's Black Community in the Antebellum Era*. Westport, CT: Greenwood Press, 1982.

Coughtry, Jay, et al. *Creative Survival: The Providence Black Community in the 19th Century*. Providence: Rhode Island Black Historical Society, 1984.

———. *The Notorious Triangle: Rhode Island and the African Slave Trade, 1700–1807*. Philadelphia: Temple University Press, 1981.

Curry, Leonard P. *The Free Black in Urban America, 1800–1850: The Shadow of the Dream*. Chicago: University of Chicago Press, 1981.

Curtis, Christopher M. "Reconsidering Suffrage Reform in the 1829–1830 Virginia Constitutional Convention." *Journal of Southern History* 74, no. 1 (February 2008): 89–124.

D'Amato, Donald A. *Warwick: A City at the Crossroads*. Charleston, SC: Arcadia, 2001.

Davis, Harry E. *A History of Freemasonry among Negroes in America.* Cleveland: United States Supreme Council, Ancient and Accepted Scottish Rite Freemasonry, Northern Jurisdiction (Prince Hall Affiliation), 1946.

Dennison, George M. *The Dorr War: Republicanism on Trial, 1831–1861.* Lexington: University of Kentucky Press, 1976.

Dyer, Elisha. "The Old Schools of Providence." *Narragansett Historical Register* 5, no. 1 (1886): 220–240.

Earle, Jonathan H. *Jacksonian Anti-Slavery and the Politics of Free Soil, 1824–1854.* Chapel Hill: University of North Carolina Press, 2004.

Eze, Emmanuel Chukwudi, ed. *Race and the Enlightenment: A Reader.* Malden, MA: Blackwell, 1997.

Fairclough, Adam. *Better Day Coming: Blacks and Equality, 1890–2000.* New York: Penguin, 2002.

Foner, Eric. *Gateway to Freedom: The Hidden History of America's Fugitive Slaves.* Oxford: Oxford University Press, 2015.

Forbes, Robert Pierce. *The Missouri Compromise and Its Aftermath: Slavery and the Meaning of America.* Chapel Hill: University of North Carolina Press, 2007.

Gates, Henry Louis, Jr. "The Trope of the New Negro and the Reconstruction of the Image of the Black." *Representations*, no. 24 (Autumn 1988): 129–155.

Geake, Robert A., and Loren M. Spear. *From Slaves to Soldiers: The 1st Rhode Island Regiment in the American Revolution.* Yardley, PA: Westholme, 2016.

Gettleman, Marvin. *The Dorr Rebellion: A Study in American Radicalism, 1833–1849.* New York: Random House, 1973.

Gettleman, Marvin, and Noel P. Conlon. "Responses to the Rhode Island Workingmen's Reform Agitation of 1833." *Rhode Island History* 28, no. 3 (Summer 1969): 75–94.

Gilkeson, John. *Middle-Class Providence, 1820–1940.* Princeton, NJ: Princeton University Press, 1986.

Gosse, Van. *The First Reconstruction: Black Politics in America from the Revolution to the Civil War.* Chapel Hill: University of North Carolina Press, 2022.

Greene, Lorenzo. *The Negro in Colonial New England.* 1942; reprint New York: Atheneum, 1968.

———. "Observations of the Black Regiment of Rhode Island in the American Revolution." *Journal of Negro History* 37, no. 2 (April 1952): 142–172.

Grimshaw, William H. *Official History of Freemasonry among the Colored People in North America.* New York: Broadway, 1903.

Grossman, Lawrence. "George T. Downing and Desegregation of Rhode Island Public Schools." *Rhode Island History* 36, no. 4 (November 1977): 99–106.

Grover, Kathryn. *The Fugitive's Gibraltar: Escaping Slaves and Abolitionism in New Bedford, Massachusetts*. Amherst: University of Massachusetts Press, 2001.

Gura, Philip F. *The Life of William Apess, Pequot*. Chapel Hill: University of North Carolina Press, 2015.

Grzyb, Frank. "The Fourteenth Regiment Rhode Island Heavy Artillery (Colored) during the Civil War. *Small State Big History*, March 2015, http://smallstatebighistory.com.

Harris, Leslie. *In the Shadow of Slavery: African Americans in New York City, 1626–1863*. Chicago: University of Chicago Press, 2003.

Herndon, Ruth Wallace. *Unwelcome Americans: Living on the Margin in Early New England*. Philadelphia: University of Pennsylvania Press, 2001.

Higginbotham, Evelyn Brooks. *Righteous Discontent: The Women's Movement in the Black Baptist Church, 1880–1920*. Cambridge, MA: Harvard University Press, 1993.

Hinks, Peter. *To Awaken My Afflicted Brethren: David Walker and the Problem of American Slave Resistance*. University Park: Pennsylvania State University Press, 1997.

Hodges, Graham Russell. *New York City Cartmen, 1667–1850*. New York: New York University Press, 1986.

Hoffmann, Charles, and Tess Hoffman. *North by South: The Two Lives of Richard James Arnold*. 1988; reprint Athens: University of Georgia Press, 2009.

Holt, Michael. *The Rise and Fall of the American Whig Party: Jacksonian Politics and the Onset of the Civil War*. New York: Oxford University Press, 1999.

Horton, Caleb T. *The Tide Taken at the Flood: The Black Suffrage Movement during the Dorr Rebellion in the State of Rhode Island and Providence Plantations (1841–1842)*. Providence, RI: Providence City Archives, 2017. https://www.providenceri.gov.

Horton, James, and Lois Horton. *In Hope of Liberty: Culture, Community, and Protest among Northern Free Blacks, 1700–1860*. New York: Oxford University Press, 1997.

Howe, David Walker. *The Political Culture of the American Whigs*. Chicago: University of Chicago Press, 1979.

———. *What Hath God Wrought: The Transformation of America, 1815–1848*. New York: Oxford University Press, 2007.

Hunt, Gaillard. *William Thornton and Negro Colonization*. Worcester, MA: American Antiquarian Society, 1920.

Ignatiev, Noel. *How the Irish Became White.* New York: Routledge, 1995.

Johnson, Leandrew L. "A Brief Historical Sketch of the Congdon Street Baptist Church of Providence, Rhode Island, 1819–1965." Providence, RI: History Committee, Congdon Street Baptist Church, 1965. Dr. Carl Russell Gross Collection. Rhode Island College, Providence.

Jones, Jacqueline. *A Dreadful Deceit: The Myth of Race from the Colonial Era to Obama's America.* New York: Basic, 2013.

Jones, Martha S. *All Bound Up Together: The Woman Question in African American Public Culture, 1830–1900.* Chapel Hill: University of North Carolina Press, 2007.

———. *Birthright Citizens: A History of Race and Rights in Antebellum America.* New York: Cambridge University Press, 2018.

Jordan, Winthrop. *White over Black: American Attitudes toward the Negro, 1550–1812.* Chapel Hill: University of North Carolina Press, 1968.

Lancaster, Jane. "Encouraging Faithful Domestic Servants: Race, Deviance, and Social Control in Providence, 1820–1850." *Rhode Island History* 51, no. 4 (1993): 71–87.

Lemons, J. Stanley. *Black in a White Church: Biographies of African American Members of the First Baptist Church in America.* Providence: Rhode Island Black Heritage Society, 2011.

Lemons, J. Stanley, and Michael A. McKenna. "Re-Enfranchisement of Rhode Island Negroes." *Rhode Island History* 30, no. 1 (Winter 1971): 3–14.

Litwack, Leon. *North of Slavery: The Negro in the Free States, 1790–1860.* Chicago: University of Chicago Press, 1961.

Litwack, Leon, and August Meier, eds. *Black Leaders of the Nineteenth Century.* Urbana: University of Illinois Press, 1991.

MacGunnigle, Bruce C. "Ichabod Northup, 'Soldier of the Revolution,' and His Descendants (Part 1)." *Rhode Island Roots* 34, no. 3 (2008): 113–132.

Malone, Christopher. *Between Freedom and Bondage: Race, Party, and Voting Rights in the Antebellum North.* New York: Routledge, 2008.

Martin, CJ. "Forever and Hereafter a Body Politic: The African Union Meeting House and Providence's First Black Leaders," *Rhode Island History* 77, no. 1 (Fall 2019): 20–46.

Masur, Kate. *Until Justice Be Done: America's First Civil Rights Movement, from the Revolution to Reconstruction.* New York: Norton, 2021.

Maxey, Edwin. "Suffrage Extension in Rhode Island Down to 1842." *American Law Review* 42 (1908): 541–577.

May, Vanessa. "'Obtaining a Decent Livelihood': Food Work, Race, and Gender in Du Bois's *The Philadelphia Negro.*" *Labor: Studies in Working-Class History of America* 12, nos. 1–2 (2015): 115–133.

McBurney, Christian. *Abductions in the American Revolution: Attempts to Kidnap George Washington, Benedict Arnold, and Other Military and Civilian Leaders.* Jefferson, NC: McFarland, 2016.

Melish, Joanne Pope. "Black Labor at the Nightingale-Brown House." John Nicholas Brown Center for Public Humanities and Cultural Heritage, https://www.brown.edu.

———. *Disowning Slavery: Gradual Emancipation and "Race" in New England, 1780–1860.* Ithaca, NY: Cornell University Press, 1998.

———. "The Racial Vernacular: Contesting the Black/White Binary in Nineteenth-Century Rhode Island." In *Race, Nation and Empire in American History,* edited by James T. Campbell, Matthew Pratt Guterl, and Robert G. Lee, 17–39. Chapel Hill: University of North Carolina Press, 2007.

Miller, Randall M., and John David Smith, eds. *Dictionary of Afro-American Slavery.* Westport, CT: Praeger, 1987.

Miller, William Lee. *Arguing about Slavery: John Quincy Adams and the Great Battle in the United States Congress.* New York: Vintage, 1995.

Mills, Quincy T. *Cutting across the Color Line: Black Barbers and Barbershops in America.* Philadelphia: University of Pennsylvania Press, 2013.

Montgomery, David. *Citizen Worker: The Experience of Workers in the United States with Democracy and the Free Market during the Nineteenth Century.* Cambridge: Cambridge University Press, 1994.

Moses, Wilson Jeremiah. *Alexander Crummell: A Study of Civilization and Discontent.* New York: Oxford University Press, 1989.

Mowry, Arthur May. *The Dorr War.* Providence, RI: Preston and Rounds, 1901.

Penn, Irvine Garland. *The Afro-American Press and Its Editors.* Springfield, MA: Wiley, 1891.

Pierson, William. *Black Yankees: The Development of an Afro-American Subculture in Eighteenth-Century New England.* Amherst: University of Massachusetts Press, 1988.

Pole, J. R. "Suffrage and Representation in Maryland from 1776 to 1810: A Statistical Note and Some Reflections." *Journal of Southern History* 24, no. 2 (1958): 218–225.

Polgar, Paul J. *Standard-Bearers of Equality: America's First Abolition Movement.* Chapel Hill: University of North Carolina Press, 2019.

Pope, Tony. "Our Segregated Brethren, Prince Hall Masons." Kellerman Lecture for South Australia. Williamstown, Victoria, Australia: Australian Masonic Research Council, 1994.

Popek, Daniel M. *They ". . . Fought Bravely, but Were Unfortunate": The True Story of Rhode Island's "Black Regiment" and the Failure of Segregation in Rhode Island's Continental Line.* Bloomington, IN: AuthorHouse, 2015.

Potter, David M. *The Impending Crisis, 1848–1861.* New York: Harper and Row, 1976.

Power-Greene, Ousmane. *Against the Wind and Tide: The African American Struggle against the Colonization Movement.* New York: New York University Press, 2014.

Price, George R., and James Brewer Stewart, eds. *To Heal the Scourge of Prejudice: The Life and Writings of Hosea Easton.* Amherst: University of Massachusetts Press, 1999.

Prinz, Deborah. *On the Chocolate Trail: A Delicious Adventure Connecting Jews, Religions, History, Travel, Rituals, and Recipes to the Magic of Cacao.* Woodstock, VT: Jewish Lights, 2013.

Pryor, Elizabeth Stordeur. *Colored Travelers: Mobility and the Fight for Citizenship before the Civil War.* Chapel Hill: University of North Carolina Press, 2016.

Quarles, Benjamin. *Black Abolitionists.* New York: Oxford University Press 1969.

———. *The Negro in the American Revolution.* 1961; reprint Chapel Hill: University of North Carolina Press, 1996.

Raboteau, Albert J. *Slave Religion: The "Invisible Institution" in the Antebellum South.* Updated edition. 1978; New York: Oxford University Press, 2004.

Rael, Patrick. *Black Identity and Black Protest in the Antebellum North.* Chapel Hill: University of North Carolina Press, 2002.

Rammelkamp, Julian. "The Providence Negro Community, 1820–1842." *Rhode Island History* 7, no. 1 (January 1948): 21–33.

Rappleye, Charles. *Sons of Providence: The Brown Brothers, the Slave Trade, and the American Revolution.* New York: Simon and Schuster, 2006.

Ratcliffe, Donald. *The One Party Presidential Ticket: Adams, Jackson, and 1824's Five-Horse Race.* Lawrence: University Press of Kansas, 2015.

———. "The Right to Vote and the Rise of Democracy, 1787–1828." *Journal of the Early Republic* 33 (Summer 2013): 219–254.

Richards, Leonard. *Gentlemen of Property and Standing: Anti-Abolition Mobs in Jacksonian America.* New York: Oxford University Press, 1970.

———. *The Slave Power: The Free North and Southern Domination, 1780–1860*. 2000; reprint Baton Rouge: Louisiana State University Press, 2009.

Robinson, Caroline E. *The Hazard Family of Rhode Island, 1635–1894*. Boston: N.p., 1895.

Rockman, Seth. *Scraping By: Wage Labor, Slavery, and Survival in Early Baltimore*. Baltimore, MD: Johns Hopkins University Press, 2009.

Roediger, David. *Wages of Whiteness: Race and the Making of the American Working Class*. New York: Verso, 1991.

Rogers, L. E., ed. *The Biographical Cyclopedia of Representative Men of Rhode Island*. Providence, RI: National Biographical Publishing, 1881.

Rogers, Patricia Dane, and Laurel Crone Sneed. "The Missing Chapter in the Life of Thomas Day." *American Furniture 2013*. Chipstone Foundation, 2013, https://www.chipstone.org.

Rusert, Britt. *Fugitive Science: Empiricism and Freedom in Early African American Culture*. New York: New York University Press, 2017.

Schantz, Mark. *Piety in Providence: Class Dimensions of Religious Experience in Antebellum Rhode Island*. Ithaca, NY: Cornell University Press, 2000.

Sherer, Robert Glenn, Jr. "Negro Churches in Rhode Island before 1860." *Rhode Island History* 25, no. 1 (January 1966): 9–25.

Ships and Shipmasters of Old Providence: A Brief Account of Some of the Famous Merchants, Sea Captains, and Ships of the Past, Together with Reminiscences of a Few Notable Voyages Made in Providence Ships. Providence, RI: Providence Institution for Savings, 1920.

Sinha, Manisha. *The Slave's Cause: A History of Abolition*. New Haven, CT: Yale University Press, 2016.

Sirgo, Henry B. "Samuel Ames." In *Great American Judges: An Encyclopedia*, edited by John R. Vile, 1:20–24. Santa Barbara, CA: ABC-CLIO, 2003.

Slauter, Eric. "The American Hermit and the British Castaway: Voluntary Retreat and Deliberative Democracy in Early American Culture." *Early American Literature* 46, no. 1 (2011): 121–156.

Smith, Kimberly. *Dominion of Voice: Riot, Reason and Romance in Antebellum Politics*. Lawrence: University Press of Kansas, 1999.

Stachiw, Myron O. *The Old Brick Schoolhouse, 24 Meeting Street Providence, Rhode Island*. Providence, RI: Providence Preservation Society, 2014.

Stark, Bruce P. "Universal Suffrage, the 'Stand-up Law,' and the Wallingford Election Controversy, 1801–1818." *Connecticut History Review* 53, no. 1 (Spring 2014): 16–44.

Sterling, Dorothy. *Ahead of Her Time: Abby Kelley and the Politics of Anti-Slavery*. New York: Norton and Norton, 1991.

Stockwell, Thomas B., ed. *A History of Public Education in Rhode Island, from 1636–1876*. Providence, RI: Providence Press, 1876.

Sullivan, Joseph W. "Reconstructing the Olney's Lane Riot: Another Look at Race and Class in Jacksonian Rhode Island." *Rhode Island History* 65, no. 2 (2007): 49–60.

Sweet, John Wood. *Bodies Politic: Negotiating Race in the American North, 1730–1830*. Baltimore, MD: Johns Hopkins University Press, 2003.

Taylor, Nikki M. *Frontiers of Freedom: Cincinnati's Black Community, 1802–1868*. Athens: Ohio University Press, 2005.

Thompson, Mack. *Moses Brown: Reluctant Reformer*. Chapel Hill: University of North Carolina Press, 1962.

Van Broekhoven, Deborah. *The Devotion of These Women: Rhode Island in the Antislavery Network*. Amherst: University of Massachusetts Press, 2002.

Van Deburg, William L. "Henry Clay, the Right of Petition, and Slavery in the Nation's Capital." *Register of the Kentucky Historical Society* 68, no. 2 (April 1970): 132–46.

Wang, Xi. "Make Every Slave Free, Every Free Man a Voter: The African American Construction of Suffrage Discourse in the Age of Emancipation." In *Contested Democracy: Freedom, Race, and Power in American History*, edited by Manisha Sinha and Penny Von Eschen, 117–40. New York: Columbia University Press, 2007.

Welburn, Ron. *Hartford's Ann Plato and the Native Borders of Identity*. Albany: State University of New York Press, 2015.

Wilentz, Sean. *Chants Democratic: New York City and the Rise of the American Working Class, 1788–1850*. New York: Oxford University Press, 1984.

Williams, Eric. *Capitalism and Slavery*. 1944; reprint New York: Perigree, 1980.

Williams, William H. *Slavery and Freedom in Delaware, 1639–1865*. Wilmington, DE: Scholarly Resources, 1996.

Winch, Julie. *Philadelphia's Black Elite: Activism, Accommodation, and the Struggle for Autonomy, 1787–1848*. Philadelphia: Temple University Press, 1988.

Wroth, Lawrence C. *The First Press in Providence: A Study of Social Development*. Worcester, MA: American Antiquarian Society, n.d.

York, Neil L. "The Uses of Law and the *Gaspee* Affair." *Rhode Island History* 50, no. 1 (February 1992): 3–21.

Index

Abigail, enslaved woman, 27, 232n49
abolitionism: citizenship rights and, 108, 181–82, 186, 248n7; colonization backlash, 125; color line and, 120; division on "white" provisions, 194–95; early allies, 26–27; Garrison's Independence Day address, 140; George Latimer and, 200; interracial ties of, 61, 132–35, 142; national movement, 117, 203; Philadelphia and, 37; presidential elections and, 206; "Second Wave," 108, 113, 117, 129; "white" provision in proposed RI constitution, 187–88
abolition laws, campaigns for, 3
Adams, Charles Francis, 206
Adams, John Quincy, 44–45, 151–52, 156, 206
Addison Hollow. *See* pogroms
Address on the Right of Free Suffrage (Luther), 149
African American convention movement. *See* Colored Convention movement
African American Studies, 203
African Society, 67, 77–79, 81, 96. *See also* African Union Meeting House
African Union Meeting House: abolitionist speakers at, 11; "African School" at the, 137–38; Black leadership class and, 51, 65–67; construction and incorporation, 78; fundraising for, 70–71, 238n20; Meeting Street Baptist Church successor, 67, 77; planning committee, 10, 53, 58, 68; planning meeting, 64–66; twenty year battle for voting rights, 201; white role in founding, 63, 65–66; women and planning, 69
African Union Meeting House school, 103
Alexander I (tsar), 44
"Algerine Law," 190–91
Allen, Edward, 23
Allen, Richard, 37, 50, 67, 234n88
Allen, Samuel V., 89
Allen, Zachariah, 93
Alpin, William, 188
amalgamation or intermarriage, 101, 133, 144, 151
American Anti-Slavery Society (AASS), 130, 132, 140–41, 143–44, 154, 159, 187–88, 205–6
American Colonization Society, 40, 71, 93, 109, 121–24
American Moral Reform Society, 136
American Prox, 52–53

253

American Revolution: African American and Native American role, 46, 123, 156; Black communities and, 16; Continental Army and Black soldiers, 21; dissenters to slave enlistment, 21–22; economic cost of, 29; effect on missionary work, 31; hope for Black citizenship, 19; offers of freedom, 16, 21. *See also* First Rhode Island Regiment
Ames, Samuel (Town Born), 167, 170–74, 177, 180–81
Ames, Wyllys, 130
anti-abolitionism, 92, 105, 133–34, 142, 152, 188
Anti-Federalists, 37, 46
anti-Jacksonians, 112–13, 116, 122, 124
Anti-Masons, 112, 154
Anti-Slavery Convention of American Women, 144
antislavery societies, 141. *See also* American Anti-Slavery Society (AASS); Rhode Island Anti-Slavery Society (RIASS)
Apess, William, 139
An Appeal from a Colored Man Whose Father Fought in the Revolution (Northup), 211
Appeal of Forty Thousand Citizens Threatened with Disfranchisement, to the People of Pennsylvania (Purvis), 155
Appeal . . . to the Colored Citizens of the World (Walker), 77, 95, 105, 113–14, 117, 120
Arnold, Benjamin, 176–77, 179, 181, 188
Arnold, Lemuel, 109–10, 116
Arnold, Welcome, 27–28
arsenal attack and insurrection (1842), 192–94
Asher, Jeremiah, 72
Atwell, Samuel Y., 162, 164, 167, 177, 182, 190
Axum, James, 114

Bailey, Primus, 56, 105, 154, 199
Balch, Joseph, 88
Barbadoes, James, 132
Barrett, George W., 68–69, 74–75
Bartlett, Irving, 65

Benjamin Franklin (ship), 129
Benson, George and family, 79, 121
Benson, Helen, 121, 239n53
Benson, Henry E., 121, 130, 134
Bibb, Henry, 206, 251n11
Bignell, Abraham, 165
Birney, James G., 147
Black freemasonry, 35–36, 67, 94, 123, 237n9
Black leadership: advocating for themselves, 66; business and intellectual elite, 68–69, 178; equitable education and, 209, 211; meetinghouse and equitable citizenship, 65; Native ancestry and, 122; Peterson's warnings against deceit, 192; petitioning campaign and, 145; sacrifices of, 202–3; voting rights campaign, 146, 148, 170, 174, 202. *See also* African Union Meeting House; Free African Union Society; Rhode Island Anti-Slavery Society
Blodgett, William P., 175
Board of Trade and Plantations (Great Britain), 7
"bobalition" tropes and broadsides, 9, 59, 90, 133, 170, 237n50
Bonner, Christopher, 8
Boston Gazette, 87
Boston Times, 133
Bourne, George, 132
Brenton, Scipio, 48–50
Brewer, Elizabeth, 125
Briggs, Aaron, 19–20
Brooks, George E., 39
Brown, Benson & Ives, 38
Brown, Bonner, 32, 34, 233n71, 233n74
Brown, Charles G., 182
Brown, Cudgo (or Cudge), 32, 34, 47, 233n71, 233n74
Brown, John A., 161, 172–73, 176–77, 180, 186, 190
Brown, John and Joseph, 20, 37
Brown, John Carter, 75
Brown, John Edwin, 130
Brown, Moses: abolitionism of, 28, 37, 234n90; African colony and, 36, 38; African Union Meeting House and, 65,

67–69, 76; friend to free African Americans, 47; and Garrison, 121; influence in elite circles, 62, 79; land sale to Noah Brown, 48, 233n74; manumission of Bonner Brown and Cudge Brown, 34, 233n71; Providence Society for the Encouragement of Faithful Servants and, 110; and Quakerism, 26–27, 75; vision of citizenship, 29; and Yamma, 35
Brown, Noah, 47–48
Brown, Obadiah, 79
Brown, Phillis, 34
Brown, William J.: African Union Meeting House and, 66–67, 82; and Barrett's military knowledge, 74; church attendance, 50; Convention for the Improvement of the Free People of Colour attendee, 135; and Dorr, 193; education of, 80–81; and Goldsbury, 72; and Hazard, 129; and Howland, 192; job discrimination and, 73; memoirist, 19; mutual benefit society and, 182; Native intermarriage and, 122; petitions and, 165; protest against taxation, 77; and Saltonstall, 83; SnowTown riot and, 114–15; taunts from white neighbors, 88; temperance campaigns, 128, 138; underground economy and, 86; voting rights and, 168; Whig Party and, 206–7; and Wyllis, 119
Brown, William Wells, 206
Browning, Peter, 94
Brownson, Orestes, 158
Brown University (Rhode Island College), 5, 33, 50
Bucktail Republicans, 153
Buffum, Arnold, 128, 144
Burges, Tristam, 1–3, 110, 155
Burgess, Samuel, 186
Burgess, Thomas, 188
Burr, Seymour, 21
Burrill, James, 56, 58

Cady, Josiah, 130
Cannon, Noah Caldwell, 145
Carpenter, Thomas, 161
Carrington, Edward, 74–75

Casey, Abraham, 31
Cass, Lewis, 206–7
Chace, Elizabeth Buffum, 128, 206
Chaput, Erik, 65, 148
Charlotte (ship), 38
Child, Lydia Maria, 173–74, 182
Childs, Joseph, 197–98
citizenship rights: Black leadership and, 209–10; color line and, 12, 144–46, 161; competing visions of, 29; Easton's address on, 92, 96–98; equitable education, 79–80, 209; free white men and, 7–8, 45; laws limiting Black rights, 204; poor whites and Black people, 195; racial inferiority and, 102; U. S. passports, 209; women and vote, 229n9. *See also* voting rights
Clapp, Henry, 204
Clark-Pujara, Christy, 24, 65
Clay, Henry, 57, 109, 123, 152, 157, 204–5
Coggeshall, Cato, 32–33, 115
Cole, Thomas, 159
colonization: Black leadership and, 16; Henry Clay and, 123; mob rule and violence, 133; newspaper editorials and articles, 123; race pseudoscience and, 124; white collaborators and Black resistance, 39; white elite and, 66, 93. *See also* American Colonization Society
Colored American, 23, 144, 152–53, 155, 157–59, 162–63, 181–82, 247n29
Colored Association of Providence for the Promotion of Temperance, 128–29
colored convention movement: Black leadership and, 120, 145; Easton and, 95–96; Niger and, 12, 94, 121; Willis and, 73; Wyllis and, 119, 121. *See also* National Conventions of People of Color
Colored Female Literary Society, 130
Colored Female Tract Society, 125, 130
Colored Ladies' Literary Society, 125
color line, 12, 120, 144–46, 159–60, 164, 170, 174, 203, 211
Columbian Phoenix, 52, 236n45, 244n34
Concord Juvenile Anti-Slavery Society, 140
Congdon, Hodge, 68, 77, 114

Congdon, Jane, 77, 114
Congdon, Prince, 166
Conley, Patrick, 41
Connecticut, 56; Black disenfranchisement, 236n38; freemanship relaxed white added, 56; Revolutionary War offers of freedom, 21
Connecticut Journal, 53
constitutional convention, 12
"Constitutionalist" Party, 151
Constitutionalist-Whig Party, 157
Convention for the Improvement of the Free People of Colour (Philadelphia), 135
Cook, Charles, 139
Cornish, Samuel, 95, 145, 152–53, 155–56, 247n29
Cottrol, Robert, 33, 62, 65, 68, 73, 80, 251n11
Coughtry, Jay, 34
Country Party, 29, 46, 52
Courier and Enquirer, 133
Crawford, James E., 159
Crawford, Lucy, 166
Creek and Seminole Wars, 192
Crown Coffee House slave market, 25
Crummell, Alexander, 12, 66, 71, 153, 177
Cuffe, Paul, 104, 238n19
Cummins, Oliver, 88–91
Cunningham, James, 23–24

Danforth, Joshua, 123–24
Dark Work (Clark-Pujara), 65
Declaration of Independence: basis for hope, 19; Black leaders use of, 5; Black soldiers' role and, 29, 122–23; children inheritors of the sentiments, 140; color line and, 178; Enlightenment philosophy, 7, 208–9; Evarts letter, 57; Evarts's letter to Congress and, 57; petition recalling, 131, 147–48; protection of ideals, 12; taxation without representation, 155; Vorhis story, 2
Democratic Party, 58, 112–13, 149, 152, 186, 188, 196, 207
Democratic-Republican Party, 44, 46, 84, 101, 154, 199–200

DeSimone, Russell J., 65
"Division of Rhode-Island Veterans," 55
domestic workers, 25, 74, 110–11
Dorr, Thomas: abolitionist, 172; about, 148; Black vote and "white," 177, 180–82, 185, 195, 248n7; Constitutionalist Party, 151; and People's Constitution, 188, 191; and People's Constitution boycott, 199–200; run for Congress, 157–58; Suffrage Association and, 12, 161; and Suffrage Party, 190. *See also* Dorr Rebellion
Dorr Rebellion (1842), 3, 8, 129, 148. *See also* arsenal attack and insurrection
Douglass, Frederick, 4, 71, 139, 145, 185–88, 200, 204–6
Downing, George T., 49, 94, 209–10
Dred Scott v. Sandford (1857), 12, 45, 101, 154, 208, 211
Drown, William, 142
Dunsmore, Lord (John Murray), 16, 20
Dwight, Sereno Edwards, 53
Dwight, Timothy, 55
D'Wolf, Bristol, 28
D'Wolf, James, 55

Earle, Thomas, 154
Easton, Hosea, 92, 95–98, 104–5, 107, 113–14, 125, 132, 242n77
Eddy, Samuel, 57
education: "Act to Establish Free Schools" (1800) for white children, 80; African Free Schools, 54; "African School," 137; Black property taxes and, 103–6, 211; citizenship rights and segregation, 79–80, 209–10; city council and Black children's schooling, 138; Pond Street School, 137–38; private schools for Black children, 80; Providence English School for Colored Youth, 137; school integration and, 103, 137, 209–11; school segregation, 5, 12; universal public school legislation, 80, 103
Eldridge, Elleanor, 69, 73, 110–11, 166, 195–96, 230n9
elite whites: Black alliances and, 17, 25, 44, 47, 50, 63, 66, 70–71, 117; Black

meetinghouse plan, 81–82; employment and, 74–75; government of, 7; and "Hard-Scrabble" shooting and trials, 91–92; Ichabod Northop and, 176; voting rights and, 202
Ellis, James E., 103, 121
Emancipator, 130, 133, 144, 157, 165, 188, 197, 200
enfranchisement and disenfranchisement: Black vote (1843), 4; Democrat control and, 207; Pennsylvania constitutional convention and, 153–56; reenfranchisement, 11; rejection of "white" in voting requirement, 203–4; shifting racial ideas and, 61–62. *See also* People's Constitutional Convention; Rhode Island General Assembly
Enlightenment philosophy, 5–7, 26
Ennis, William, 198
enslaved people: colonial laws and, 7; naming of, 31–32, 232n66; proof of, 233n71; South Carolina planned slave rebellion, 87; in territories of Arkansas, Florida and D.C., 130–31; urban and rural occupations and conditions, 25–26; Virginia slave insurrection (1831), 114
Erickson, George, 115
Esterbrook, Prince, 20
Evans, George Henry, 158
Evarts, Jeremiah, 57

Fairbanks, Asa, 195
Farrier, Arthur, 90
Federalist-African American alliance, 229n4
Federalist Papers, 178
Federalist Party: allies of northern Black communities, 2–3, 10; aristocrats of, 109; Blacks and elite alliance, 55–56; failure of, 84; gradual emancipation, 54, 200; push to broaden rights (1811), 54; rejection of "white" in voting requirement, 52–53; Revolutionary War ideals, 51, 55; understanding of liberty, 44; voting and property ownership, 112; and voting rights, 52, 55–58, 60, 62; waning of influence, 9, 11; and William Jones, 43. *See also Providence Gazette*
Fenner, Arthur, 52
Fenner, James, 52, 109, 112, 198, 201, 204
Fillmore, Millard, 207
First of August celebration, 159, 210
First Rhode Island Regiment: Battle of Rhode Island, 22; Black soldiers in, 10, 27, 35, 123; Bristol Rhodes in, 50; descendants of, 46; Greene manslaughter conviction, 23; Ichabod Northop, Sr. in, 175, 211; legislation forbidding Black enlistment, 22; Oswego campaign, 22; Pine's Bridge (Yorktown), 22; Stoddard manslaughter conviction, 23–24
Fogg, William, 153
Forten, James, 238n19
Forward, William, 154
Foster, Stephen, 185–87
Fourteenth Rhode Island Heavy Artillery (Colored), 211
Francis, John Brown, 190
Free African Society (Philadelphia), 36–37
Free African Union Society, 15–17, 85, 233n82
Free African Union Society, Newport chapter, 10, 31–32, 36–38
Free African Union Society, Providence chapter, 32–35, 37, 40, 47, 67
Freedom's Journal, 95, 113, 152
"freeman" system, 11
Free Soil movement, 4, 58, 206–9, 251n11
Free Soil Party, 206
Freetown, Sierra Leone, 38
Frieze, Jacob, 150, 158
From Slave to Citizen (Barlett), 65
Fugitive Slave Law (1850), 206–7

Gabriel, Claude, 43–45, 48, 63
Gardner, Caesar, 165
Gardner, Caleb, 31, 232n60
Gardner, Cato, 32, 233n68
Gardner, Newport, 16, 30–31, 37–38, 49, 93
Gardner, Winsor, 138–39, 141
Garnet, Henry Highland, 66, 71

Garrison, William Lloyd: at the African Union Meeting House, 127; attack by colonizationist movement, 133; and Charles Lenox Remond, 143; defense of Black voting, 173; and Goodell, 195; Independence Day address, 140; influenced by Black abolitionists, 120; marriage to Helen Benson, 79, 121, 239n53; New England Anti-Slavery Society founder, 125, 129; People's Constitution and, 182; popularity of, 152; Providence visit, 127; and RIASS, 205; Suffrage Association and, 185–86; *Thoughts on African Colonization*, 124; trip to British Isles, 130. See also *Liberator*
Genius of Universal Emancipation (Lundy), 120
Gibbs, Abraham, 68, 76–78
Gibbs, William, 60
Gilbert, Nathan, 130, 135
Gilkeson, John, 70
Gilmer, George, 105
Goldsbury, Asa C., 68–69, 71–72
Goodell, William, 171, 195–97
Gorham, Charles, 129–30
Gosse, Van, 7
Graham, Thomas, 68, 78
Great Britain: emancipation of Caribbean slaves, 114, 134; First of August celebration, 159, 210
Green, Frances Whipple, 110, 171, 195–96
Greene, Christopher, 22
Greene, Henry, 67–68, 72–73
Greene, Prince, 23
Gumes, James, 182

Hall, Christopher "Old Kit," 83–85, 89, 91, 93, 106, 240n3, 241n28
Hall, Prince, 35, 67, 123, 233n82, 237n9
Hamilton, Alexander, 54
Harris, James, 68, 77, 165
Harris, Stephen, 78
Harrison, William Henry, 152, 161, 190
Hartford Convention on secession, 52, 56
Hayden, Lewis, 71

Hazard, Benjamin, 99–102, 113, 142, 150–52, 154, 156, 167, 208
Hazard, James, 120, 129–30, 165, 177, 182, 192, 197, 201–2
Head, George, 165–66
Herald of Freedom, 140
Herndon, Ruth Wallace, 47
Hilton, J. T., 139
HMS Gaspee burning (1772), 19–20
Holbrook, Felix, 32, 35, 42, 233n71
Hopkins, Samuel, 26, 30–31, 35–39
Hoppin, William, 208
Horton, James and Lois, 5, 17
Howell, David, 28
Howland, Thomas, 12–13, 138, 165–66, 182, 192, 201–2, 205, 207–9
How the Irish Became White (Ignatiev), 54, 235n29
Hubbard, Ezra, 90
Humes, Gilbert, 90
Hunter, William, 55

Ignatiev, Noel, 54
In Hope of Liberty (James and Lois Horton), 5
Irish immigrants, 54, 84, 143, 158, 235n29

Jackson, Andrew, 84, 93, 95, 109, 122–23, 130, 136, 152, 158, 192, 240n19
Jackson, Charles, 169, 197–98
Jackson, Henry, 65–66, 71, 79, 81–82
Jay, John, 54
Jay, Peter, 60
Jeffersonians, pro-slavery, 44, 52, 54, 229n4
Jim Crow, 145, 187
Jocelyn, Simeon, 128
John Carter Brown Library, 75
Johnson, James W., 139
Johnson, Nathan, 138
Johnson, Richard, 115
Jones, Absalom, 37, 234n88, 238n16
Jones, Martha S., 126
Jones, Robert, 129–30
Jones, Rosanna, 166
Jones, William, 43–44, 52, 56, 63, 93
Jordan, William, 115

Kansas-Nebraska Act (1854), 207
Kelley, Abby, 182, 185–88
Kent County Female Anti-Slavery Society, 157
King, Samuel Ward, 161, 190–91, 193
Kinnicutt, Anthony, 40–42, 53, 200
Knight, Nathaniel, 193
Knight, Nehemiah, 60
Knight, Nehemiah R., 93
Know-Nothing Party, 208

"Lancasterian plan," 81
Landholders Convention, 163, 182, 185, 197
Landholders court case, 190
Lang, Solomon, 133
Latimer, George, 200
Law and Order Party, 190–91, 194–96, 201, 204–6
leadership class, 5, 68. *See also* Providence leadership class
Leavitt, Joshua, 197
Lee, William, 166
Lemons, J. Stanley, 65
Lewis, John W., 72, 82, 120, 136–40, 145, 159, 230n15, 238n25
Lexington (steamer), 135
Liberator: African Union Meeting House resolutions, 121, 123; agents for, 12, 106, 121, 143, 154; citizenship petition and, 117; on the Colonization Society, 124; Dorr endorsement, 157; Dorr Rebellion and, 188; founding of, 120; on Henry Clay, 204; Lewis advertisements, 137; nationwide circulation, 128, 152; on Pennsylvania developments, 153; political leanings of, 188; Providence antislavery society and, 129, 134; Providence Colored Ladies Society essays, 125–27; Suffrage Association and, 159; on Thomas Dorr, 248n7
Liberia, 12, 91, 93, 122–23, 209
Liberty Party, 4, 147, 204, 206, 251n11
The Life of William J. Brown of Providence, R.I., 66, 72–73, 82, 128, 241n28, 251n11
Litwack, Leon, 8
Locke, John, 5–7, 208

Locofoco Democrats, 158, 161–62, 190, 204
Lopez, Aaron, 31
Lundy, Benjamin, 120
Luther, Seth, 113, 149, 158
Lyman, Theodore, Jr., 59
Lyndon, Caesar, 31

Macauley, Zachary, 38–39
Malone, Christopher, 62
Martin, Henry, 130
Marycoo, Occramer. *See* Gardner, Newport
Massachusetts: antislavery petitions, 152; Black exclusion voting (1821), 59; "civil and religious liberty" petition, 35, 104; disenfranchised citizens in, 149; electoral qualifications, 151
Massachusetts General Colored Association, 125
Masur, Kate, 7
McCarty, George, 57–58, 68–69, 76, 82, 104, 118, 162, 202
McCarty, Terisa, 76
McCarty petition (1840), 159, 164–65, 167, 177, 183
McKenna, Michael, 65
McKenzie, James, 32, 35–38
Melish, Joanne Pope, 18, 61–62, 160, 203
Memoirs of Elleanor Eldridge (Green), 195–96
Messer, Asa, 109, 112
Metcalf, Nathaniel, 90–91, 240n3
military service: American Revolution and, 75, 83, 211; Black defense of country, 211; Black Union troops, 211; Dorr Rebellion and, 75; Militia Act of 1792, 46, 229n8; Minuteman companies, 16, 20–21; War of 1812, 74. *See also* First Rhode Island Regiment
Missouri statehood question, 11, 57–59, 236n46
Monroe, James, 93, 187
Morristown committee, 87
Mosher, Caleb, 173, 248n45
Mowry, Nathaniel, 176
Mumford, Cato, 32, 34–35, 233n71

Mumford, Nathaniel, 34, 233n71
mutual aid societies, 15, 85, 203. *See also* Free African Union Society

Narragansett Indians, 231n13
National Anti-Slavery Standard, 159, 173, 182, 191, 200
National Conventions of People of Color, 128–29, 147
Native Americans: Indian removal policy, 122; intermarriage and, 122; temperance campaigns and, 139
Native Son (Wright), 75
Naturalization Acts (1790s), 45
Negro Election Day (Rhode Island), 17–19, 25, 40, 49
Nell, William Cooper, 159
New Age, 158, 161–62, 165, 167–68, 172, 186–87
New England Anti-Slavery Convention, 76
New England Anti-Slavery Society, 125, 129
New England Temperance Society of Colored Persons, 139–40
New-England Union Academy, 137
New Jersey, 229n9
Newport: Black leadership of, 24, 33; Black population of, 18–19, 44; British occupation of, 21, 28; colonization plan, 36–38, 93; enslaved people of, 25; Free African Union Society, 15, 31, 36, 47; General Assembly in, 231n28; John Williams and, 129; links with Providence, 35; mobs at Kelley rallies, 188; old aristocrats of, 100, 151–52, 157, 185; People's Constitutional Convention and, 164; suffrage question and "white," 180, 196, 200; white religious allies in, 10
Newport Mercury, 93, 241n27
New York: birthright citizenship, 111; constitutional convention, 60; disenfranchised citizens in, 149; property requirement abolition campaign, 153
New York Advocate, 60
New York Gazette, 133

New York Manumission Society, 66
Nichols, Richard, 205
Niger, Alfred: attempt to vote, 170, 172–74, 200; barbering and, 142; Black and white non-freeholders, 148; Black leadership and, 118, 121, 135, 147, 202, 206; forcible removal from voting booth (1841), 200; future leaders and, 82; *the Liberator* and, 134; "mustard seed," 148; national convention movement, 119; petition writing, 104–7, 127, 160, 162, 164, 177, 183; Prince Hall mason lodge and, 94, 123; RIASS and, 141, 145, 185; Suffrage Association and, 12, 171–72; and Whipper, 136, 138–39; and Wyllis, 131–32
Nightingale, Joseph, 34–35
Northup, Catherine, 175
Northup, Cato, 128
Northup, Ichabod, Jr.: Black leadership and, 120, 176; future leaders and, 82; military service and, 123, 211; petition writing, 177, 182, 197, 202, 210; Prince Hall mason lodge and, 94; real estate holdings of, 165; writings of, 127
Northup, Ichabod, Sr., 175
Northwest Ordinance fugitive slave provision, 236n46
Nubia, Salmar, 15–16, 31–32, 93

occupations: artisans and Black people, 48; artisans and enslaved people, 230n4; barbering, 49; Black limitations, 142–43; Blacks barred from apprenticeships, 142; niche opportunities, 48
O'Connell, Daniel, 143
Olney, Bristol and family, 32–34
Olney, Jeremiah, 22, 24, 49
Olney, William, 37
Ormsbee, John, 81

Paine, Aramancy, 206
Parker, Clementia, 210–11
Parker, Ransom, 82, 120, 137–38, 165, 177, 200, 210
Paul, Nathaniel, 68–71, 113
Pearce, Duttee J., 90, 92, 164, 188, 190

Pennsylvania: constitutional convention and Black voter qualifications, 153–56; disenfranchised citizens in, 149, 185–86
Pennsylvania Freeman, 140
People's Constitutional Convention (1841): Black voting question, 176–77; call for delegates, 168; comparison to General Assembly petition, 182; Niger attempt to vote, 170; People's Constitution and "white provision," 171–73, 179–81, 186, 188; petition for Black voting, 177–79; response to General Assembly, 163; RIASS meeting and, 186; Suffrage Association and, 167
People's General Assembly, 191
Perry, Oliver Hazard, 184, 249n12
Peterson, Abraham, 192–93, 205
Peterson, Susanna, 133
philanthropic whites, 3, 10, 29, 54, 65–66
Phillips, Wendell, 185
Pierson, William, 17–18
Pillsbury, Parker, 92, 187–88
"Pinkster" festivals (New York), 17
Pitcairn, John, 21
pogroms: Addison Hollow, 87, 89, 91–93; backfire on white mob, 145; in "Hard-Scrabble" and "Snow Town," 11, 64; in "Hard-Scrabble" and trial, 83–86, 88–91, 240n3, 240n14; "Snow Town" and, 85, 108–9, 113–17, 127, 134, 166, 175, 243n86
Polk, James, 204
poor and artisan whites: antebellum rioting by, 240n19; competition for citizenship rights, 9–10, 95; disenfranchised whites and, 113, 158; freeman/ slave to white/Black, 150; political setbacks and, 108–9; Providence Anti-Slavery Society and, 130. *See also* pogroms
Potter, Elisha R., 102, 107, 190, 198
Potter, Ray, 130, 132, 141
Potter, Thomas Hazard, 22
Powell, William P., 135, 139
Prentice, John, 130, 132
Prescott, Richard, 22–23
presidential elections, 149, 204, 206
Price, Augustus, 136, 138
Prince Amy, 17
Princeton University (College of New Jersey), 30–31
Proffitt, John, 111
property ownership, 3, 6–7, 53–54, 73, 76, 85, 92, 107, 202
Providence: city government charter, 117; destructive riot, 64; school systems for Black and white children, 99
Providence Abolition Society, 79
Providence African Society for Mutual Relief, 92, 94, 123
Providence Anti-Slavery Society: abolitionism and voting rights, 134; American Anti-Slavery Society and, 140; beliefs of, 130, 146; interracial ties of, 132–33; Pawtucket Anti-Slavery Society and, 141; petition for abolition, 131; RIASS and, 165; Suffrage Association and, 150; suffrage movement and, 150
Providence Anti-Slavery Society "committee of the colored people," 130
Providence Black community: alliance with dominant political party, 205; Black leadership occupations, 70, 72–73, 75–78, 82, 94, 166, 238n19; Black population of, 18–19, 43–44, 64, 85, 109, 230n12; Black property ownership and businesses, 70, 83–84, 94, 238n19; Black treatment after city defense, 194; disenfranchised whites and, 91; Howland nominated as election warden, 208; liquor licenses, 242n52; Native intermarriage and, 122; petition for removal from tax rolls (1831), 104; self-liberation in place, 212; shadow community, 203, 250n1; tax rolls and, 99; underground economy, 86; Whig Party and, 206
Providence City Directory, 91, 142, 166
Providence Colored Ladies Society, 125–27
Providence Female Anti-Slavery Society, 125
Providence Female Juvenile Anti-Slavery Society, 135, 137

Providence Gazette, 27–28, 51
Providence Journal: Black population reporting, 109; colonization and, 244n34; colonizationism and, 133; color line articles, 171–72; defense of Clay, 205; Easton's advertisements in, 114; editorials on Black voting, 196–97; free education editorial, 103; General Assembly petition news, 107; Hall obituary, 83; Primus Bailey and, 199; school integration and, 210; Suffrage Association and, 170, 181; Whig Party and, 206; "white" clause" editorial, 180; Wyllis eulogy, 119
Providence Ladies' Anti-Slavery Society, 135
Providence leadership class, 8, 10
Providence Literary Cadet, 1, 83
Providence Patriot, 52–56, 59–60, 86–87, 109, 112, 133, 151, 244n34
Providence's Black leaders, 9
Providence Society for Abolishing the Slave Trade, 37–38, 79, 121
Providence Society for the Encouragement of Faithful Servants, 110
Providence town council, 40–42, 87
Providence Union Anti-Slavery Society, 159
Pryor, Elizabeth Stordeur, 144
Pullman porters, 75–76
Purvis, Robert, 155–56, 185–86

Quakerism, 2, 19, 26–27, 34, 124, 141
Quamine, John, 30–31, 35, 49, 233n82
Quaque, Philip, 30
Quincy, Josiah, 54
Quom, 55

Rammelkamp, Julian, 65
Randolph, John, 57
Randolph, Richard K., 152, 167, 185, 191, 194, 197–98
Ray, Charles B., 145, 163
religion and churches: African Methodist Episcopal church, 50, 67, 136; African Methodist Episcopal Zion church, 136; Baptists and abolitionism, 141; Black churches, 237n16; Christ Church (Episcopalian), 165; discriminatory treatment in white churches, 67; First African Baptist Church (New Orleans), 72; First Baptist Church, 64, 66–67, 73, 79; Freewill Baptist Church, 119; Freewill Baptist congregation, 136; missionary work, 3, 30–31, 35, 39; Protestant Christianity, 7; Rhodes's church services at home, 51; Second Great Awakening, 69, 79; segregation in, 142; toleration toward all Christian denominations, 69. *See also* African Union Meeting House; Quakerism
Remond, Charles Lenox, 135, 143–45, 159, 200
Remond, Sarah Parker, 143
repatriation and emigration, 10, 36, 38–40. *See also* Free African Union Society; Sierra Leone settlement
republican citizenship, 5, 8
republicanism, 96, 108, 136, 148, 167, 170
Republican Party, 52, 54–58, 62, 112, 208
Revolutionary War pension, 40, 46, 50–51
Rhode Island: abolition of slavery in, 16; Black soldier enlistment Continental Army, 21–22; disenfranchised citizens in, 149–50
Rhode Island American, 52, 54–55, 57–58, 60, 87, 92, 102–3, 110, 123
Rhode Island Anti-Slavery Society (RIASS): antislavery petitions, 151; Black civil and political rights, 125–26, 135; Black leadership support and, 205; equal rights in the state, 145; founding of, 141; Fugitive Slave Act (1850) and, 206; Harper's Ferry (1859) and, 206; member votes against new constitution, 189; new constitution vote, 200; Niger and, 147; People's Constitutional Convention and, 182, 185–86; Quincy Adams letter, 156; Suffrage Association and, 12; ties with the Black community, 142–43
Rhode Island colony, freeman voting rights, 41
Rhode Island constitutional convention (1824), 86

Rhode Island constitutional convention (1841), 162–63, 167–69, 187, 189
Rhode Island General Assembly: acted as a court, 232n49; "An Act in Relation to Blacks and People of Color" (1841), 162; antislavery petitions (1834), 151; Anti-Slavery Society petition (1839), 157; anti-slave trade resolutions, 37, 234n90; colonial laws carryovers affecting Black people, 46–47, 235n13; constitutional convention and poll tax (1842), 198; constitutional convention and tax rolls (1842), 197; constitutional convention and "white provision" (1842), 197–200, 203; constitutional convention for "all male native citizens" (1842), 193, 196–97; constitution to voters (1842), 198–99; education of children born to enslaved mothers (1784), 28–29; formal opposition to slavery (1779), 27; freemanship removal petition (1829), 241n45; freemanship requirement, 85–86, 95; gag rule on antislavery petitions, 151–52; general suffrage bill (1818), 56–57; land ownership and suffrage, 169; liquor purchases and licenses, 26, 102, 242n52; McCarty petition (1840), 160; out-of-state sales of enslaved forbidden (1779), 27; petition for Black voting rights (1841), 182–85; petition for citizenship rights (1828), 102–3; petition for gradual abolition (1784), 28, 64, 80; petition for removal from tax rolls or free education (1831), 104–6, 120, 242n52; petition for removal from tax rolls or free education (1841), 162; petition repudiating previous petition (1841), 164–67; petition to free any enslaved persons brought to Rhode Island (1775), 27; post-nati (after-birth) emancipation act (1784), 24, 46–47; public school legislation (1828), 98, 103; rotating meeting location, 231n28; state constitutional amendment, 150–51; taxation exemption repeal (1843), 200–201; warning out system, 47; "white" provision (1841), 187; whites only general suffrage bill, 45, 52–53, 58–62; Will the General Assembly Put Down Caste Schools (1858), 210
Rhodes, Bristol, 50–51
Richmond, Gilbert, 130
Richmond Enquirer, 59
Rights of Colored Men to Suffrage, Citizenship, and Trial by Jury (Yates), 155
"Robert the Hermit," 1, 83
Robinson, Martin, 130
Rodman, Samuel, 177
Roediger, David, 95
Rogers, Nathaniel P., 185
Rousseau, Jean-Jacques, 5, 208
Royal African Company, 7
Ruggles, David, 145

Salem, Peter, 20–21
Sally (privateer), 40
Saltonstall, Leverett, 83
Sayles, Welcome, 181
Schantz, Mark, 65, 79, 239n51
Scott, James, 134, 142, 244n37
Second Party System, 149
Second Treatise of Government (Locke), 5
Sessions, Horace, 93
Seward, William, 207
Shaw, James, 116
A Short History of the African Union Meeting and School-House (Jackson), 65–66, 68–69, 82
Sidney, Joseph, 54
Sierra Leone settlement, 36–38
Simmons, James F., 157, 162, 194, 196, 198
Simmons, Mary, 34
Sinha, Manisha, 39, 117
Sisson, Jack "Prince," 22–23
Sisson, Susan, 188
skin color, 9, 71, 106, 170
Slave Power, 204, 206–7, 211
"Slave Representation" (Dwight), 53
Smith, George J., 68–69, 75–76, 94, 177
Smith, James McCune, 66
Smith, Perry, 194
The Social Contract (Rousseau), 5
the South and southern slaveholders, 54, 57–58, 93, 101–2, 105, 151, 160, 204

Spear, London, 32–33
Stanton, Henry B., 141, 245n51
Stead, Thomas, 196
Stevens, Thaddeus, 154
Stevens, Zingo, 16
Stewart, Maria, 126
Stiles, Ezra, 26, 30
Stober, William, 32–33
Stoddard, Fortune, 23–24
Strong, Caleb, 53–54
Suffrage Association (Rhode Island): abolitionists in, 168; African Americans' role in, 8; agitation among poor and artisan whites, 174; alienating Black leaders, 168; binding referendum on "white" qualification, 187; constitutional convention, 12; Democratic leanings, 55, 186; exclusion of Blacks, 200; founding of, 158; ignored by the *Liberator*, 159; Irish vote and, 178; Niger's vote denial, 170–73; People's Convention delegates, 167; political crisis of, 3; position on Black suffrage, 148, 161, 163, 168–71, 176, 181, 185, 193; taxation without representation principle, 162
suffrage movement: freemanship removal petition, 99–100, 241n45; free white men and, 95, 99, 112; presidential election years and, 149; report on suffrage petition, 99–101; right for all Black Rhode Island men, 148
Suffrage Party, 190–92, 195–96, 199–200, 204
Sumner, Charles, 209
Sweet, Jesse B., 88–89
Sweet, John Wood, 18, 23, 62, 117
Sweetland, Warwick, 67–68, 73
System of Doctrines Contained in Divine Revelation (Hopkins), 35

Taber, Constant, 75
Taber, Henry, 68, 75
Tallmadge, James, 57
Taney, Roger, 45, 101, 154, 208
Tappan, Arthur, 130
Tappan, Lewis, 133, 141–42, 147

taxation without representation, 5, 10, 19, 41, 120, 123, 155, 162–63, 167, 247n29
Taylor, Anthony, 32
Taylor, Nikki, 203, 250n1
Taylor, William, 91
Taylor, Zachary, 206–7
temperance campaigns, 3, 7, 26, 119, 127–28, 146. *See also* Colored Association of Providence for the Promotion of Temperance
"Temperance Convention for People of Color in New England," 138–39
Thomas, George, 49–50
Thompson, George, 134–35, 141
Thompson, Thomas, 53, 68, 73–74
Thornton, William, 36
Thoughts on African Colonization (Garrison), 124
Tillinghast, Charles F., 197
Tillinghast, Joseph L., 89, 91–92
Tillinghast. Wilbor, 130
To the Friends of Equal Rights in Rhode Island (Northup, Parker), 210
Townsend, Lucy, 80
Treadwell, James, 114
Treatise on the Intellectual Character, and the Civil and Political Condition of the Colored People of the U. States (Easton), 95
Triangle Trade route and slave import duties, 24–25
Turner, Nat, 114, 117, 123
Tyler, John, 190–91

Underground Railroad, 138, 145
U. S. Congress: gag rule on antislavery petitions (1836), 151–52; Maine and Missouri statehood bills, 58; Missouri statehood debate (1819), 57–59, 236n46; U. S. Navy enlistment bill and "whites," 194
U. S. Constitution, 5, 7, 29, 53–54, 131, 155, 236n46

Van Buren, Martin, 60, 153, 157, 206–7
Van Rensselaer, Thomas, 144

Vesey, Denmark, 87
Vine (brig), 93
Virginia, 16, 20, 95
Volunteer Police Corps, 193
Vorhis, Alley (wife), 1–2
Vorhis, Robert, 1–3, 9, 13, 83–84
voting rights: Black and white non-freeholders, 148; Black leadership and, 4; Black voter in Little Compton, 56, 105, 154, 199; Black voting states, 100; editorials and articles on, 59, 112–13; Federalists and, 55; Fogg lawsuit in Pennsylvania, 153; military service argument, 183, 185–86; native citizens argument, 178, 183; property ownership and, 112; push to broaden rights (1811), 52–54; re-enfranchisement, 176, 248n2; "substance" or intelligence and, 151; tax-payer argument, 184; white qualifications, 9, 11, 52, 58–61, 176. *See also* property ownership; suffrage movement

Walker, David, 77, 95, 105–7, 113, 117, 120, 125, 131–32
Wanton, Newport, 16
"warned out," 34–35, 47, 50
War of 1812, 52, 55–56, 74–75, 156, 192, 249n12
Washington, Bushrod, 93
Washington, George, 16, 21, 93, 156
Washington Globe, 196
Waterman, George, 103
Waters, Peter, 68, 78
Wayland, Francis, 99, 127, 196, 210
Webb, James Watson, 133
Webster, Daniel, 191
Weeks, Joshua, 68, 77
West African settlement (1794-1795), 36
"We Would Ask, Why Deny Us Our School Rights?" (Northup, Parker), 210
Wheatley, Phillis, 35, 90, 233n82
Wheeler, Henry T., 89, 91, 107, 240n3
Whig Party: anti-gag resolutions and, 157; Black leaders and, 4, 12; Black political participation, 152; Black voters and, 204; Brown, Hazard and Gorham for, 129; "Conscience faction," 207; elections (1840), 161; end of, 207–8; principle of propertied citizenship, 112; Providence and Newport split on racism, 156–57; voting rights position, 149
Whipper, William, 135–36, 138–39, 147
Whipple, John, 157, 162, 190
White, Aaron, 186
white supremacy: Black communities and, 87–90; definition of white, 53; effect on Black people, 3, 84; founding philosophers' vested interest, 7; "inside walk" and, 87–88, 90–91, 240n18; post American Revolution, 45–46; self-fulfilling ideas of, 6; struggle against, 4, 13, 122
Whitman, Prince, 49–50
Wicks, Josiah, 78
Wilberforce settlement (Canada), 71
Williams, Augustus, 115
Williams, Catherine, 166
Williams, Derry, 68, 77
Williams, John, 129–30
Williams, Roger, 51, 69, 180
Willis, George C., 67–68, 72–73, 76, 82
Winch, Julie, 9
Wolmsly, Stephen, 68, 77
women: African Union Meeting House and, 68; Black women's savings, 69, 111; Christian respectability and, 126; Enlightenment view of, 46; first petition signers (1841), 166; franchise and, 55; property ownership and, 229n8; property ownership and businesses, 6–7, 68; Providence Colored Ladies Society, 125; Providence Female Anti-Slavery Society, 125; voting rights and, 100, 229n9
Workingmen's Party, 113
World Anti-Slavery Convention, 143
Wright, Richard, 75
Wyllis, George C.: about, 119; Black leadership, 118, 120, 127, 145, 206; call for action by, 121; Convention for the Improvement of the Free People of

Wyllis, George C. (cont.)
　Colour attendee, 135, 139; and *Freedom's Journal*, 113; petition writing, 104, 107, 132, 160, 162, 164–65, 177, 183, 202; presidential candidate support, 207; Prince Hall mason lodge and, 94, 124; temperance association and, 129, 140

Yamma, Bristol, 16, 30–32, 35–36, 49, 233n71, 233n82
Yates, William H., 154–55
Young Men's Union Friendly Association, 128

Zion's Herald, 133